CROSSWALK

CROSSWALK
One Nation under God
2nd Edition

Rodrick Purves

TATE PUBLISHING
AND ENTERPRISES, LLC

Crosswalk
Copyright © 2015 by Rodrick Purves. All rights reserved.

No part of this publication may be reproduced, stored in a retrieval system or transmitted in any way by any means, electronic, mechanical, photocopy, recording or otherwise without the prior permission of the author except as provided by USA copyright law.

The opinions expressed by the author are not necessarily those of Tate Publishing, LLC.

Published by Tate Publishing & Enterprises, LLC
127 E. Trade Center Terrace | Mustang, Oklahoma 73064 USA
1.888.361.9473 | www.tatepublishing.com

Tate Publishing is committed to excellence in the publishing industry. The company reflects the philosophy established by the founders, based on Psalm 68:11,
"The Lord gave the word and great was the company of those who published it."

Book design copyright © 2015 by Tate Publishing, LLC. All rights reserved.
Cover design by Nino Carlo Suico
Interior design by Jake Muelle

Published in the United States of America

ISBN: 978-1-62746-448-2
1. Religon / Christian Life General
2. Religion / Christian Life / Spiritual Warfare
15.01.06

Contents

Forward 9

1. Crosswalk California 19

2. Walking into Downtown San Diego 25

3. San Diego the Journey Begins 27

4. Walking to Carlsbad 31

5. Walking on to Carlsbad 33

6. Carlsbad to Oceanside 35

7. Entering into Oceanside 37

8. Entering Capistrano Beach 53

9. Dana Point 71

10. Entering Laguna Beach 77

11. Entering Laguna Beach 81

12. Laguna Beach to Newport Beach 91

13. Laguna Beach to Newport Beach 97

14. Coming into My Native Hometown
    Corona Del Mar and Newport Beach 105

15. Entering into Huntington Beach 121

16. Walking into Seal Beach 127

17. Long Beach 129

18. Long Beach to Los Angeles. 133

19. Road to Redondo Beach 137

20. Redondo and Hermosa 141

21. Los Angeles. 145

22. Walking Up to Ocean Beach Pier 155

23. Santa Monica Heading to Malibu PCH
    (Pacific Coast Highway) 159

24. Malibu to Point Mugu Naval Station 163

25. Walking from Point Mugu to Oxnard. 167

26. Walking from Oxnard to Summerland 169

27. Summerland to Santa Barbara. 171

28. Santa Barbara headed to Gaviota State Park. 177

29. Gaviota State Park to Lompoc 179

30. San Luis Obispo to Morro Bay 189

31. Carmel Highlands to Monterey. 193

32. Seaside to Marina City 197

33. Off to Aptos 207

34. Walking to Santa Cruz 211

35. Soquel to Santa Cruz. 217

36. Walking from Santa Cruz to Ano Nuevo Beach 221

37. Ano Nuevo Beach to Half Moon Bay 225

38. Half Moon Bay to San Francisco. 229

39. El Granada, Moss Beach, and into Montara 231

40. Pacifica to San Francisco 237

41. Walking through Daily City 239

42. Entering San Francisco 243

43. Sausalito 247

44. Salt Point to Anchor Bay. 251

45. Gualala 253

46. Anchor Bay to Manchester 257

47. Point Arena. 259

48. Walking into Manchester 261

49. Manchester to Elk. 263

50. Elk to Mendocino. 267

51. Little River 269

52. Leggett to Garberville. 271

53. Smithe Redwood Reserve 275

54. Richardson Grove State Park. 279

55. Richardson Grove 281

56. Garberville to Stafford. 287

57. Headed to Weott. 295

58. Heading to Redcrest 299

59. Stafford to Eureka. 303

60. Reaching Fernbridge 305

61. Headed to Eureka 307

62. Eureka to Crescent City 313

63. Somewhere in the Great Ohio Valley
    Year of our Lord 1625 325

64. The End of Crosswalk California 339

References & Topical Index 341

Forward

The path and the cross we must bear!

If God has called you to do something it is best to say yes, and that is my story. I searched my heart to understand the calling? While in the search, my life moved in many directions. I finally surrendered to His calling, and all I can say is it is hard to walk by faith because the road maps are not always evident. But even in the worst of times, our Father is always patient, loving, and kind. When times get tough just remember that God carefully made each one of us, and knows exactly what it is going to take to move us. However, it's just so hard sometimes to turn away from this crazy world, to pick up our personal crosses, and follow after Him. Yet this is the only way we will ever find peace and true joy in our lives through our Lord Jesus.

The way of the cross
A Preparatory prayer

My Lord Jesus Christ, Thou hast made this journey to die for me with love un-utterable; and I have so many times unworthily abandoned Thee. However my Lord of my heart knows I love Thee, with my whole heart, and because I love Thee, I repent sincerely for having offended Thee. Pardon me, my God, and permit me to accompany Thee in this journey. Thou goest to die for love of me; I wish also, my Jesus, I will live and die always united to Thee!

My name is Rod, I'm 49 and I am a 15 year Navy man and a plank owner meaning Commissioning crew, aboard the first Arleigh Burke class destroyer DDG 51. This has little to do with our story, however The Admiral himself had a motto, we have come to fight and you better know how! Admiral Arleigh Burk was a WWII class destroyer commander, who moved quickly through the ranks by his fortitude, honor and ability to command. He became CNO of the Navy. This American father is in heaven today forever watching over us. It is my prayer that what he sees in me will bless his heart, also that he will pray for me before the throne room of the Holy Trinity. And in the body that is, God the Father, Christ his Son our Lord, and the Holy Spirit would again bless us in America and heal our land.

Our story opens and finds me working on the USS Sumner in the Yellow Sea, in oceanographic research as an A/B. I was standing watch when the captain and first mate came to me asking this question: If you could, how would you change the world?

These were men of position and power asking me such a strange question! And it was asked in such a way, as if they really wanted to know? The answer was a simple one: America and all Christian nations should start preaching Jesus, and go back to teaching creation once again in our schools. Besides; isn't that what we are finding out here? They listened as I continued answering their question. "Gentlemen you know as well as I do that the science and research we are doing all over the earth only reveals creation! Every piece of it is dripping creational designer. Since that is the truth of it; are we not duty bound to tell the people to repent and turn back to God? Anything else is vanity. Or are we to seek our own glory by hiding truth?"

My answer made them nervous and a bit uneasy, and I could tell that I had said something that would affect the rest of my life. I had no idea just how much this life that I once thought was mine would change? From that point on the spiritual battle was underfoot. Everywhere I turned, I was walking on egg shells!

I had been working at sea all of my life. I am a Catholic man of faith, and I love our Lord. I share a wonderful relationship with our King. I enjoyed Jesus showing me His creation while traveling the oceans and countries of the world for the past 22 years: I served in the US Navy for 15 years, then as a fisherman boat skipper, and now as a merchant sailor...

Then all at once that peaceful time of work and discovery was about to end. I was to learn what it would mean to surrender my will all self-interests, and desires for my life. Now I was to begin to walk and to serve our Lord. I was instantly made aware that it was His life that He would take over from that point on.

I quickly left my lifelong career on the sea, returned home to Newport Beach CA, and began to seek Godly counsel to help explain what was happening to what I thought was my own life. Then the Lord spoke verbally to me pick up and carry my cross. What did that mean? I questioned it without getting an answer. So I studied scripture to find the meaning of such a calling.

The Dream

I didn't find any answers quickly. I did notice the more I studied the Word of God to find answers, the more I was building a passion for teaching His Word. I couldn't stop and I loved it. Then one night I had a premonition or a dream. In the dream I was carrying a full size cross physically up Highway 1 in California. I woke up and asked myself, "Who does that?!" I just went back to sleep wondering what the dream could be all about?

At times I thought he must want me to start a new church or movement; however being a Catholic that is not an option. I certainly wouldn't want to be responsible for any more division of Christ's church. What could this mystery be I wondered? Month after month went by as thoughts of the crosswalk up the coast kept nagging at me!

Each time the thought came to me, I would argue with our Lord. I am not wise or knowledgeable enough to do such a thing, nor do I know scripture well. Besides, there are so many well-trained pastors and priests who could do a much better job. Why me, Lord?

Then I had another dream; Satan came as a dragon, roaring into my life, and stabbing me to death. That was the first time I ever felt the torment of Satan. This much was obvious he wanted me dead and out of his "territory."

I was living with my brother after 22 years at sea in Palos Verdes Estates. We had been separated all that time. Upon my return, I was sad to hear that my brother—who was baptized, raised Catholic and educated at a Catholic school claimed to be an atheist. I told him that was impossible because there is no such thing as a true atheist. He was caught up in the lie of this world. I began to pray for my brother that our Father would change his heart. God was to answer my prayers, because Steve turned back to the Lord in 2003, ultimately back to the Catholic Church, and today spends most of his free time working in lay ministry.

What I realized was my brother was just an example of what had happened to the entire state of California and sadly enough most of our nation, while I was at sea: Many have walked away from their faith and heritage, and the fruit of this error was every-where. I couldn't believe what was on television, also driving down the street shown on billboards for all to see, or what girls wore on the street! What had happened to my small little Newport Beach surf town? What happened to our Christian nation?

All of this drove me to find answers. I searched the Word of God and prayed constantly. I noticed that my passion to share the Word of God with others continued to grow. How strange, I thought, since sharing the Gospel with others was completely out of character for me. By nature, I am a quiet guy. Or so I thought perhaps this was the answer to my dream. Through my church, I started going to all the local piers with a worship team. At

Balboa, Newport Beach and Huntington Beach, we played worship music and prayed with all the people who would respond. We prayed in privet behind a garden wall as not to be in the open. While I enjoyed these evenings tremendously, it never felt like it fulfilled my calling.

Throughout this time I felt quite alone, as I had always desired a normal life. You know a wife, children and a white picket fence. I deeply wanted to be married but I did not know where to start. So my brother said he had a friend who recommended Mariners' Church. So I went there, a great church, but as a Catholic, I felt at times that I was in the wrong place. Still I stayed, eventually getting married to Ronda. After marriage she immediately wanted to move to another church California Victory Church which was Pentecostal.

California Victory was an enjoyable experience. However, as I would pray, I was always reminded of my calling to do the crosswalk. I finally shared my dream of the crosswalk with my pastor and wife Ronda. They both embraced the idea as God-inspired but never thought the time was right. Months passed, and still the church Pastors and Ronda would both say: not yet! Simultaneously however this time I was being drawn to my Catholic roots. There was a real struggle going on in my mind about what to do?

Then I had another dream about the crosswalk. It was clear that if I didn't go right then, I would be making the crosswalk from a wheelchair! I immediately awoke, knowing my fate. I knelt at the side of my bed and pleaded with the Lord: How can I do this in a wheel chair? Father I'm married with a step-son and a foster daughter in tow how can I leave them to walk up the coast of California? Even knowing that I had to go, how does one commit to such a thing?

The next week when I was at work, a man in a big truck dropped off supplies to our jobsite. I saw he was crying out in pain over something so I walked over, said that I was a Christian, and asked what was bothering him. I was surprised to find out he was having marital problems just like me! So we prayed together, he said thank you and told me the prayer helped him feel much better. Thinking I had done my good deed for the day, I went back to work. While climbing up a tall ladder to install a large lighting fixture, the ladder collapsed. I had shattered both knees and left ankle! The vision had come true!

All kinds of things began to go through my head, and I began pleading with the Lord: I am only a sailor, not a scholar, priest, preacher, nor prophet. Who am I? That the Lord would seek someone like me? Surely there are more qualified people, given all these churches located in Southern California!

Though I knew I had to go, I did nothing due to fear and a lack of understanding. I was focused on my recovery and the challenges of workers' compensation procedures. My family and I suffered greatly; under this stress, the problems which already existed in our marriage grew. A year later, I was able to return to work in a small lumber company, trying to recover from the resultant financial mess. In the midst of these challenges, the walk was in the forefront of my life, in my thoughts and in my dreams, but I let the worries about my marriage and life, overtake me.

As my body healed, I was getting strong again. Then one evening I was working on a table saw. One of the teeth broke off and flew into my neck, almost ending my life. I was out of work again. After this incident, my wife looked at me and said it was time to get on the road before it got worse!

Then it became real. I was going! WOW! Now what? I built a cross and cart with my brother. It came together quickly, as things do once you finally enter into the will of God. It wasn't fancy however it worked on the way to covering 1100 miles, with a little help from the kindness of strangers. Well that's another chapter. Through this four year period of arguing and questioning God, with all that happened, I was being prepared spiritually and mentally for the journey. And a message that I was to give to those I met on the cross walk was being formed in my heart.

The Message—One Nation under God!

The message was a simple truth to be given to our country. I knew I had no choice but to get on the road, and let the Holy Spirit speak though me to all who would listen. It was time to surrender, and trust the Lord. The message specifically, was that it is time for the Body of Christ to unite and heal our great Christian nation. Centuries ago God used great Christian men and women at great risk to their lives and families to found a free nation, the United States of America. He inspired our Constitution, and Bill Rights to ensure the United States of America would always remain free. Our Father has placed each of us in this incredible country with clean water, plentiful food, beautiful lands and a powerful Constitution designed to protect the freedom of his children. This message is for the sleeping giant, the Body of Christ, who has fallen asleep, and let our free land slip into bondage.

Christians make up the majority of our American citizenry yet our lives and our children are under attack, while we do nothing. Jesus is the only one that can save and protect us, and the teaching of this truth has been systematically removed from our schools, universities, court rooms, hospitals, even our military, to a great extent, even "watered-down" in our modern Churches. The true history of our great Christian nation has been altered while we've been asleep. It has come to the point where our American brothers are being oppressed for mentioning his name. I pray we all wake up soon before it's too late and the United States of America becomes like the other Christian nations of the world that have surrendered to the enemy. Let us not forget that Iraq and Northern Africa were the heartland of Christianity before they fell asleep.

The majority of "We the People" of the United States of America love Jesus! The media, our universities-colleges-public schools, the liberal branch of the government, the world all deny it. However, We the People say, "Yes we do," yet our voice is not heard. This sad reality that the Body of Christ remains weak is due to division. With a weakened opponent, the enemy has his way in the media, educational system and in our government. There are many new Churches across the nation and tens of thousands of new people joining the body but we still remain weak. Our churches are active in their individual ministries and mission work but each one is an island unto itself; and sometimes, the goal is to furiously fight to maintain spiritual influence over a local area. Competition among churches for influence or fame is vanity.

Intuitively, all Christians know we have one enemy, and his army is not divided. The army of darkness is well-honed, strong and organized across the world and has been for thousands of years. His goal is to lie, steal, kill and destroy the Body of Christ. All his efforts are to keep the body weak, and divided while he wages war against our children and the structure of the American family.

One battleground which has raged without impunity has been our educational system. Originally strong in teaching foundational Christian precepts, it has succumbed to theoretical reasoning over facts, and promoted philosophical premises over moral absolutes, entrenching in our society the age-old secular humanist errors founded in ancient Greece. Or fractured teaching Hummed from some libertarian exuded secular reality. Sadly this slide of hand, new reality comes into play by falsely and maliciously constructing a new reality formed by want and personal desire. The end result is performed by removing solid reason, while hiding from the hard facts. Which is the system of lies and temptation built to miss guide us!

This system has convinced us that we are great thinkers, unique individuals who can succeed under our own strength. We can be rich, powerful, smart, and famous, that this is the end-all goal, and this self-absorption leads to "happiness".

Unfortunately, our churches have not been immune to this. So now we live in a world where not only the Churches stand alone because its leaders are individual thinkers, but all the people who attend are also individual islands unto themselves. It is time for the army of light, the Body of Christ, to unite in our efforts and fight back in a single voice of love. As Arleigh Burke said "we have come to fight and you better know how". This is what I have been asked to share from the reality of the holy cross. I was not chosen because I'm smart or a great speaker, but rather because he knew I'd do it. And that I'd walk a thousand miles to tell of his love for his people.

Those who God appoints, he anoints. When the Holy Spirit convicted me of this mission, I could not sit any longer. Through a series of crazy events, God placed it on my heart to carry a cross and the American flag from Mexico to the Oregon border with this message, and for it to be heard across the country. It's time for the country to unite as "One Nation under God". Please know this, Our God is a God of love, kindness and forgiveness but he is also a jealous God and a God of wrath. He has given us a wonderful gift as he did Israel. We have turned from our God to worship other idols such as money, education, clothes, fame, homes, cars and sports, in other words "the world". He wants us to turn back to Him. He wants us to love each other, our families and our communities. Remember his words,

James 4:4.

You adulterous people, don't you know that friendship with the world is hatred toward God? Anyone who chooses to be a friend of the world becomes an enemy of God.

He is asking that our nation become Christian again, a United Nation under God! This all begins with prayer. Each morning, pray for your family that Jesus will change our hearts and guide us back into truth, peace, joy and happiness. Pray we will no longer believe the lies of Satan that have caused the Church to splinter. Pray for wisdom and discernment to combat Satan's plans. I pray we all can turn off our televisions, put down our newspapers and video games and go back outside with our families, friends and communities. We need to witness to the incredible nation we have been given as strong united Christian communities. It's time to work together, pray together, vote together, and rise up new leaders, telling our government:

WE ARE NOT GOING TO TAKE IT ANY MORE!

So the journey began. Join me as I recall the journey of someone responding to his call. Pray as you read this message and be open to the Father's love presented here.

1

Crosswalk California

Here is what I received and learned along the 1100-mile journey:

On Saturday Memorial Day weekend of 2005, I left from Imperial Beach. My plans were to walk alone, with about $200, an American flag, some clothes, a little camping gear and a lot of faith, trusting that all would be well.

The first leg of the walk, my family, brother, and friends joined me in a day of sending-off. Immediately the first group of people that we came up to asked me what I was doing. I told them I was walking from Tijuana to the Oregon border, and shared the message of unifying the Body of Christ and healing our nation. This message is for every Christian, of all denominations, that believes, and therefore has been saved by the blood of Jesus.

To my surprise, after hearing the message, they asked if they could sign the cross. I wasn't sure, so I quietly prayed and felt no conviction about this. In fact I heard in my heart "why not sign the cross, the testimony of their signature is for all to see". Besides, it really is our cross anyway! After all, Christ is God and he sacrificed himself for the redemption of fallen man on that cross, creating the path in which we can be reconciled back to the Father. That is how signing of the cross began, culminating in tens of thousands of signatures: a testimony of their love for Jesus. Moments later an 18-year-old boy with his family came to us, moved to give his heart to Jesus; at that same time, a man was watching the event from his hotel room. His name was Ken. He literally ran from his room and asked me what I was doing. When I told him, he dropped everything in his life and committed to walk with me, which he did, up to San Simeon. I could not have made the distance without Ken's help. Obviously, it was God once again.

All that day as I walked through Imperial Beach the message of "One nation under God" rang true with almost everyone who spoke with us, including the American Legion Hall that took pictures for their newsletter. As evening came, my family that I love so much said their goodbyes and headed for home. It was just the two of us; Ken and I, off on the greatest adventure of our lives.

A little later that day, the front tire on the cart went flat, and Ken volunteered to get a new tube, and he ran ahead. I kept pushing the cross with the flat tire. Many people stopped and asked if they could help or donate to the walk. The people of Coronado seemed very kind, helpful and warmly received the cross. It was getting late as I came across a guard shack at the Coronado keys community entrance, where Ken had stopped much earlier to call for help. The guard explained, when the bike shop heard the situation, they agreed to stay open until Ken arrived by city bus. The bus driver heard what Ken and I was doing, and took him off route, directly to the bike shop. Thank you again to everyone who helped us. God is good all the time, as we will find out as this story unfolds.

I waited at the bus stop until Ken returned. Meanwhile I shared with those nearby about the Love of Christ for us. A while later Ken returned with a new tube. It was a great feeling to see my new friend again and to be back on the walk.

About two miles up was the Coronado state beach where we camped for the night, right on the Mission Bay waterfront. It was a wonderful spot but Ken and I were very tired, and we knew we had a long day ahead. So we prayed together, and had some barbeque chicken for dinner. As we put up the tent, we began to share about our lives. It turned out that Ken and I were both struggling with marital problems. In addition, I found out that Ken was in San Diego, checking him-self into rehab, when he saw me go by with the cross. While on the phone with his mother, speaking of repentance, he was amazed to see this huge cross at that same moment! He dropped everything, and you know the rest of the story. We laid our heads back under the stars and shared about God's love.

Life is hard on all of us at times. I am a sinner, in constant need of forgiveness from my friends, family and the Lord. In order to be forgiven by my Lord I must forgive, and this is so hard sometimes. We are all tested, and make all kinds of mistakes, sometimes missing God completely.

The good news is Christ came for our sins. And, while God judges us, he is our Father first and foremost, and loves us as such. Let's never forget, he is looking for willing souls to serve him, not perfect ones!

As we awoke the next day, we started a quick bible study and found ourselves in Hebrews:

Hebrews 6

Therefore let us leave the elementary teachings about Christ and go on to maturity, not laying again the foundation of repentance from acts that lead to death, and of faith in God, instruction about baptisms, the laying on of hands, the resurrection of the dead, and eternal judgment. And God permitting, we will do so.

It is impossible for those who have once been enlightened, who have tasted the heavenly gift, who have shared in the Holy Spirit, who have tasted the goodness of the word of God and the powers of the coming age, if they fall away, to be brought back to repentance, because to their loss they are crucifying the Son of God all over again and subjecting him to public disgrace.

Land that drinks in the rain often falling on it and that produces a crop useful to those for whom it is farmed receives the blessing of God. But land that produces thorns and thistles is worthless and is in danger of being cursed. In the end it will be burned.

Even though we speak like this, dear friends, we are confident of better things in your case—things that accompany salvation. God is not unjust; he will not forget your work and the love you have shown him as you have helped his people and continue to help them. We want each of you to show this same diligence to the very end, in order to make your hope sure. We do not want you to become lazy, but to imitate those who through faith and patience inherit what has been promised.

The next morning, we walked past the Coronado Naval base and met many of our service members. They loved to see the flag and cross together. I reminded them of the Revolutionary War battle cry, as I yelled, "No King but King Jesus". This was when the revolutionaries took a stand against King George, of course. I explained that our flag's colors and symbols represent the Kingdom of heaven itself. As for the flag's colors, the red is for the blood of Jesus, the white is for the Holy Spirit, and the blue field is the river of life. As for its symbols, the stars are to remind us that we are citizens of heaven, children of light, actually living in the Kingdom of heaven. I quietly asked myself, why don't they teach that in school? I explained to them that I am a retired Navy cook who studied American, Christian, Islamic, and Judaic history as I fought through 15 years at sea "one meal at a time!" I shared with them that I had spent the majority of those years living outside of the United States, and could not believe we have fallen so deeply asleep here at home. This walk was a wake up call for all who would listen to the truth. We discussed the removal of the name of Jesus from military prayer, and as I spoke to them I was reminded of Revelations 19.

Revelations 19

"Let us rejoice and be glad and give the glory to Him, for the marriage of the Lamb has come and His bride has made herself ready." It was given to her to clothe herself in fine linen, bright and clean; for the fine linen is the righteous acts of the saints.

Righteous acts is to repent, turn from all sin and live holy lives

Then he said to me, "Write, 'Blessed are those who are invited to the marriage supper of the Lamb.'" In addition, he said to me, "These are true words of God." Then I fell at his feet to worship him. However, he said to me, "Do not do that; I am a fellow servant of yours and your brethren who hold the testimony of Jesus; worship God. For the testimony of Jesus is the spirit of prophecy."

I spoke this as proof of the communion of saints, and if they are not preaching Jesus they are all too often false prophets. Without Jesus, without the cross, without the resurrection, our faith is worthless!

We said our goodbyes as Ken and I continued our walk through the city of Coronado. There was an outdoor art festival taking place in the park. Ken and I met a young Hispanic woman, about 19 years old. She felt that the Lord had been calling her and her mother to repentance and back into Church. I asked her some questions about her faith. She was seeking and checking out some Christian Churches in the area but had not made Christ her Lord and Savior yet. I asked if she would like to.

She said yes and we began to share about God's Son, and we let her know the seriousness of her decision to follow the Lord, Praise God! So I reminded her that a commitment to Christ demands that we live as Christians always to the best of our ability. I could see the light of the Lord shining on her face as we read the prayer of commitment of faith and I held this young woman in my arms as she wept for joy. I reminded her that God the Father had fearfully and wonderfully created her and that God has now called her into the Kingdom of heaven by God the Father through his Son Jesus. I also told her to find a Church to serve in as soon as she could, in order that she may be mentored. I also shared about how Jesus was now her husband, and that one day Christ would bless her life if she would be faithful to serve.

Ken, I, and the young woman shared our good-byes, and we began walking into the park, and further on through the art festival. Many people surrounded us and received prayer. For doing this we were greatly blessed by God's wonderful family. Us all of us we are all his after all!

There were all types of people there, so we received some persecution, mostly political based upon the "separation of Church and state" myth. I indicated if that were so, we would have to restructure our entire nation: we would need a new flag, Constitution, Bill of Rights and burn the historical documents, all of which mention God and religious principles. If, indeed, we were not founded as a Christian Nation, where did all of these things come from? Our nation's written documental structure, these statuettes which some people would seek to tear down? Again why?

Moving on we arrived at the ferry docks. Just then the funniest thing happened: I ran into an old surfing friend from my childhood. He was surprised, based on the Rod he knew from days gone by. We shared old surfing stories of lonely giant waves surfed in our younger days. You know, God and his power to save, even when we make poor choices.

We had a few laughs and took the ferry across the bay from Coronado.

2

Walking into Downtown San Diego

Where the ferry landed, there were many handicapped, marginalized, and less fortunate, along with too many homeless. We stopped to pray with them, giving each of them a couple of bucks from the little we had for food. We prayed for hope and restoration. At the end of the line of these people, we entered a shopping area. Just then, a family came over to us that had been watching. The father shared with us that we had so spiritually affected their daughter by our act of faith, and the love we showed for the helpless, that they had to come over. This young woman, his daughter, received Christ on the spot. The father gave us twice what we had just given away, as he had been trying to win the case for Christ in his daughter's life for some years. There is just no way to understand the intricacy of God's planning. This plan began at her birth! Every day it amazes me to watch Him use a sinner like me.

We walked all around the Bay, getting many remarks, both praise and persecution. Some people were mad at us because of their own sin, which uncomfortably convicted them in their hearts. Christ convicts us unto repentance. It saddens me to see so much hatred and fear in our nation. It is all around us, I thought to myself. However, praise God that he who is in us, is greater than he that is in the world. Also his love endures forever!

Surprisingly to me, many bystanders indicated that the flag and the cross were parts of a dying fantasy which I was crazy to uphold, and also, that I would not complete the walk safely. However, Ken and I pushed on in confidence that the walk would be finished, if it is God's will. Yet, I had no real understanding of what God's overall plans or intentions were. It certainly was a walk of faith!

With no place to camp, we used our remaining cash for a small hotel room. The next morning at about 7am, Ken and I started walking west on Mission St, when we ran into a man holding a piece of an olive branch. The olive branch is a sign of peace in biblical teaching. He asked why we were walking. I softly replied, out of obedience to the calling and that we were just messengers standing for Christ our Lord! He smiled, gave us a gift offering, and we gratefully shared a little prayer before heading north on Mission St. towards Mission Beach.

In God's timing, we walked in as the controversy over the cross on Soledad Mountain was occurring. Some of the people were trying to have the great cross at the Veterans' memorial taken down. The people of the city thought Ken and I were walking to support the cause of the cross. God used the walk to support the faith of the people of San Diego and they rallied together around the cause of keeping the cross on Soledad. We experienced amazing joy and excitement in the people we met, as the drivers passed by waving and thanking us. I said "Thank God, we were just walking His cross!" I later heard that 79% of the people in San Diego voted to keep the cross, and the cross is still there. Praise God! It was then I knew that it was God's perfect plan to be walking the cross on the day before the vote. God's timing is amazing to me!

3

San Diego the Journey Begins

Entire families were running to sign the Lord's cross, from little babies reaching up and making a mark with a pen, to the great-grandparents married for generations. We encountered everything from persecution to profound blessings from block to block. One cannot express the great joy a soul can experience witnessing such an event!

On Memorial Day, we entered Mission Beach. When we arrived on the boardwalk, there was a news reporter there. It was a live television and the story was about Mission Beach on Memorial Day weekend.

Here enters two people, pushing this cross with an American flag, surrounded by hundreds of curious people. The reporter quickly came over with the obvious question "So, what in the world are you two doing?!" The Lord allowed me to explain the great founding of our Christian nation and the relationship between God and the US flag on live television on Memorial Day, wearing my Navy cruise jacket and standing under a twelve foot cross! We serve an awesome God. I felt truly blessed. We spent the rest of Memorial Day praying for many families and people, winning souls but still suffering some persecution from non-believers.

We had a long, hilly walk through La Jolla and on to Torrey Pines. We walked late into the evening, not being able to find an affordable place to stay. We were very hungry and tired, when suddenly a car pulled up, and a man and his wife got out who'd seen us on the news. The couple took us to dinner at a great restaurant. We were very blessed. As if that were not enough, the wife of this fine couple started up a conversation about the Lord that ignited the whole restaurant with the presence of the Holy Spirit. The waiters, servers and all the customers in the restaurant signed the cross after our wonderful dinner. We shared and witnessed before many who were standing around the cross. Now we had the strength to make it the rest of the way to the campground in Solana Beach. We arrived at about 2 am where we camped out, played worship songs and slept under the stars. It had been a very long and eventful day!

The next morning we ran into Pam from Christian Fellowship Church in Cardiff by the Sea. She walked with us to Encinitas as we witnessed to many people. While going by the Real Surf Shop, some young employees came out, signed the cross, and gave us some great T shirts. There were many people seeking prayer, and there were several new converts on their way to salvation along the Coast Highway that morning. Finally we arrived in Encinitas where Pam treated us to breakfast. We had a great time fellowshipping with her and the wait staff. After breakfast we parted ways, and Ken and I were off once again.

As I was walking, the Holy Spirit was placing into my heart some discernment about what problems were over an area. We prayed spiritual deliverance prayers over the land and experienced strongholds falling down to the glory of God the Father! Strongholds my fellow Americans are placed over places and regents strategically placed over an area to cause satanic takeover. First a legion spirit is put into place and if the spirit is not challenged, legends of satanic powers are placed to setup a stronghold of satanic influence. When in beaded the darkest powers of hell, are sent to attack the Hearts and souls of unsuspecting men and women. When a Stronghold of satanic power is in place, the people of that surrounding area are tempted by these powerful influence's drawing them into all kinds of sin, they are mainly working to create sin against the Holy Spirit.

The deadly sins are Pride, Covetousness Lust, Anger, Gluttony, Envy, and Slothfulness.

These deadly sins begin by human hearts falling into all types of sub sin and havoc in order to destroy all that is good on God's green earth, in-order to drag as many human hearts and souls as possible into the path of destruction So the cross is the power of deliverance it is the holy cross which destroyed the Strongholds all alone my path not me or Ken! Please understand how much Jesus loves you all Holy men and women, and sinners' turn away day by day try to practice these Virtues a little each day. Also if you do not attend a church find a good one, and find a mentor that can help you be free and learn to become true disciples of the living God in Christ Jesus. I am Catholic it is my hope for unity of Gods church, also my beloved friends if it is placed on your heart attend the mass and seek the counsel of the holy priesthood. I am sure there love, and solid counsel will place your hearts In right order, and alignment with God do this to help your selves find the greatest deliverance, and the purest of Peace that a soul can achieve in this life. And to obtain the promos of heaven! The Holy Eucharist is the gate key to heaven!

This is my purest hope that you the readers can help me. Just try a little day by day, my beloved fellow Americans, and Californians I am called to this penitence, this walk to suffer in your behalf, and for my own sin's! As I am only one of your own a human soul a man, once again because this is so real and very dangerous to us all! Strongholds my fellow Americans are in placed over places and regents strategically placed over an area to cause satanic takeover.

So the cross is the power of deliverance it is the holy cross which destroyed the Strongholds. Please understand how much Jesus loves you all work together in order to turn away from all forms of darkness day by day try to practice these

Eight Beatitudes

1. *Blessed are the pour in spirit; for there's is the kingdom of heaven*

2. *Blessed are the meek; for they shell possess the land.*

3. *Blessed are they that mourn; for they shall be comforted.*

4. *Blessed are they that hunger and thirst after Justus; for they shall be filled.*

5. *Blessed are the merciful; for they shall obtain mercy.*

6. *Blessed are the clean of heart; for they shall see God.*

7. *Blessed are the peacemakers; for they shall be called children of God.*

8. *Blessed are they that suffer persecution for Justus sake; for there's is the kingdom of heaven.*

This is my deepest hope that is you the readers can help me. Just try a little day by day my beloved fellow Americans and Californians I am called to this to suffer in your behalf, and for my own sin's! As I am only one of your own, this is the only path back to repentance. Also these types of things were to take place for the next 1100 miles. Praise the Lord of all of Heaven's armies; forever we do serve an all-powerful God!

At times I could see the powers of darkness peering around corners of building's cowering at the power of the holy cross. I felt deep sorrow for these lost spirits for they are lost forever. I mostly found these lost spirits with in our city limits most often around college campuses and schools. A warning, I believe that satanic forces are after our youth! Your families, so I bid you to stand my friends stand in the love and power of the holy trinity! All nations worship and Praise the Lord of all of Heaven's armies; forever we do serve an all-powerful God! Every Nation raise and tong sings praises to our God and King!

4

Walking to Carlsbad

People were coming out of their places of business, praying with us, and thanking us for stepping out in Christ! People of all nations' races and tongues were worshipping the living God Ken and I found this to be true wherever we walk through! I thank God for our open borders here in America because we are a Christian nation. God has moved people from all over the globe for us to witness and to love. Where else in the world do you have people of all nationalities serving the Lord? In the blessed United States of America we have people from Jerusalem and all other Middle Eastern nations, Indians from India to Pakistan, Hispanics and Latinos, all nations of Asia, Africa, Native Americans and many others—all praising Jesus!

Of course there are also many from these nations that choose to not praise Jesus. I pray for the day that the Bible, Quran, Book of Mormon and all other religious beliefs are taught side by side based upon their true history without any revisionism. Let our children decide based upon the facts, not the historical revision that is taught today in our schools. I told them that we as Americans have the right to worship the living God freely and without persecution, anywhere at anytime! In addition, that it is wonderful and exciting to serve such a loving father of us all.

So let us rejoice, my brothers and sisters in the Lord Jesus. I pray that Father God renews our hearts, and that we will speak boldly about our Lord and Savior, Jesus Christ.

Most of the persecution we encountered at this point was coming from the unsaved people from other countries. Some of them shouted at me, telling me that religion is what is wrong with this nation. Most were Muslim and new arrivals to America.

I had to agree with them, based on their humanistic definition of religion. Our fathers founded this Christian country on religion, but not on just any religion. They founded this country on faith and trust in God, his Son Jesus Christ and the Holy Spirit—the Holy Trinity. This is what the United States of America's core truth is based upon, not "religion" alone. We have gone too far with this, truth-is-relative, equality movement;

James ch1 v 27:

> *true and undefiled religion is to care for widows and orphans,*
> *feed the homeless, help the suffering, and to teach the good news*
> *that Jesus still lives and heals.*

The origin of "religion" comes from the Bible, so Jewish and Christian faith is religion, only when these actions are held in the hearts of the lay religious, and becomes the daily practice of the whole.

All others are teachings of governments or the individual humanistic enlightenment of one of God's creations. They are not religion, based upon the original or definition of the word of God.

5

Walking on to Carlsbad

As we entered the state campground, I was surprised at the persecution we received from the state park attendants, who were very young. We have turned far from the truth! They did not want us to stay at the state park with the cross. I had to remind them of our right to freely express our faith and our protected freedom of speech based upon the constitution of California:

ARTICLE 1: DECLARATION OF RIGHTS

SEC. 2. (a) Every person may freely speak, write and publish his or her sentiments on all subjects, being responsible for the abuse of this right. A law may not restrain or abridge liberty of speech or press.

SEC. 4. Free exercise and enjoyment of religion without discrimination or preference are guaranteed. This liberty of conscience does not excuse acts that are licentious or inconsistent with the peace or safety of the State. The Legislature shall make no law respecting an establishment of religion. A person is not incompetent to be a witness or juror because of his or her opinions on religious beliefs.

After some discussion, they let us in, and we rested two days worshipping, witnessing and answering questions. To not offend others, we always acted and spoke in a quiet, reverent manner.

As I mentioned before, I am a Catholic. My Californian heritage traces back to the time of the building of the missions with Fr Serra! Each day it becomes ever clearer to me that our Father in Heaven is not trying to start anything new. His goal is to restore California and the United States of America back to our rich, glorious Christian heritage. Of course he can do this in an instant, but this is not the way he typically works. Through years of trying it my way, he has caused me to submit my will to his. Now he has me walking as a beacon of light, in hope others will submit to his desire for us, and to "choose" to pursue our freedom from the bondage caused by satanic strongholds again which our state and country has fallen into.

6

Carlsbad to Oceanside

As we got closer to Camp Pendleton Marine base, we stopped after praying with many hurting people to get something to eat. When we entered the restaurant, we met a man in his 50's who was sitting down, waiting for his take-out order. He asked for prayer. He told us that he had been in great torment; we prayed and shared the Gospel of Jesus with him through lunch. After he finished he got up without a word, went outside and sat on a bus stop bench just outside the front door of the hamburger stand.

Ken felt the urge to run out to the man and re-engage the conversation. I said, "Let him think and rest a while," so he agreed with what I said. The cooks and the owner talked with us about Jesus while we finished. They were Catholics. I shared with them that I too am Catholic and always will be, even though I am serving in a Pentecostal Church called "California Victory Church" in Newport Beach to be in agreement with my wife. The owner bought our lunch and thanked us. We prayed that God would further bless his business.

When we went outside to talk to the man we had prayed with, he readily announced that he would give his life to Jesus! We prayed together and this 50-year-old man started crying tears of joy! I could see God removing his pain. Ken and I were truly so touched by the Spirit of God, as we witnessed the deliverance this man was experiencing, by the saving power of Christ

Jesus. We said that he now must find a good teaching Christian Church that can explain the word of God and the workings of the Holy Spirit. He agreed. After that, he signed the cross and we went down the road. As we were walking along the beach, many people were touched and we prayed prayers of agreement with so many. In addition, some just wanted their name on the cross as their private confession of faith.

At one of the parking lots along PCH in that area, we met a 91-year-old woman. She was born in Germany and lived there through the rise of Hitler and the Third Reich. Her testimony was one of serving Jesus Christ from the age of 12 in Frankfurt. As Hitler rose to power, the persecution of the Jews in Germany had become brutal and inconceivable. She shared with us that the Nazi government killed her parents, and thousands of others as well thus she became an orphan along with so many other lost children at that time forced to live in the streets because of the brutal human imposed petulance of the axis anti-Jewish movement of the Third Empire. These manufactured circumstances forced this young girl to find a living as best as she could while living in pre WWII Germany.

This strong woman had lost everything: parents murdered, without a home; all she had ever come to know and love was stripped away. And, in spite of it all, this fine, loving lady gave the glory to God for her blessings in life. God enabled her to come to the Christian USA through the kindness of an American soldier, who literally saved her from the fallen life in Germany during the war. She said God blessed her, and God bless America! I agreed, we prayed and hugged each other, and on we went.

God, I thank you because this woman's testimony so blessed my heart that I cried out for joy. And yet, this joyful moment was tempered, because I was spiritually witnessing the attack and demise of the fallen faithful. Her story reminded me that the same attack is happening here in America. Are Christians again going to sit on our hands as the same socialistic, Nazi, Liberal ideology takes hold of the United States of America, as it did in Germany?

7

Entering into Oceanside

I saw a very young woman who sadly had been overcome by circumstances and given into prostitution. This poor young girl was crouched down sitting along the side of a dark back street. I walked over. As I got closer, I noticed she was quite lovely, though she couldn't have been over 15—a child really. How this child was thrown away and under Satan's control, I'll never know. I asked her if she knew how much Jesus loved her? Moreover, did she know that he was here with us to deliver her from such pain, and willing to forgive all of her sins?!

She began crying so hard it was heart-wrenching. We spent some time praying, for her future joy and happiness and began to share about the love of Jesus. It was easy to see she had been very frightened. Well, Jesus called her, and she accepted Christ into her heart; then she got up, and left with a smile, and a joyful thank you. After spending some time in conversation, I believe she was going home, to her parents—home to seek Love and protection, home to seek a change for her life within Christ's church, the true home of us all.

Ken and I continued walking and found a hotel just outside Camp Pendleton Marine base. God so moved this young woman working in her office that she ran out to sign the cross. She wanted to help us any way possible by discounting hotel rates and finding a safe place for the cross, too. Ken and I were very tired;

still we sat up and prayed for the names of the people who had signed the cross. All the glory goes to God the Father forever, for the softening of hearts encountered along our journey thus far, knowing we had only begun. May HIS patience guide us as a nation to even greater national repentance!

The next morning we awoke with nothing at all to our names, wondering what to do for breakfast. Out of the blue, a business woman came running across the street and handed us a financial gift offering. She told me that the Holy Spirit had told her to give this amount to us. So we shared our testimony of faith together and were blessed by the Holy Spirit. It was about 7 am, and we were just about to enter the south entrance to the base, so we pulled the cross in front of a Denny's restaurant to get some breakfast. So without the offering we would have had to wait to eat. Once again this was just another example of God's provision given unto obedience.

A group of Marines from the base stood nearby, and asked about the cross I was carrying. I told them that we were walking to Oregon, lifting the name of Jesus on high walking to reminding people that we are a Christian nation, but that we have forgotten who we are! Our American sons prayed together with us, and signed the cross. These young Americans told me that the U.S. Military was deploying them to Iraq in a couple of weeks. God bless our troops! Let our people of this nation remember that our armed forces are in place in order to protect Christians and people from genocide and American harm all over the world, we are a peace force fighting for Justus for all, not just American standards and policies. It is not about oil Amen! Civilians have missed the mark due to their many fears. I constantly wondered what ever happened to the land of the brave.

Romans 13

Let every person become loyally subject to the governing (civil) authorities. For there is no authority except from God by His permission, His sanction, and those that exist do so by God's appointment. Therefore he who resists and sets himself up against the authorities resists what God has appointed and arranged in divine order. Moreover, those who resist will bring down judgment upon themselves receiving the penalty due them. For civil authorities are not a terror to people of good conduct, but to those of bad behavior. Would you have no dread of him who is in authority? Do what is right and you will receive his approval and commendation. For he is God's servant for your good. However, if you do wrong, you should dread him and be afraid, for he does not bear and wear the sword for nothing. He is God's servant to execute His wrath (punishment, vengeance) on the wrongdoer. Therefore one must be subject, not only to avoid God's wrath and escape punishment, but also as a matter of principle and for the sake of conscience. For this same reason you pay taxes, for the civil authorities are official servants under God, devoting themselves to attending to this very service. Render to all men their dues pay taxes to whom taxes are due, revenue to whom revenue is due, and respect to whom respect is due, and honor to whom honor is due.

Then we started walking toward the main gate of the base. As we approached, a young woman, standing her watch as gate sentry, began walking toward us with a stern expression. I wondered what she would ask me. This young private quickly answered that question; she asked, "Just where do you think you are going with that cross?" She showed very little reverence to our Lord Jesus. Barely 20 years old, her actions saddened me.

I then explained that we were walking the cross across the length of our state of California, border to border. She was enraged at the statement and said I could not walk through the base. It was then that I showed her my I.D. This young guard found I was retired Navy, with my full rights and privileges to enter the base, and walk the designated bike path. She began to get a little angry. Not at me, but at the thought of the cross entering what she proclaimed to be "her" base? I then tried to share with her that God places people in government in order to protect the Christians and civil populace. I began to share the rich Christian heritage of America, and the true meaning of the flag. The young woman became outraged just at the thought of what I was saying to her, and then she began yelling at me. "Get that cross off my base!!!"

I did not confront her any farther. The sergeant in charge heard the commotion and inquired about what was going on. She approached the sergeant. She expressed her outrage about the cross. The young sentry expressed her dislike of that the cross entering the base because it would "cause a riot." The sergeant asked me to move up toward the guard shack. Then the officer of the watch called the base duty officer to get permission to let Ken and I receive a day pass. The Duty officer then ordered the personnel at the gate watch to let us pass. He instructed us to stay to the bike path as we intended, and in we went, cross and all, to walk the 22 mile expanse of the base.

We first encountered a couple of seasoned Marine wives, their families serving for many years. They just stopped and stared at the cross without moving. I approached them and they began to worship Christ, breaking into tears. They were military wives with a lifetime of service and submission to their husbands in the United States Marines, God bless them for their sacrifice! I know that a military wife's job is not easy. In fact, wives of military men have to humble themselves in so many aspects of their lives. They must submit to their husbands and our country in order to help the men be a better servant of God, in the armed forces and to our nation. Church wives in general could learn much by these women's ability to submit. They also can learn by the word of God. God's word is the place where God blesses this is the very establishment of womanhood by their willing submission. This is where their real power is, in accordance to the word of God.

Genesis 2:18-25

The LORD God said, "It is not good for the man to be alone. I will make a helper suitable for him." Now the LORD God had formed out of the ground all the beasts of the field and all the birds of the air. He brought them to the man to see what he would name them; and whatever the man called each living creature, that was its name. So the man gave names to all the livestock, the birds of the air and all the beasts of the field. But for Adam no suitable helper was found. So the LORD God caused the man to fall into a deep sleep; and while he was sleeping, he took one of the man's ribs and closed up the place with flesh. Then the LORD God made a woman from the rib he had taken out of the man, and he brought her to the man. The man said, "This is now bone of my bones and flesh of my flesh; she shall be called 'woman,' for she was taken out of man.' For this reason a man will leave his father and mother and be united to his wife, and they will become one flesh. The man and his wife were both naked, and they felt no shame.

So the wives of these men and I prayed for restoration of faith, that it would strengthen our nation and that we would be a true Christian people, submitted to truth and the order of God. Also that the Kingdom of Heaven would truly open and deliver us from evil, let there be an open heaven over our nation, and that God would richly reign over us once again, so that we Christian Americans can truly be a light to all the people around us and in fact the world!

We agreed to submit to God, to speak boldly about our Lord our Savior at all times, as Paul taught us to do! Then we moved on further into the base, where we observed the Marines preparing for deployment to Iraq, and getting their equipment ready. The young men and women soldiers were seeking prayer and blessing at the foot of the cross. Others were lifting their Bibles up in their hands as we passed, if only to show that they were reading, and believing that God will protect them by their faith.

Much of the base was open land, and very quiet; so we prayed over it, as the Spirit would lead. We also prayed for all the hearts and souls of the people who had already witnessed the cross of our Lord's Passion, and especially for those who signed it. May God richly bless them in Jesus' mighty name! Moreover, the Lord led me to tell the Marines to read and learn about the prophecy found in the Bible, which foretold the battle in Iraq. For the purpose of this summary, I will just explain it by chapter & verse, revealing some of the mysteries through the Holy Spirit—the power of Trinitarian faith!

Jeremiah ch50 thru ch52

The word that Jehovah spoke concerning Babylon, concerning the land of the Chaldeans, by Jeremiah the prophet: Declare ye among the nations and publish, and set up a standard; publish, and conceal not: say, Babylon is taken, Bel is put to shame, Merodach is dismayed; her images are put to shame, her idols are dismayed. For out of the north there cometh up a nation against her, which shall make her land desolate, and none shall dwell therein: they are fled, they are gone, both man and beast. In those days, and in that time, saith Jehovah, the children of Israel shall come, they and the children of Judah together; they shall go on their way weeping, and shall seek Jehovah their God. They shall inquire concerning Zion with their faces thitherward, saying, Come ye, and join yourselves to Jehovah in an everlasting covenant that shall not be forgotten.

We see a lot of this prophecy in our news today about Iraq. Before entering into war with Iraq, America and by the Holy Spirit inspired leadership of our beloved President George W. Bush, Joint Chiefs of Staff and the House, worked to set and publish a standard of peace, which was not to be the case. We must not conceal, or forget the truth that America has taken Babylon, while our nation sat in front of our TV sets and bore witness to the fulfilling of this wonderful prophetic promise of God's mighty Hand. So for the love of you, mighty God, and Father, I seek thee O my God may America, and all the Christians around the world, rejoice that God's word is true and will not return void.

We all sat before our television sets and watched our American soldiers pull down the statues and idols of Babylon with ropes, as the gates of Babylon burned, just as God declared would happen through Jeremiah! Moreover, we all experienced the Iraqi warriors fleeing in every direction. Also, as the joint chiefs set the invasion in motion, we attacked mainly and first from the North. This is why reading the word and teaching it in our schools is so important—we would have true answers for our children, and all citizens of the America! We are one nation under God, though we have forgotten who we are. How did we become deceived so quickly?! 233 years is not long to have fallen so far from God's truth most of the falling in the past 30 years.

Jeremiah 51 v7

Babylon hath been a golden cup in Jehovah's hand that made all the earth drunken: the nations have drunk of her wine; therefore, the nations are mad. Babylon is suddenly fallen and destroyed: wail for her; take balm for her pain, if so be she may be healed. We would have healed Babylon, but she is not healed: forsake her, let us go every one into his own country, for her judgment reaches unto heaven, and is lifted up even to the skies. Jehovah hath brought forth our righteousness: come, and let us declare in Zion the work of Jehovah our God.

It was and is Babylon that intentionally started and fed the lie of humanistic faith, i.e., atheism! Yes, humanistic atheism is an idolatrous faith. You must have *faith in humanism* to believe it is true. The Bible teaches us this; we confess with our mouths that we are wise and yet we become utter fools, not seeing or accepting the truth of God's creation and design in all things, which GOD created.

Jeremiah 51 v11-14

Make sharp the arrows; hold firm the shields: Jehovah hath stirred up the spirit of the kings of the Medes; because his purpose is against Babylon, to destroy it: for it is the vengeance of Jehovah, the vengeance of his temple. Set up a standard against the walls of Babylon, make the watch strong, set the security guards, and prepare the ambushes, for Jehovah hath both purposed and done that which he spoke concerning the inhabitants of Babylon. "O" thou that dwells upon many waters, abundant in treasures, thine end is come, the measure of thy covetousness. The Lord of Heavens Armies has taken this vow and has sworn to it by his own name: Your cities will be filled with enemies, like fields swarming with locusts, and they will shout in triumph over you."

Remember the picture of Desert Storm, as we entered into HIS-story? People, today, are blaming the president for his part in fulfilling prophecy. We do not study scripture nor do we allow ourselves to understand it! What is the use of an educational system that does not educate about things of such importance?

Jeremiah 51 v24-27

Behold, I am against thee, O destroying mountain, saith Jehovah, which destroys all the earth; and I will stretch out my hand upon thee, and roll thee down from the rocks, and will make thee a burnt mountain. And they shall not take of thee a stone for a corner, or a stone for foundations; but thou shalt be desolate forever, saith Jehovah. Set ye up a standard in the land, blow the trumpet among the nations, prepare the nations against her, and call together against her the kingdoms of Ararat, Minni, and Ashkenaz: appoint a marshal against her; cause the horses to come up as the rough canker worm. Prepare against her the nations, the kings of the Medes, the governors thereof, and all the deputies thereof, and all the land of their dominion. And the land trembles and is in pain; for the purposes of Jehovah against Babylon do stand, to make the land of Babylon a desolation, without inhabitant. The mighty men of Babylon have forborne to fight, they remain in their strongholds; their might hath failed; they are become as women: her dwelling-places are set on fire; her bars are broken. One post shall run to meet another and one messenger to meet another, to show the king of Babylon that his city is taken on every quarter: and the passages are seized, and the reeds they have burned with fire and the men of war are affrighted.

We sat and watched on many news broadcasts as American forces crumbled Saddam Hussein's armies and decimated his communications. CNN for one told us of the dictator who was running and hiding, proclaiming the fall of the once mighty city in the "mother of all wars". What is still going on today just look around you in any direction? This is the fall of our American populace.

Jeremiah 51 v32

All the escape routes are blocked the marshes have been set aflame and the armies are in panic.

I believe this prophecy was fulfilled with the lighting of the oil fields in the first Gulf War. Again I would suggest praying about these passages, reading them over and asking the Lord for eyes to see! Think about who you are in Christ and whether you have allowed yourself to be separated from the truth of his word. Scripture warns of the subtlety of this, and the severe effect it can have: "O" wicked, perverse, and blind Generation! 2000+ years have passed and most Christians are still drinking spiritual milk, when truth is the strong meat as St Paul described. Our school systems have become incorporated by humanistic theology into its curriculum, and removed truth, history, and scripture from the shelves. How blind, and wrong it is to purposefully mislead our American children in schools today. I pray America repents, and returns to our roots of the Catholic Church and all that is Christ's Christian faith community. As I do stand for freedom of religion; however, to stand in truth, some reading is required. And in fallowing the fullness of truth all completed journeys end in the roots of the Catholic church and Judean values.

We were walking further into the base, which is approximately 23 miles from the main gate to San Clemente. Ken and I were about three quarters of the way through, when one of the Marine captains stopped me, thanking us for what he witnessed in his heart, the cross, and the flag. What a message!

The Birth of the American Flag: Betsy Ross made The American Flag at 239 Arch Street, Philadelphia, in 1776, out of fine, unused linen. It was adopted to be our flag by Congressional Resolution on June 14, 1777, as the national Standard of the United States. We were to recognize this flag as the Emblem of Liberty. This Liberty includes the ability to worship the Living God as per your faith, without persecution—not Liberty to do anything we want or to act without responsibility. Remember, sin is bondage; spiritual enslavement to all wickedness is bondage by becoming in slaved to the strongholds of darkness, the total opposite of freedom, which is liberty!

We as Americans, more often than not, confess Christ and serve God the Father of all creation, and his Son King Jesus. Our red stripe of the flag represents the blood of Christ, the blood of martyrs, and the blood of patriotic Americans who died for our country, and freedom in Christ Jesus. (Remember sin is bondage) Our white stripe represents purity, knowledge, and wisdom of the Holy Spirit. Our blue field represents the river of life, which is a cleansing supernatural river of life that gushed forth from the side of Christ Jesus our King the river which flows through the nation, and the whole of the world, holding our land together as brothers and sisters under the command of King Jesus to his body! The battle cry of our American ancestors was, "One King, King Jesus!" This battle cry resounded across the battlefields, all

CROSSWALK

across America and around the world found in time which is the truth found in history, as your founding fathers bravely gave their lives so that you could worship Jesus Christ here in America. Moreover, the literal reason for the stars is certainly not to count the number of states in the nation, but more symbolically, to be an ever-present reminder that we actually live in the Kingdom of Heaven. We are to live as citizens of light, to become a people that worship the true God. We Americans and all Christians around the world make up the body of Christ, a band of loving brothers and sisters. Are we not the land of the brave any longer? Haven't we become a land of false pride, and fearful of everything that surrounds us? Recall for a moment that God threw Satan out of heaven because of such pride!

The captain of the Marines did not have the true understanding of the flag as to what it represented, which we attribute to the degradation of our school system! This was caused by the systematic removal of the teaching, and heart felt understanding of the Gospel in our schools today. The respectful proclaiming of the Pledge of Allegiance is formative, in order to becoming a true Christian nation; it is not to worship a rectangular piece of cloth! It is a declaration before Jesus to strive to create a brotherhood of national singleness of heart, no matter what church you serve in. After we shared, we prayed that God, and Christ would open our eyes in this nation, and guide us forward unto the right path. This is why I was carrying the flag with the cross, to be a reminder of how far we have turned from God here in America. I joined the armed forces in 1998 and all of this would not have been necessary because our grandparents knew all of this and practiced it. We turned down our path of defilement and distillation somewhere in the 60s it became evident. Truly I am not saying that we have not achieved some fantastic social battles. Such as equality for all Races and women! No much of these victories are of God the father. All I am saying is the new path of my idea of freedom for each individual person is slavery to sin and bondage. The way free and the path of freedom and the true American way is the path of compassion, protection of all life and our American brothers and sisters living under the statues of our God given Constitution! I all manner being respectful to all person's around you. And try to meet and learn God and good from each other's past and personage. We all have a history and a story. We should share and listen to our stories and find the good in all that is found around you each day. Peace be with you.

Here is a prayer for America, per the Roman Catholic Daily Missal, and what the church truly believes about America:

"Before Thine eyes, O lord we bring our sins, and we compare them with the strips we have received If we examine the evil we have wrought, what we suffer is little, what we deserve is great. What we have committed is very grievous, what we have suffered is very slight. Surly we feel the punishment of sin, yet withdraw not from the obstinacy of sinning? Under Thy lash our inconstancy is visited, but our sinfulness is not changed. Our suffering soul is tormented, but our neck is not bent. Our life groans under sorrow, yet amends not in deed. If Thou spare us, we correct not our ways; if Thou punish, we cannot endure it. In time of correction we confess our wrong doing after Thy visitation we forget that we have wept. If Thou stretches forth thy hand, we promise amendment; if thou strikest, we cry out for mercy; If Thou sparest, we again provoke thee to strike. Here we are before Thy, O Lord confessedly guilty; we know that unless Thou pardon we shall deservedly perish. Grant then O' almighty Father, without our deserving it, the pardon we ask. Thou who has madest out of nothing those who ask Thee; Through Christ our Lord. Deal not with us, O Lord, according to our sin's neither reward us according to our iniquities.

Let Us Pray: O' God Who by sin art offended and by penance pacified, mercifully regard the prayers of Thy suppliant people, and turn away the scourges of Thy wrath, which we deserve for our sins. Through Christ our Lord. Amen!"

Ken and I once again began walking and praying these prayers over the land's deception, which is being systematically implanted, in order to turn us from the truth of God.

It was about 4pm when we reached the other side of the base and entered into the San Onofre state beach camp-ground as we walked. Many people were in their motor homes and tents lining the side of the parking lot. We had entered a place of mixed emotion, of the surrounding public. Again, many people began to feel persecution just at the sight of the cross. What really reached into my heart were the babies, and toddlers who extended & stretched their little arms out to our Lord's Passion, this Passion for our hearts, which he accepted. He embraced the cross for our salvation.

We could see their little spirits bearing witness to the love of Christ; they were too young yet still unable to talk, however, their little faces spoke volumes. Sadly their 20 to 25 year old parents would pull them back, as if to say, you want nothing of what that man has to offer! You could see the pain in the faces of the deprived children. It broke my heart because all we could do was pray for their deliverance in Christ, O Lord that you would change the hearts of man and women so that their parents' eyes would be open, that once again we the people can start to fight the good fight of faith here in Southern California. And across our land in unity!

Catholic, Orthodox, Jewish, Lutheran, Methodist, Protestant, Anglican, Episcopal and non-denominational, all are Christian baptized children of God. In spite of our divisions, our children still know the truth. The children wanted prayer, and to sign and live the way of the holy cross; and so it was in many cases we witnessed while walking the cross, while the adults came to hear the message of salvation and what the Holy Spirit was saying. Hundreds of us in times 1000's! We all joined hands, and began to pray,

"Father, please forgive us for turning from You, Holy Lord, and Your truth, of your Son Jesus that he reigns over all the earth, and that he sets the order over all things and especially over the family. We as fathers want to act in your likeness. You are forever calling us to become fathers who are willing to love their wives as Jesus Loves his Church, to lead with love and kindness, to have and possess forgiving hearts. Teach us to live a Christian-representative life, to remember that our wives are a crown to our heads, goodness to our bones, and that God fearing wives willingly surrender and submit to their loving husbands. God, teach us to repent of our own will, and to continually seek Your Will for our lives. We ask Thee O' Lord to guide and watch over our families; Show us how to become good Stewards of the Kingdom. Teach us O' Lord that our children are truly a gift from you, and actually belong to God himself. Teach us to raise our children in the fullness and wonderful love and knowledge of our Lord and Savior! We want to be true Fathers and mothers over our families. We are tired of the lies and deception of Satan. Here in America, we stand for right action in Christ and we pray that we would truly repent and turn back to you dear Father God, as you planned it from the beginning. It starts with me, a poor sinner. Christ Jesus, be our light.

We pray that we will serve You Holy Father God, and moreover, that we will speak boldly our individual confession of faith in Christ at all times.

All of us prayed this prayer, for thousands of families as Ken and I walked through southern California. Almost every time they came to pray with us, they would say that they had forgotten how to pray. Dear merciful father deliver us from our slumber!

So many Americans answered that they never gave thought about the order of God over their families. Therefore, I reminded them that is why we need to be in fellowship in a good, biblical, Spirit-filled Church, even more important, is that we read the word of God to our families every day! Just turn off the TV, read a little, and you will find out just how wonderful that is for your family. I present to you the only instruction book to all of life's questions and problems, because as fathers and mothers our first pastoral calling is to minister over our families! Moreover that one day either in this life or the next, God the righteous Judge will Judge us on how we treated our families and children, which he gave to us in Jesus. Let us be Christ-like to our families. Men and Fathers, remember we are Love to our families; to lead by loving them, just as Christ leads us by his true and perfect Love, and as God is Our Father in Heaven, and Holy is his name.

8

Entering Capistrano Beach

We stayed at a little hotel modeled after the Hindu culture, obviously used as a brothel by the adult movies that were in the dresser drawers. However, we began to worship in our room and prayed against the wicked spirits of fornication and all types of deception over that area. The Holy Spirit gave us the wisdom and knowledge to discern the spirits that were working overtime, to blind and bind us! Weapons formed by the tempter to lead us into sin would block us from the Holy Spirit's Power.

You see, God is in control, and what is happening all around us will occur, whether we choose to see the war going on or not. The war is not with God, but rather, over our souls and our human hearts. One way to measure this is to ask yourself, do you truly love God, no matter what transpires in life? It is all a great test of your hearts; whether or not you truly love Him. It is all about personal relationship, and if we believe His word and trust in his Church!

Ask yourself, why you are sick? While there may be a number of reasons, one source could be un-forgiveness. The Gospel teaches us that God healed us of all sickness by the lashing of Christ; Our Father heals us by God's skin ripping off from His Body. Satan is here to kill, steal and destroy your life. God healed you only if you believe in the life of Christ and that you continue to fight the good fight of faith. Another reason may be for God's Will; every time God uses our sickness, healing or sufferings, it is to glorify the

Son, who suffered and died for us. This is definitely a bitter lesson to be received through Christ's Church. The role sickness plays in our lives is one to be explored. And the hardest of all is our handy capped the savvier the problem the harder to understand the plan of God? It is however a wonderful place to pray for healing with each other, and to receive the outcome with great compassion

However, it is safe to say that in order to receive God's promises, we must live according to God's plan. How are you ever going to receive if you are not a part of Christ's Church, (which is the sanctified body of Christ), who believes and practices obedience by becoming a functional disciple of a local Trinity-teaching Community of Church believers? Have we failed to put God first in our lives, pursuing worldliness? The reason these demons are here in the first place is that we have let them in by our own choices. Some of these choices include weakening of the understanding our faith, participating in syncretic beliefs (theology + mythology), such as horoscopes, "Christian" yoga, and other popular pagan activities, or pantheism, that all religions lead to God. And, let's not be ignorant to think that all monotheistic faiths are equal: Islam is one of Christianity's most fearsome enemies! Remember *Jeremiah 50 to 52?*

Yes, it is hard to stop sinning. The demons are getting stronger since we've laid down our "armor", and forgotten how to fight! Alternatively, perhaps we just quit because it is too hard for the young Christians, and too easy to walk the "wide path." In physical warfare, it's called treason, punishable by death!

Treason to God's kingdom is also punishable by death. Have we forgotten the seven deadly sins? Pride, Covetousness, Lust, Anger, Gluttony, Envy. Now think about sickness' seemingly coming from nowhere. Remember the word of God teaches that He is the righteous judge, that He judges all sin right now, today, not only when you leave this world. Now ask again, why am I sick?—speaking to your conscience. All sickness is not only of the body, but also first rooting itself in the mind; it is sickness caused by these demons that will lead to natural or physical illness. As warriors for Christ, we need to take care of ourselves, body, heart, mind and spirit! So, get into Church to find the answers for your life! This will allow us alleviate our communal and national sin, to become the nation under God as God intended us to be, once again or perhaps, truly for the first time.

Later on that night in the hotel, I had a dream. God brought me into the spirit world, which looked something like a supernatural courtroom, filled with angelic beings standing around a center table. All the room shone of finely polished marble. Then a man in a suit stood next to me, chanting something in my ear, but whatever it was somehow was blocked. He then fell to the ground, and I fell over him, grasped his chest, and prayed franticly: "the blood of Jesus compels you." I repeated said this, holding firm to his heart. Then I saw his black heart, with thick red veins, trying to keep beating. Just then, the heart stopped, and I continued praying! Then his mouth opened, and hot, thick, black smoke began bellowing from his mouth, as he died. When I awakened, I continued in prayer for some time after that, and into the next morning!

When I got up, I noticed Ken was speaking to a man in his mid 40's outside the room. I got dressed, and went to find out what was happening. It turns out the man lost his family due to his own dealings with drugs. The whole drug culture led him ultimately into relationships with other women. Fornication is such a devastating sin to marriage, and it led the wife into the same sin with the intention of paying back the injustice. After hearing of his situation, I asked if he had ever known Jesus. He told us that as a young boy he attended Catholic Church but fell away as a youth. He began to weep because of the pain and disillusionment of his life choices. In his tears, he said that there could be no forgiveness for him, and no relief for the pain he was experiencing. The weight of sin and the condemnation of Satan were so overwhelming. In spite of this, he somehow wanted his family back, and was willing to pray to God for a second chance.

God opened my heart to share with him that I was Catholic and I did not know how it would turn out. However, I know who does, and that his name was above all, both in heaven and on earth, that being Jesus Christ, Son of God! Then I asked if he would like to sit with me, and we would study the word of God in the hotel room in order to learn more about our Lord and the Kingdom of heaven together. Then the Holy Spirit witnessed to his heart, and hope began to enter into this man's life. We sat down in a couple of chairs around a small table and opened the Bible together.

John ch3 v16

For God so loved the world that he gave his only begotten Son, that whosoever believeth on him should not perish, but have eternal life.

After I read this scripture to him, tears of Deliverance from his condemnation were pouring out his eyes and down his face. He began to say "I can't be forgiven!" over and over, and I rebuked the demons over him by the Archangel Michael, and by the Kingship of Lord Jesus. Then, Ken and I began to softly plead the Blood of Jesus over him, and he gained control. Although he was still weeping and weak, I began to read and share more about our Lord, his power and willingness to forgive. Moreover, we shared the Love of Christ just a little more.

John ch7 v37-38

Now on the last day, the great day of the feast, Jesus stood and cried, saying, if any man thirst, let him come unto me and drink. He that believeth on me, as the scripture hath said, from within him shall flow rivers of living water.

We all then sat and read the message of salvation and the testimony of Jesus Christ. As we had just read that Jesus was standing there crying before the people, surely he was crying because of his understanding of the weakness of our flesh. He personally understands the torment and the painful deception of Satan's lies into our lives. This is the reason Christ became human, to bring a future and a hope to fallen man. We stayed in the book of John for a while. Then we shared in the first letter of John the apostle.

First John 01: v5-7

And this is the message, which we have heard from him and announce unto you, that God is light, and in him is no darkness at all. If we say that we have fellowship with him and walk in the darkness, we lie, and do not have the truth: but if we walk in the light, as he is in the light, we have fellowship one with another, and the blood of Jesus his Son cleanses us from all sin. If we say that we have no sin, we deceive ourselves, and the truth is not in us. If we confess our sins, he is faithful and righteous to forgive us our sins, and to cleanse us from all unrighteousness.

We then began to share testimony of my sinful nature, all that I was delivered from, and how the love and knowledge of God entered my life. We shared about God as light and that God is truth and love. We shared about living a life in Christ, which reunites us with the Father and that through the Son we can stand strong by our relationship of the Holy Spirit!

Stand strong is what He asked us to do. Then the Spirit had me share this scripture. So precious is the word of God to our lives!

First John 3 v1-17

The Father has loved us so much! He loved us so much that He called us His children. We really are his children. However, the people in the world do not understand that we are God's children, because they have not known him. Dear friends, now we are children of God. God has not yet shown us what we will be in the future. However, we know that when Christ comes again, we will be like him. We will see him as he really is. Christ is pure. Moreover, every person who has this hope in Christ keeps himself pure like Christ. When a person sins, he breaks God's law. Yes, sinning is the same as living against God's law. You know that Christ came to take away sins. There is no sin in Christ. The person who lives in Christ does not go on sinning. If he goes on sinning, he has never really understood Christ and has never known him Dear children; do not let any person lead you the wrong way. Christ is righteous. To be like Christ, a person must do what is right. The devil has been sinning since the beginning. Anyone who continues to sin belongs to the devil. The Son of God came for this purpose: to destroy the devils work. When God makes someone his child, that person does not go on sinning. The new life God gave that person stays in him. Therefore, he is not able to go on sinning, because he has become a child of God. So, we can see who God's children are, and whose children are of the devil. Those who do not do what is right are not children of God. In addition, no one who fails to love his brother is a child of God.

So I asked him if he was ready to receive Christ into his life and to overcome evil by receiving Jesus into his heart? He said yes and we all prayed together.

Dear God, I know that sin has separated this man from you. Therefore, I thank you that you sent your Son Jesus Christ to die in our place, therefore, I ask Jesus Christ to deliver this man from all deception, because Christ has nailed all our sins to his passion on the cross, and by his shed blood we are forgiven, if we will only believe in the name of Jesus. He said he did believe. And so Father we ask in the name of your Son Jesus that You will receive this man into your kingdom, and that his name be written in the Lamb's book of life. Forgive our sins and come into this man's life, please direct his life. I thank you for giving us eternal life in Jesus the Christ Amen.

At that moment his tears changed! Now tears of forgiveness began to flow down his face. We could witness the pain of sin being lifted off of him in the presence of the Holy Spirit which had filled the room. That morning was powerful. Then, the Holy Spirit led me to read this chapter and verse of the word of God in intercession for this man

First John ch1 v 9-14

Someone says, "I am in the light." However, if he hates his brother, he is still in the darkness. Whoever loves his brother lives in the light, and there is nothing in him that will cause him to do wrong. But whoever hates his brother is in darkness. He lives in darkness and does not know where he is going. The darkness has made him blind.

I write to you, dear children, because God has forgiven your sins through Christ. I write to you, fathers, because you know the One who existed from the beginning. I write to you, young men, because you have defeated the Evil One.

I write to you, children, because you know the Father. I write to you, fathers, because you know the One who existed from the beginning. I write to you, young men, because you are strong; the word of God lives in you, and you have defeated the Evil One. Do not love the world or the things in the world. If anyone loves the world, the love of the Father is not in him. These are the evil things in the world: wanting things to please our sinful selves, wanting the sinful things we see, being too proud of the things we have. However, none of those things comes from the Father. All of them come from the world. The world is passing away. In addition, everything that people want in the world is passing away. However, the person who does what God wants lives forever.

Now I said, to become a complete creation in Christ, you must return to his Church; surrender to God's will and become discipled into the service of Christ's family. By his Church, I felt, a return to the Catholic faith—his first love—was best! The way to begin restoring his family was to sell himself out to the teachings of Christ, show them in his life, and persevere in this. We shared that all things are possible in Christ! Seek ye first the Kingdom, and then God will increase all these things unto you!

Because he was seeking his family back, I showed him what was required of the family according to God's standards.

Wives and Husbands

Be willing to obey each other, Do this because you respect Christ. Wives, be under the authority of your husbands, as of the Lord. The husband is the head of the wife, as Christ is the head of the Church. The Church is Christ's body; Christ is the Savior of the body. The Church is under the authority of Christ. Therefore, it is the same with you wives. You should be under the authority of your husbands in everything. Husbands, love your wives as Christ loved the Church. Christ died for the Church to make it belong to God. Christ used His word to make the Church clean by washing it with water. Christ died so that he could give the Church to himself like a bride in all her beauty. He died so that the Church could be pure and without fault, with no evil or sin or any other wrong thing in it. Husbands should love their wives in the same way. They should love their wives as they love their own bodies. The man who loves his wife loves himself. No person ever hates his own body, but feeds and takes care of it. That is what Christ does for the Church, because we are parts of his body. The Scripture says, "So a man will leave his father and mother and be united with his wife. And the two will become one flesh." This mystery is very important. I am talking about Christ and the Church. Each one of you must love his wife as he loves himself. In addition, a wife must respect her husband.

Then lifting my eyes to meet his, I asked him what He was going to do the rest of the day? He had no plans. I said you should go and submit to a good spirit filled Church. Learn to die in Christ, and become the husband that St Paul teaches us here in Ephesians. Moreover, that the Bible is the instruction booklet for life. As Catholics we are presented with the Daily missal, the

Catechist, and the Magnificat to help guide us in understanding the teaching, so as not to get off track. He said he was baptized a catholic and his mother was trying to call him back to the church for many years. He was going to her to find a Church that would help him that day! Then he got up, turned his face to me and asked, appearing a little dumbfounded, peering deep into my eyes and asking, "Why would you spend so much time with someone you never met?"

Waiting a moment in quiet contemplation to the question poised to me, I then replied, "Because you, sir, are precious in the sight of our Father. And God will bound over the mountains for the one that has lost his way! That is why I am walking with our cross." "Our cross?" he asked. Know that Jesus Christ is God, and He had no need to have his flesh torn from his body. Or slathered to be hung on a cross! It was for our sins instead, that He willingly underwent that scourging. It was not for Himself that He hung on the cross but for payment of our sins, to justify us, to be a witness of His love and faithfulness, and to teach us how we are to live and submit to Christian living, if we only ask Him! He will send the helper the Holy Spirit to reside in our heart!

Know to enter into eternal life in Christ we have to know it is really our Cross. Jesus is the narrow gate of Salvation! I said, God bless you, that Ken and I must start walking again, we have far to go, and we departed from there.

We packed up the cart and headed up the PCH to the Sugar Shack café for breakfast. It was just up the street. The people at the restaurant were astonished at the big cross, as we pulled into the parking lot. We went inside and sat at a table with a window over looking the cross. Then the wait staff asked us what we were doing.

I humbly replied we were walking in obedience to the call of our Lord Jesus, walking the cross from Tijuana to the Oregon border. The looks on their faces were wonderful and warm and their faces alone were worth everything we were to endure, they were very gracious to us. God was changing my heart as well. I was starting to Love people as never before. I could only begin to love people as Jesus does. The Spirit showed me that it is mostly the little things that really excite our Lord, such as the flush glow of happiness on a woman's joyful face of hope, the radiance of the heart of a child, the hope of the future found in the eyes of our youth, and the strength of faith found in the faces of men!

As we waited for our order, we peered out at this huge cross through heavy paned glass windows.

We sat and watched as the cross bore witness to itself, drawing a crowd. We could all feel the mixed emotion of the different people by the expressions on their faces. Many were amazed as they were literally held captive by all the names signed on the Cross. Still others were angry and even brought to curse the witness of just looking at it. The cross brings conviction to some people; however, all were touched by the grace of Christ and walked away wondering.

Personally speaking, I will never forget the faces of everyone in the café as we were all sitting and watching Christ witness of himself his passion! It was really exciting! No one spoke a word, just the Power of the cross and the living witness of the Holy Spirit, pronouncing HIS glory, HIS alone, to all of our hearts.

The Lesson was learned. After that, I often walked away from the cross and cart. It was always a touching experience letting go of myself; just to watch God at work in people's lives. I was looking down at the people's faces and wondered how many lives would be touched over the miles ahead. Sitting there, I silently watched His passion and truth at work within the minds, hearts and Spirits of His on looking public. This witnessed to my heart so deeply, and gave new light to Ken and myself. I could not help but think to myself about what a wonderful gift Christ had called me to share with Him as we walked, and shared His grace, and Love in His earthly kingdom. It is truly awesome to be Catholic and to live a life in Christ!

We then walked through the rest of Capistrano Beach. Many passers by would honk and yell out in the joy of this sight. Yet, too, many were angry and spoke profanity against the witness of the cross. So many people were saying, "Get a job and stop convicting us!" as if I am at fault for them feeling convicted of sin. That is how far we have fallen in America today. Satan is the one that condemns us in our sin; Jesus sets us free. To true freedom in deed God bless America.

O my Lord and God, I cried out, give us eyes to see and ears to hear! Please deliver us from this wickedness and blind deception!

Some scriptures on conviction

Romans ch7 v7-13

You might think that I am saying that sin and the law is the same thing. That is not true. However, the law was the only way I could learn what sin meant. I would never have known what it means to want something wrong if the law had not said, "You must not want to take your neighbors things." And sin found a way to use that command and cause me to want every kind of wrong thing. Therefore, sin came to me because of that command. However, without the law, sin has no power. I was alive without the law before I knew the law. However, when the law's command came to me, then sin began to live. And I died because of sin. The command was meant to bring life, but for me that command brought death. Sin found a way to fool me by using the command. Sin used the command to make me die.

So, the law is holy, and the command is holy, right, and good. Does this mean that something that is good brought death to me? No! Sin used something that is good to bring death to me. This happened so that I could see what sin is really like. The command was used to show that sin is something very evil.

Just remember, God is always there to encourage us—with miracles, signs, and wonders—by all that wanted a word from God, ranging from Salvation to marriages. Every mile they approached us with prayer requests. We do serve an awesome God!

We left Capistrano and entered Dana Point. We walked along the oceanfront when we met up with a brother in Christ. He was so excited to see and hear what we were doing that he started ministering to us. The word he imparted to us spoke of the end of times, and it was inspiring, as it bore witness to our spirit. The following is what he spoke.

Revelation 14 v14 The Earth Is Harvested

I looked and there before me was a white cloud. Sitting on the white cloud was One who looked like a Son of Man. He had a gold crown on his head and a sharp sickle in his hand.

Then another angel came out of the temple. This angel called to the One who was sitting on the cloud, "Take your sickle, and gather from the earth. The time to harvest has come. The fruit of the earth is ripe." So the One that was sitting on the cloud swung his sickle over the earth. And the earth was harvested.

And this man shared with us that the Spirit showed him in a dream some time before in the desert that this end time harvest is upon us and we were just a couple of gatherers preparing the way of the harvest of the Church!

Then another angel came out of the temple in heaven. This angel also had a sharp sickle. Then another angel came from the altar. This angel has power over the fire. This angel called to the angel with the sharp sickle. He said, "Take your sharp sickle and gather the, bunches of grapes from the earths vine. The earth's grapes are ripe." The angel swung his sickle over the earth. He gathered the earth's grapes and threw them into the great winepress of God's anger. The grapes were crushed in the winepress outside the city. And blood flowed out of the winepress. It rose as high as the heads of the horses for a distance of 200 miles.

This revelation empowered us to walk 1100 miles, even if only one person was saved from the terror of this prophecy, or could come to understand the teachings of prophecies. Like the three days of darkness, and the lighting of the holy candle in order to survive the days of Christ's judgment and wrath, it would be worth all the walking. I am not a false prophet; I do not know the exact time—it can be tomorrow or ten thousand tomorrows from today—I do not know. This is a real warning for all times.

So stand in your own and other's defense by reading your Bibles and outfitting yourselves in prayer, outfitted with the full armor of God, and prepared for the just battle, because the day of our Lord is at hand! There was much more, but that was the main topic discussed. We prayed for all the Christians around the world, over our nation, and Californians and especially that the Church would awaken to plainly see the times and seasons that are upon us today.

No one knows the day or the hour, but only the season. It might be tomorrow, but it could be 100 years from now. But it will come, and God and His Church are calling us to be ready every day by taking right action.

He could come for any of us individually on the day of our death. At the day of one's death, their whole life seems like it was just yesterday. It is always yesterday when one is dying. "Yesterday I did that!" Our Lord may not come in our lifetime yet when we pass from this life to the next we best be ready with Holiness, piety, and true faith in Jesus—his Son—the narrow gate!

Study His Word and live the life that is required! Yet living a full life in Christ is fun actually. If we could come together, in singleness of heart and love, this walk would not have been necessary and all the people would actually be rejoicing. I am as one crying out in the wilderness! Make way the Kingdom of Heaven for the Day of our Lord has come. Stand still and listen to your hearts, America, because it is in the stillness of the heart that God speaks to us. Satan and his devils speak lying slanders in our ears!

God our Father is calling us to himself saying "Dear children, today I am calling you to open yourselves to God the Father for as much as you open yourselves to the Father the more he can pour out his Holy Spirit into your lives and you will bear the fruits thereof." Do not set your sights on the things of this world be rather on the truth of heaven. Seek first the Kingdom of Heaven then God the Creator of all things will be able to use you to fulfill his purposes. God only requires us to be willing souls, for Him to Live His Life in our bodies, or at least for us to be His children.

Then we crossed PCH and entered into Doheny State Beach. It was packed with summer vacationers, with locals as well as people from all over the U.S. We walked by the first camp site and asked if they would like to sign the cross? A harsh, "No!" was the response, as well as some stern looks.

Again my heart was grieved, just after the conversation we had just shared. We saw that children of all age groups were running from the beaches and campsites, to ask us what the cross was about. We shared with them about what we were doing, and all the children wanted to sign, and become a part of the blessedness of the cross of our Savior. Note how the little children are the first to respond. It is the children which we are to be come like; their running with such a pure faith. No wonder Jesus loves the little children. After all had signed, we gathered children and parents into a large group and started to pray.

Blessed are the children for they are like the Kingdom of heaven. Moreover, we asked that the Father of all creation would protect and keep them from temptation. We especially prayed that the young boys would save themselves for fatherhood, in order to show themselves Holy vessels of honor before our Lord our Christ and King.

We also asked that God would keep them in the Church, to stir up the gifts within each one, as He has purposed in his heart. For we are not our own, but bought with a price! Fathers and mothers gathered around to see what was happening and to hear the spoken word of God. Blessed are the true worshippers. May all the Fathers always remember to love their wives as Jesus Loves us, "all of HIS sanctified bride". Wives remember that your true power lies in your submission to your husbands. Let yours and their hearts become one, constantly focused on raising the children in the full loving knowledge of our Lord. Then we began laying hands upon each child's head. We reminded them that each one is special in the Sight of God, and it is Him who we are to serve with all of our hearts. Many of the parents promised to serve the Lord Jesus and to raise their Families in the Light of the Kingdom of Heaven! Even in the darkest of times, the light will always shine forth, and the truth will lead us to repentance.

Many said they never heard anyone pray like that, ever! I reminded them it is only because we have forgotten who we are. Moreover, we shared with them that it was the Father's duty to read scriptures to the family and lead his family into the Kingdom.

For all the single moms, we prayed that Jesus would be their Husband, that they would rest in HIM, and that he would send the Holy Spirit to teach their children. The Lord Jesus is the husband and Loving Father to us all.

Then we prayed for those who were seeking a Godly Husband to lead their families. We asked God, if it was His Will, that He would prepare the woman for a God-fearing, loving husband, and that he would Love them as Jesus Loves his Church. We also prayed that there would be a hedge of protection placed around their lives. Blessed be the little children for the Kingdom of God belongs to such as these. Then we prayed with them and were blessed with literally thousands of children's smiles that day in Jesus' mighty name! I am so blessed. Nothing is more tender or loving than the heart of a child, so pure, so kind, and so gentle.

After that, every hundred feet or so, a new group would come up seeking prayer. We were having Church right there in Doheny Beach State Park. About half way through, Norm and Scott, very close friends of mine from California Victory Church, came to witness what the Lord was doing!

It was at that moment when a group of young men were screaming and cursing; we could hear it rising over the park as they were preparing to fight. The group gathered on a walking overpass, which crossed over our heads and over the I; 5 freeways when I shouted back up at them. What are you doing cursing, and yelling like that young men? Come up here and make us, they yelled down at me!

Therefore, I heard the Spirit tell me to go up there, and so I did. I was walking up the stairs to where they were. They seemed a little shocked that I took them up on their offer. When I was just about there, one of them shouted, "Why don't you just leave, this is none of your business." I replied to the youths, "See all the people down there, families having a good time, enjoying their days off before returning to work? You boys want to strike fear into everyone." I then reminded them of the young men and women that were currently giving their lives for peace and freedom to serve Christ in America. That I had served for eighteen a half years myself, I promised them that it was not so that hoodlums could go around scaring all of the children of heaven. Then I said, "See the Cross down there and all the children looking up at you? Obviously, your lives are broken so what do you really want those children and people to think about you?"

They began to listen and quiet down. Therefore, I asked what it was all about anyway. The story was horrific. One of the boys said that an intruder kidnapped one of his sisters and raped her one night. Coming from praying for families and children and literally floating in the spirit to the disgust of the gutter, I could not comprehend the anger of such an event.

Right then the Holy Spirit had me ask if any one of them had any real proof of the persons actually involved in this act. As it turned out, it was only the anger of this event and no one had any proof of personal involvement, and the situation solved itself. I explained to the young people that when we do things like this in anger and violence, as many gangs do, this is just some of the things Satan wants to have happen, because he wants to kill you.

In addition, I went as far as to say that, as of today we must bring an end to gangs and the valance caused it was time to be over! We adults and citizens of the United States will come after all of you and you will not stand! We will stop all of the raping of our children! We will not tolerate this behavior any longer! Then I told them to pass the word that I am not kidding. The military is in place to protect the Christians and all citizens of America and if you do not stop, you will be punished by men with real guns.

I told them that I have a 7 million-member family of military brothers and sisters that will stop them! They agreed with me. I said that violence and anger are the devil's play ground. Moreover, I asked that the Holy Spirit change these young hearts! They wanted out of the deception. Therefore, I shared the love of Jesus and all of us joined hands and said the sinner's prayer. I walked back to the cross and the violence ended at that minute. Praise God!

We started pushing on through the park. So many people were amazed at how easy it was to love in the Holy Spirit, which Jesus taught us to do. They were amazed at how this actually worked and it radically changed the situation. Hundreds of people engulfed us, seeking peace, deliverance, prayer, and order in the family. By the time we passed through the park, I was in shock to see the number of hurting Christians here in America today! I know that Christ is cleaning up his Bride and the righteous judgment of God is true but more than this, He is patient. Moreover, His mercy endures forever, but it is HIS judgment that leads his children to repentance. In other words, God is judging the Church so that we might repent and let God prepare us for the return of our Lord Jesus. Amen!

Just then my brother called me. He had come down and got us a great room at the Holiday Inn Express, in San Juan Capistrano beach. Our feet were sore, so the timing was impeccable! My Brother and Norm, Scott, from our church, and I were fellowshipping over dinner and we had a wonderful time! We ate at a little restaurant called the Rib Place on PCH, and we were so hungry. It tasted great!

The fellowship and our dinner of ribs, salad and corn bread were the greatest. God, it is all about you, thank you Lord all over again! I never want to stop singing Your praises; Blessed are You my Lord; Praise you for such a wonderful brother, and friends, and all the souls that we encountered that day. Surely I am not one that I should boast, for I am just a mortal man, a sinner and I fall and make mistakes. So again I had to just stop, and thank you, Lord, for every name on the cross. Please richly receive them into your Kingdom, and May the Spirit of the Lord descend upon each life. May the old dream dreams, and the young prophecy in your precious name! Moreover, I prayed He would lead each one into the Church or Parish He would have each of them serve.

Then, a bigger question was nagging me. What do we do for them, as our Churches of today have so much confusion due to doctrinal differences? O Lord, I do not know where to refer the people to best serve You because I am only a sailor, the very least of your servants.

9

Dana Point

Once we entered Dana Point, we came by a Starbucks coffee shop across the street. The Holy Spirit wanted me to go over there and I, with all wonder, thought maybe God was going to bless me with some coffee, since it was morning anyway. Being a Navy man, well I do enjoy my coffee, yes probably too much. Ken and I left the cross at the Salt Creek Street light and went to enjoy a good cup. However once I walked into the coffee shop, I noticed that the place was full of people standing in lines, so I asked Ken to get us the coffee. He ordered the Vinte caramel frappuccino and I ordered as I always do the Vinte mild coffee black. I was walking to the restroom when I came across a young Haitian woman with that famous Haitian candor, wearing a full dress with her beautiful braided long black hair sticking out from her hat. As she was staring out the window, somehow I could sense great fear in the young woman. I asked her, "How are you this morning?" Slowly we began a light conversation between us. I knew immediately that she was the reason we were to enter Starbucks, not because of coffee!

No this woman was truly hurting. In the Navy, I had been in Haiti many times, and have seen this fear in their people. When people are practicing Voo-doo or any type of black magic of any type in their lives, it can bring great pain and suffering through frightening false visions and internal paranoia!

I asked if something was bothering her. She replied, "That cross, across the street, that huge cross! It is so big! Why is it there? They are trying to kill me," she said. I let that last comment pass for the moment. Then I shared with her that Ken and I were carrying the cross to the Oregon border. She asked why we would do such a thing! I told her, to be a witness of Jesus, our Reigning Lord and King!

She began to calm herself and asked many questions. She shared with us that she is a Christian, "outside" of Christ's Church and she felt she was the last Christian on earth. It turns out that it was quite the opposite of what she said. She had been practicing other religions, rituals that released Satan's demon armies to destroy her and our Christian Land. Seeking idols opens doors for Satan's powers and princely world to enter into our land and homes. It is when the people are seeking God that the lands are blessed, I explained to her!

Isaiah 57

The good men perish; the godly die before their time and no one seems to care or wonder why. No one seems to realize that God is taking him or her away from evil days ahead. For the godly that die shall rest in peace. But you come here, you witches' sons, you offspring of adulterers and harlots! Who is it you mock, making faces and sticking out your tongues. You children of sinners and liars! You worship your idols with great zeal beneath the shade of every tree and slay your children as human sacrifices down in the valleys, under overhanging rocks.

Sacrificing babies is this exactly it is not choice it is pagan sacrificing to the God of their own Lust! Again as I read this portion of scripture, it rings out about abortion in our own country and time. This is part of the reason I am praying for God's forgiveness and say that we are an adulterous people in America today; let's read on.

Your gods are the smooth stones in the valleys. You worship them, and they, not I, are your inheritance. Does all this make me happy? You have committed adultery on the tops of the mountains, for you worship idols there, deserting me. Behind closed doors, you set your idols up and worship someone other than me. This is adultery, for you are giving these idols your love instead of loving me. You have taken pleasant incense and perfume to Moloch as your gift. You have traveled far, even to hell itself, to find new gods to love. You grew weary in your search, but you never gave up. You strengthened yourself and went on. Why were you more afraid of them than of me. How is it that you gave not even a second thought to me? Is it because I have been too gentle that you have no fear of me? Then there is your "righteousness" and your "good works", none of which will save you. We shall see if the whole collection of your idols can help you when you cry to them to save you! They are so weak that the wind can carry them off! A breath can puff them away. However, he who trusts in me shall possess the land and inherit my holy mountain. I will say, rebuild the road! Clear away the rocks and stones. Prepare a glorious highway for my peoples return from captivity. The high and lofty One who inhabits eternity, the Holy One, says this: I live in that High and Holy Place where those with contrite, humble spirits dwell; and I refresh the humble and give new courage to those with repentant hearts. For I will not fight against you forever or always show my wrath; if I did, all humanity would perish the very souls that I have made. I was angry and smote these greedy men. However, they went right on sinning, doing everything their evil hearts desired. I have seen what they do, but I will heal them anyway! I will lead them and comfort them, helping them to mourn and to confess their sins. Peace, peace to them, both near and far, for I will heal them all. But those who still reject me are like the restless sea, which is never still, but always churns up mire and dirt. There is no peace, says my God, for them!

Remember the prayer for America?

This passage blessed her heart, the entire crowd around us was listening to the teaching of Isaiah, and they were all shining by the Holy Spirit as they stood in line for coffee.

Then a story about a very scary past-life, full of gang violence and old boyfriends trying to kill her came out, and how the spirit world was trying to destroyer her. I knew that Voo-doo was the problem. Voo-doo is witchcraft. I just calmly asked if she wanted to be free from this bondage.

"Yes, Oh yes," she replied but she felt it was too late for her, that she had to fight the good fight of faith all alone. Misguided, she was torn between two realms of reality good and evil. Can a person serve two masters? She did not trust anyone, had no faith in the Church or any person on earth. I asked if I could pray for her. She said, "Yes." As we prayed she began to feel the real peace of the Lord, and started to weep. But she still could not accept the truth, so we started to leave. The young woman did thank us for caring enough to stop, and to spread a little joy into her life. She said she was not ready to let go of all the pain. Sometimes we hang on to sin because it is "familiar"; scripture warns us against the enemy's familiarity with our weaknesses. Why do we reject God's Love only to hang on to our pain and suffering, only to serve false gods? He wants to deliver us and grant us peace, yet we suffer because of our own foolish pride, instead of submitting to the Lord God and HIS plan for our lives. The peace I am talking about is one that resides in our hearts, not that life is wonderful all the time.

Even when life is tough, in those times of painful testing and pruning, we have the Lord's peace in our hearts and souls. See if your mind is focused and filled with light; if so, all hell can break loose around us, yet persons with a Christ-centered heart and mind can survive great persecution and sufferings. Darkness cannot penetrate the light, even during the darkest of times! Our Lord is talking about peace in our hearts and minds.

CROSSWALK

Some of the people that were witnessing the attempt at conversion in Starbucks came over to us asking many questions, about evangelism and serving God! Moreover, they came and signed the cross. Then we were off headed north once again.

10

Entering Laguna Beach

The enemy spirits were rattling their sabers and were strongly felt as we entered Aliso Beach. A woman ran out of a store, over to the cross and thanked God for our obedience, to stand against the powers over that area. We prayed together and a small gathering began to form around us. We stood and prayed over the families and people in that area of Laguna Beach. However, the sad part of the walk was beginning to materialize.

I started to see and understand that women had become the main force of prayer; even early on in the walk this was evident. Where are the men, Lord? I asked. They were asleep in their sinful nature so proud or afraid; too many were following the way of the Nicolaitans' doctrine! That revelation saddened me for I could see it was true.

So once again, we prayed for men to rise up, and take their place. We prayed that sons and daughters would awaken from this terrible slumber. We asked that the Lord would awaken the Church from the deception of falsehoods "in Christ". We prayed that God would deliver us unto his true righteousness by the power of our Lord and Savior Jesus Christ. We prayed for deliverance from the Nicolaitans' spirits and doctrines, the Churches teaching the duality of man, those confessing Christ but abusing Paul's doctrine of grace. By the name of Christ Jesus, I do pray!

Nicolaitans

God commends THE CHURCH AT EPHESUS (Rev. 2:6) for hating the "deeds" of the Nicolaitans, while He blames the Church at Pergammum for having them who hold their "doctrines" (Rev. 2:15). They were seemingly a class of professing Christians, who sought to introduce into the Church a false freedom or licentiousness, thus abusing Paul's doctrine of grace (Compare 2 Pet. 2:15, 16, 19), and were probably identical with those who held the doctrine of Balaam (q.v.), Rev. 2:14.

As John the beloved wrights to us in Revelations

Revelation 2

"To the angel of the Church of Ephesus write, 'These things says He who holds the seven stars in His right hand, who walks in the midst of the seven golden lamp stands: "I know your works, your labor, your patience, and that you cannot bear those who are evil. Moreover, you have tested those who say they are apostles and are not, and have found them liars; and you have persevered and have patience, and have labored for My names sake and have not become weary.

Nevertheless I have this against you, that you have left your first love. Remember therefore from where you have fallen; repent and do the first works, or else I will come to you quickly and remove your lamp stand from its place unless you repent. But this you have, that you hate the deeds of the Nicolaitans, which I also hate." He who has an ear, let him hear what the Spirit says to the Churches. To him who overcomes I will give to eat from the tree of life, which is in the midst of the Paradise of God."'

Father God, bless the Churches and, I beseech Thee O' Lord, to awaken Christ's holy Catholic and apostolic Church. Bring us under your wing, and deliver us from all fear. Send the Archangel

Michael to slay the beast and grant us peace, in Jesus' Name we pray!

I myself at this point stood, returned to my first love of the Catholic Church, and confessed my own fornication with false doctrines. The woman was in disbelief that we would walk in, in order to reclaim the land, for fear has gripped the people. Once the land of the brave, a land of strong Christians has now become the land of the lost in sin. If Christ is for us, who can be against us? First, you must seek Christ, and surrender all to Him, for it is in God that we trust!

11

Entering Laguna Beach

Walking into Laguna Beach, a practicing homosexual asked me "what the hell" I thought I was doing, "with that big cross?" When I shared with him, he got very disgusted at us. Yet he listened to what I was saying, because I truly cared for the man, showed him respect and explained Christ's love for sinners. Specifically, I shared what Paul had taught us about homosexuals and how it destroys entire nations. We told him that no gene has been found to produce homosexuality, and nothing in nature has forced him to be homosexual, as man would teach, but rather it is a curse possibly from generations past. In the Old Testament it is thought that the sins of past generation come to visit us to the third generation. So Jesus said he did not come to end the Law but to fulfill it so it is highly possible we are setting ourselves up for a huge fall even to the generations yet to be born. Moreover we told him that God could fully restore him by Christ's Love and protection! Here is what St Paul teaches us in the book of Romans about this particular sin. Look at it as a path that leads to destruction of our individual lives, and the warfare it invites into our nation, and world!

Romans 1

For I am not ashamed of the gospel of Christ, for it is the power of God to salvation for everyone who believes, for the Jew first and for the Greek. For in it the righteousness of God is revealed from faith to faith; as it is written, "The just shall live by faith." For the wrath of God is revealed from heaven against all ungodliness and unrighteousness of men, who suppress the truth in unrighteousness, because what may be known of God is manifest in them, for God has shown it to them. For since the creation of the world His invisible attributes are clearly seen, being understood by the things that are made, even His eternal power and Godhead, so that they are without excuse, because, although they knew God, they did not glorify Him as God, nor were thankful, but became futile in their thoughts, and their foolish hearts were darkened. Professing to be wise, they became fools, and changed the glory of the incorruptible God into an image made like corruptible man and birds and four-footed animals and creeping things.

Therefore God also gave them up to uncleanness, in the lusts of their hearts, to dishonor their bodies among themselves; who exchanged the truth of God for the lie, and worshiped and served the creature rather than the Creator, who is blessed forever. Amen. For this reason God gave them up to vile passions. For even their women exchanged the natural use for what is against nature.

Likewise also the men, leaving the natural use of the woman, burned in their lust for one another, men with men committing what is shameful, and receiving in them-selves the penalty of their error, which was due. And even as they did not like to retain God in their knowledge, God gave them over to a debased mind, to do those things, which are not fitting. They were filled with all unrighteousness, sexual immorality, wickedness, covetousness, maliciousness; full of envy, murder, strife, deceit, evil-mindedness; they are whisperers, backbiters, haters of God, violent, proud, boasters, inventors of evil things, disobedient to parents, undiscerning, untrustworthy, unloving, unforgiving, unmerciful; who, knowing the righteous judgment of God, that those who practice such things are deserving of death, not only do the same but also approve of those who practice them.

This man became outraged at the truth and he began yelling at me and cursing us. However The Lord gave me great grace and I told him that I was not angered by his statements, and that I only read out of a part of the Bible written 1988 years before our conversation. Moreover, I told him that God destroyed Sodom and Gomorrah for this same sin, and the flood of Noah's time was because of this same sin. Moreover, this is the reason we all suffer; before we can commit grave sin, we would have had to commit previous sins, as we gradually lose God's protection through disobedience. Remember what we just read in

Romans 1:

Therefore God also gave them up to uncleanness, in the lusts of their hearts, to dishonor their bodies among themselves; who exchanged the truth of God for the lie, and worshipped and served the creature rather than the Creator, who is blessed forever. Amen.

Most have fallen short of the glory of God through desires of the flesh. We also said that forgiveness and redemption are available, through repentance and returning to the love of Christ. We shared with him how he to could return to his first love. Repent, for the Kingdom of Heaven is at hand! Serve God through the Lordship of Christ his Son. He calmly asked to see my bible and sought for a verse that would defend his sin—try as he might, it was not to be found! And of course not, for the word does not contradict itself; as some would say.

The Love of Christ calmed him, but he did walk away. I was very sad for him, however the Holy Spirit quickened my heart, and I knew that a seed had been planted. I pray for his eyes to be open, knowing that all types of sin leads us unto destruction, but that life in Christ is wonderful and exciting, and there is no better life. Then we pushed on. California has been a Christian state for centuries, starting with the Indians who loved Christ in the missions. I come from an original Californian family and have the ability to back up this statement!

Revelations 2 v14-15

But I have a few things against thee, because thou hast there them that hold the doctrine of Balaam, who taught Balac to cast an obstacle before the children of Israel, to eat things sacrificed unto idols, and to commit fornication. So hast thou also them that hold the doctrine of the Nicolaitans, which thing I hate. Repent, or else I will come unto thee quickly, and will fight against them with the sword of my mouth.

I would only guess that is what I was sent to do on this cross walk. All sex outside of marriage is sin and not tolerated in the Kingdom of Heaven, which we are the foot-stool thereof. Partly due to this self-indulgence, in these last days the people of the world are becoming more engaged in the demonic.

These are the driving forces behind man's fallen nature that is brought on by satanic forces, which are constantly pulling us into temptation. The less we seek God in prayer, the stronger the demonic invasion will become. We are turning to humanism and science (nothing is wrong with science itself, but many people possessing atheistic hearts have tried to support their false beliefs using science as a twisted source false knowledge. In fact, when research of the whole thought to a complete end well studying science and making scientific discovery is appreciating God's artwork! The problem lies within, when these theories are turned against God's word or used to discredit His creation.

In addition, the soft, "clubhouse" Christian movement often teaches false doctrine about God's word! All too often without knowing, they have become like the Nicolaitans!

2 Peter 2

But false prophets also arose among the people, just as there will be false teachers among you, who will secretly bring in destructive heresies, even denying the Master who bought them, bringing upon themselves swift destruction. And many will follow their sensuality, and because of them the way of truth will be blasphemed. And in their greed they will exploit you with false words. Their condemnation from long ago is not idle, and their destruction is not asleep.

So then a strong Christian needs to stand firm, know God's word, and put on the full armor of God every day, continuing to fight the good fight of faith, and stand against Satan's last onslaught! When God calls you to a Christian life, truly live it, because the battle rages and it is real! The Godly and the angels are fighting against sin and the devil throughout every generation. That is the life of the fallen world, which pertains to all people who are not in the body of Christ Jesus Lord of all.

When we come to salvation, we become a new creation, called by God unto repentance and Christ's holiness. God calls all Christians to strive for and stand in holiness. However, God does not expect us to be immediately perfect, but He gently calls us unto repentance, eventually perfecting our lives through right action, and building a strong prayer life. God calls all Christians to pray without ceasing. How often do you pray?

We proceeded north to my friend's house in Laguna Beach. It would be wrong of me to say Laguna is a bad city. Far from it, there are many Godly people there. God bless them. I pray for all the deceived because they are lost and hurting.

It is the passion of Christ that convicts many young and old alike, without saying a word. Just the sight of the cross can bring conviction and for some conviction feels like persecution to a person. Not to hurt us, but rather to bring us to remembrance of our sin, then unto repentance. Sin is what hurts us, not the awareness of it!

Still Ken and I did have great results with many people of the city. Please remember: rejoicing in the heavens is for today, the only thing stopping us is sin. Again, many families approached us, signed the cross, and received prayer for their wives and children. God bless America once again for we are a big part of heaven's armies.

Praise HIM Father God the Holy one that created the whole earth. Do not fall into the trap of Middle Eastern and Far Eastern governmental and spirituality teaching. Just do a little studying before you make that leap.

Know that it is God, who allowed foreigners to move here in greater numbers, some we have evangelized already and others are just waiting for their Christian brothers and sisters to bless them, and welcome them home. Of course, some are not, as we well know.

So remember, God chose people to come here and test our faith. Do you know scripture? You had better, because they are watching to see if you live what you preach! Some of the Middle Eastern people know the Bible better than us. And, most notably, the Hispanic people were, by far, the most willing to stop their hard work, reach out to sign the cross, and receive a kind word and blessing. How do we treat them? God will bless them and, as we are becoming weaker and weaker in our faith, God help us. The next person we talked with was a middle age woman and her older son. He had taken her to doctors, since the poor woman was fighting cancer, and she believed very much that God would heal her, if it was HIS will. Suffering is a very hard teaching but, during our suffering, if we will give it up to Our Lord and seek HIS face, it will become a blessing unto us and often for others as a sin covering.

We prayed in agreement, enjoyed a great conversation about the beauty of southern California, and watched the children playing in the sand on the beaches. I could not help but ponder on what style of life are we setting up for the children. I can not help but shudder at the thought! We as a nation are moving more and more into a proud and greedy society, even to the point of destroying our children in the lie of "protection" and contraception. Morality and chastity must be valued in society, and are established from a complete and structured family unit, a committed father and mother who are actively engaged in their faith and in the faith instruction of their children! Nothing less works! Scripture describes the curses brought upon families and nations who do not support the family unit, and the bearing of children out of the sacrament of marriage. Children today may not have any idea, nor any point of reference for this.

Then Ken and I walked up to my friend's house and received a warm welcome. We have known each other from birth and we enjoyed staying there overnight with their young sons. They were truly in amazement at what we were doing as a labor of Christ's love. They were asking questions and their minds and hearts were open wide for the love & knowledge of God's Kingdom! Ken and I really got into the love and kindness of our Lord, as the boys just wanted to serve us and make our stay comfortable. "Come as little children." God commands us to be like children, for such are like unto the kingdom of heaven. We prayed for the whole family just before we left. The eyes are the window to our hearts, and children's eyes are so clear and pure, just shining with kindness and purity.

Romans 1 v19

Because what may be known of God is manifest in them, for God has shown it to them.

I found this to be very evident and true in children by their eagerness to hear about God and His Kingdom. And how they are always ready and willing to receive a word of knowledge or a blessing from God! The Holy Spirit made it so apparent to me, in the way we can slip away far from the pure knowledge of God, as we grow older, and how our sins separate us farther and farther from God. This takes place if we are not living repentant lives! Please remember again that our Children are like the Kingdom of Heaven, pure and holy. It is what we teach them, which can lead them either astray or down the right path of righteousness.

What if fathers realized that we are all God's children and that our wives are our sisters before marriage, and that our children actually belonged to the Lord? What would our nation look like then? We would be a nation that would pray, and serve God working to build HIS Kingdom. We would submit ourselves and realign our behavior to model Christ our Lord. For those who are single, they would be praying to be in God's will, regardless of whether He sent a spouse into our lives. For those who will be married one day, or who are already married, we would be praying for our spouses Then, we would be praying for the blessing of children, before their birth, during, and ever after. We would be praying every day over each child without favoritism over a son's or daughter's because all are God's children created for His purpose.

God gives us stewardship over their lives, not control. We are to fill them, and guide them into God's Kingdom with all heavenly knowledge. However, we can not teach what we do not possess. So we as God's people must study all of Gods Kingdom principles, in order to pass them to our children and extended families and friends. We must understand that God is the righteous judge and the judgment of God is coming to us all.

Truly it is better to make changes now, and live the life that God has set before each one of us. This is the simplicity of Christian living: Taking right action with great love and compassion for all people, and giving God the honor and glory from our hearts.

Matthew 10 v12-26

*"Behold, I send you out as sheep in the midst of wolves._
Therefore, be wise as serpents and harmless as doves. But
beware of men, for they will deliver you up to councils and
scourge you in their synagogues. You will be brought before
governors and kings for My sake, as a testimony to them and
to the Gentiles. But when they deliver you up, do not worry
about how or what you should speak. For it will be given to
you in that hour, what you should speak; for it is not you who
speak, but the Spirit of your Father who speaks in you. "Now
brother will deliver up brother to death, and a father his child;
and children will rise up against parents and cause them to be
put to death.*

*And you will be hated by all for My names sake. But he
who endures to the end will be saved. When they persecute you
in this city, flee to another. For assuredly, I say to you, you will
not have gone through the cities of Israel before the Son of Man
comes." A disciple is not above his teacher, nor a servant above
his master. It is enough for a disciple that he is like his teacher
and a servant like his master. If they have called the master
of the house Beelzebub, how much more will they call those of
his household! Therefore do not fear them. For there is nothing
covered that will not be revealed, and hidden that will not be
known.*

This is where the demonic spirits work to destroy the family
unit and the Church! Let us see the war as it is, in order to be able
to resist the devil. The Lord teaches that a disciple is not above
his teacher, nor a servant above his master. He is teaching us to
have patience and to submit to spiritual authority. Man's biggest
problem is we don't want to submit to our teachers, or to anyone
for that matter!!

Today mostly the problem lies in our individual pride and lack
of patience and trust; we do not even trust the creator.

Love, Trust, Patience, and Submission are impossible without a healthy understanding of the power and joy God has for us. We need to practice these Quadrants, which are the foundational building blocks of Faith. What do I mean?

Love others in small and large ways, living each day, one day at a time, reading God's instruction manual as a guide. Trust in Christ that He has forgiven your sins, after you have accepted Christ. Find and submit to spiritual authority i.e. Christ's Church leadership. Moreover, find a person to disciple under for mentoring and spiritual guidance. After this, have patience for the Lord to perfect the work he started in you! For a healthy understanding of these Quadrants of life, think and pray about these things, and release your worry and suffering to God daily, and surrender yourself unto the Father as we become a living sacrifice to Christ who is our Lord and King forever. I brought this teaching out at this time to help show the stand we were called to deliver and the war we all are fighting! And hopefully come to personally understand how to fight to win the battle you might be experiencing in your life.

12

Laguna Beach to Newport Beach

When we were just about to leave Laguna, we met a man, a homosexual who had open sores all over, and almost void of muscle mass. I asked if he had heard of Jesus Christ, and he started weeping just by hearing the name of our Lord! He was demonically tormented and dying of Aids! He was tender-hearted and open to the Gospel teaching of the curse of homosexuality, in comparison to the man we talked with when we'd entered town. Here was a person ready to hear the hard truth. Because of the AIDS he was fighting, and the hard reality of sin, and what it does to our natural bodies, he understood. I then showed him that Jesus breaks the curses of generations past, and redeems us by his shed blood. Through first choosing Jesus as your Lord and savior then the person must spend time to become a disciple! Where in the catholic faith it takes a year before training even begins sometimes then a year to two depending on the date you enter the church. Once fully trained turn and stand in the fullness of faith, if it be His will, He has power to heal through His grace and His love. We must want to repent, turn to him, and begin to serve Him to help lead others into the Kingdom and away from sin and decay! We as fallen humanity are all sinful, but living our lives as HIS living representatives is what our Lord requires. Generations of Americans, who lived before us, understood this truth. Most all of us have grandparents that have spoken the truth of Christ Jesus to us but far too often, we are hard of hearing and of heart to receive the wisdom of their love!

Romans 2

If you think that you can judge others, then you are wrong. You too are guilty of sin. You judge people, but you do the same bad things they do. Therefore, when you judge them, you are really judging yourself guilty. God judges those who do wrong things. In addition, we know that God's judging is right. You judge those who do wrong, but you do wrong yourselves. Do you think you will be able to escape the judgment of God? God has been very kind to you, and he has been patient with you. God has been waiting for you to change. However, you think nothing of his kindness. Perhaps you do not understand that God is kind to you so that you will change your hearts and lives. But you are hard and stubborn and refuse to change. Therefore, you are making your own punishment greater and greater on the day God shows his anger. On that day, all people will see God's right judgments. God will reward or punish every person for what he has done. Some people live for God's glory, for honor, and for life, that has no end. They live for those things by always continuing to do well. God will give life forever to them. But other people are selfish and refuse to follow truth. They follow evil. God will give them his punishment and anger. He will give trouble and suffering to everyone who does evil to the Jews first and to the non-Jews. But God will give glory, honor, and peace to everyone who does well to the Jews first and to the non-Jews. For God judges all people in the same way.

People who have God's law and those who have never heard of the law are all the same when they sin. Those who do not have the law and are sinners will be lost. In addition, in the same way, the law will judge people who have the law and are sinners. Hearing the law does not make people right with God. The law makes people right with God only if they obey what the law says. (The non-Jews do not have the law. However, when they freely do things that the law commands,

92

then they are the law for themselves. This is true even though they do not have the law. They show that in their hearts they know what is right and wrong, just as the law commands. In addition, they show this by the way they feel about right and wrong. Sometimes their thoughts tell them they did wrong. In addition, sometimes their thoughts tell them they did right.) All these things will happen on the day when God will judge the secret thoughts of people's hearts. The Good News that I preach says that God will judge everyone through Christ Jesus.

Therefore, I explained Romans 1 to him, that we are judged and condemned by our sin that breaks God's law. The progression is from sin to sickness to decay or death. Then, in Romans 2, we see clearly that through repentance and right living under God's leadership through Christ our Lord, we receive His redemption and love. God is not a man that he should deceive any one. But moreover He will perform his truth in every life. His promises are true, but they require a response from us to activate the offer.

I shared with him my testimony that in my teens before I came to Christ I was also a blasphemer and a sinner that confessed God but lived hard after the things of the world. Because I gave myself over to temptation and sin; I came under God's Judgment through His Law. I told of how Christ healed me, delivered me, and made me whole, even when I had earned death.

I thank God for HIS Son Jesus, who delivered me and stood me upon a rock. Moreover, that was why I was there on that day, to bring the glory and light of the true knowledge of our Lord Jesus Christ to yet another sinner. I shared how God used me to bring the love of Christ to my Father, how he himself was also dying of cancer, and how he turned to the Lord at age 67. That night he accepted Christ he was supposed to die, the doctors had said that there was a cord wrapped around his liver that was killing him, and it would take a miracle if he survived 24 hours. He was putrid green because that cord was strangling his liver.

Then I prayed for him for Christ's grace to enter in and heal him. The next morning, he awoke, feeling much better. Christ had answered our request! The doctors were baffled and amazed by this miracle of Christ's redemptive power. God took my father home 2 years later. I thank God that we shared the love of Christ together. Before this, Christ was a cause of separation between us. We prayed together, read scriptures; and I was able to share with him the one thing that the world could never offer: the gracious Love of Christ.

After losing my earthly father, I often wondered whether he made it. One day not long after his death, I was serving on the worship team at Church, and in the middle of worship I sought out knowledge of our heavily father to grant me the peace of knowing if my father made it. Then I looked up and the heavens opened only for a moment, only a glimpse of the throne room of God could I see, then there was a vision of my father, worshipping Our King, standing right next to me.

The majesty of the moment, the very foretaste of the promised future glory of the Kingdom of Heaven, broke me into tears. The majesty of His Court, not just my father being next to me, grasped my heart of hearts and, for that one moment of true glory and splendor, there are no words!

In addition, I know I will serve the LORD JESUS our creator forever, because of this moment in space and time!

For me, I continually ponder on what it must have been like for John the Beloved to sit before the Lord Jesus in his Court of angels, to have received the entire book of revelations, and how a man could stand in the magnificence of His Glory. I read revelations a little differently now, how it expresses the majesty of the heavens, and how can we experience heaven today.

I realize that I am only a man, only one of thousands proclaiming his glorious testimony. This man received Christ and we began praying for his healing, then he proclaimed Christ as HIS King and Lord and went to find a Church in which to be belong. The Lord made another disciple that day. I know it! May the Lord bless and keep his newfound sheep! Moreover, heal him of all his earthy afflictions, especially AIDS!

The Parable about a Lost Sheep (Luke 15:3-7)

"What do you think. If a man has a hundred sheep and one of them strays, he leaves the ninety-nine in the hills and goes to look for the one that has strayed, does not he? If he finds it, truly I tell you that he rejoices over it more than over the ninety-nine that have not strayed. In the same way, it is not the will of your Father in heaven that one of these little ones should be lost."

I also felt something strange in my spirit entering into Laguna. The first homosexual was very different, with his stony heart, and upon exiting, the second was open and receiving. Could it be more than circumstance? Perhaps, by walking and spreading the truth of Christ, strongholds were destroyed over the area, I pray that they were in Jesus' name, I feel that they were! All Glory is due unto the Lord our God, I am but a lowly servant pushing his victory up the coast.

13

Laguna Beach to Newport Beach

We walked to Scotchman's cove where a woman pulled over, asking for prayer and deliverance. Again, another Christian woman locked in Fear and torment, because of the sinful nature of men, and the price of that sin over us all. Please notice that our women are weeping before the Lord! Where are the men? This time it was not so much what we were doing, but that two Men were willing to take the territory by the power and authority of Christ, as HIS witnesses! I shared with her that it is time for the true Sons and Daughters to stand up and take their rightful place! I told her that I feel its God's time to raise us from ashes! Then I showed her Romans 8.

God's Spirit Helps Us

For I consider that the sufferings of this present time are not worth comparing with the glory that will be revealed to us. For the creation is eagerly waiting, for God to reveal his children, because the creation was subjected to frustration, though not by its own choice. The one who subjected it did so in the hope that the creation itself would also be set free from slavery to decay in order to share the glorious freedom of God's children. For we know that all creation has been groaning with the pains of childbirth right up to the present time.

However, not only creation groans, but we, who have the first fruits of the Spirit also groan inwardly as we eagerly wait for our adoption, the redemption of our bodies. For we were saved with this hope in mind. Now hope that is seen is not really hope, for who hopes for what can be seen. But if we hope for what we do not see, we eagerly wait for it with patience.

She hugged our necks and drove away, delivered from fear and happy about the good report of redemption! Walking a little further, another man pulled over. He asked if he could take a picture, but found that he had forgotten his camera. He drove back into Corona Del Mar to buy one, then came back and photographed the event, praying with us and confessing his Love for Christ. He is a Catholic attending at Our Lady Queen of the Angels parish, Corona Del Mar. So many people have such wonderful faith. God, I pray that we would all have the faith and Love that this man displayed.

This brought the question of unity of the Churches to my mind. What if we were all one, worshipping the Lord around one tabernacle, with one shepherd, with love in our hearts and a fire burning within us? The Lord says; "You will all be one, worshipping Me around one tabernacle, with Love in your hearts, and a fire burning within you. I shall accomplish My priestly prayer, and My Kingdom on Earth shall be as it is in Heaven."

This walk had forced me to evaluate my own faith. I saw this multitude of faith-filled people, these brothers, and sisters in Christ. I saw how they received in their hearts only by the sight of the cross. It forced me to deeply evaluate myself and ask: What would I have done if I were driving by and seeing the same sight? What questions would I have asked, if any? Would I have stopped at all? How would it affect my life in the end? I can only guess the answers to these questions. However, I received peace, and far deeper understanding daily just how far we have turned from God here in America.

In fact Christ is my resource, and His love has set me on a quest to share His truth, and the Holy Spirit strengthens me, and compels me to keep walking. It was Jesus' way of showing me His truth, and fervent Love for all mankind.

I was learning just how very vital we are to each other's spirits. It was humbling to be sure, but I found there is such great joy and rejoicing found in simple, humble acts of love and kindness!

I can only answer that I found greater love. I also received a better understanding of the tormentor Satan, how the enemy entraps us, and encages us by our unrepented sin. We are not as different as we may think. Romans 2, remember? Well, Praise God that he is gracious and kind. We tend to be captured and lost in our own pain and suffering. Random acts of true love—shared in humility toward our fellow man—there is the remedy to our personal suffering, this is the greatest way we Christians can bear our own crosses every day. Yes, war must, and will continue until we, the faithful, figure this out. That ever lasting peace will come to us as the final trumpet sounds the return of our Lord! When we find peace within ourselves...

Luke 19

Some of the Pharisees in the crowd said to Jesus, "Teacher, tell your disciples to be quiet." He replied, "I tell you, if they were quiet, the stones would cry out!"

When he came closer and saw the city, he began to cry over it, saying, and "If you had only known today what could have brought you peace! Now it is hidden from your eyes. For the days will come when your enemies will build walls around you, surround you, and close you in on every side. They will level you to the ground—you and your children within you. They will not leave one stone on another within you, because you didn't recognize the time when God came to help you."

Please know the times and the seasons are upon us here in California and across our nation. Please Know that it is from a heart of compassion that I am doing such a thing as carry the cross open our eyes, Lord, so we can see the warning that this walk brings! Also the Love that you are to us all for an out pours of mercy upon us and for the whole world. Unity and peace over man kind Amen.

I was constantly brought into prayer by my spirit asking God for right words and the humility to understand the suffering, or the Joy of each person that came before the cross.

I found in the first 90 miles of the walk that I realized sub-mission is the most drastic problem in the Church, even from the beginning of the early Church. It has always been man's will, or greed, or controlling spirit that divides the Church, detract-ing from the powerful effect of our Lord's commission to spread the gospel message. Some leaders of entire Church movements are literally fighting to steal other Christians in order to build up their Church. Pray about a heart of submission, it is Christ's Church after all; is anyone more capable or more anointed to teaching a doctrine or message, better than one of his chosen vessels over another? A simple challenge for all the churches, I would have only one request perhaps we can all down load a copy of the Catechism of the Catholic church read it digest it along with the holy bible. If only to see where we can stand together in unity, and Love together as one in Christ Jesus.

John 16 v13-14

Yet when the Spirit of Truth comes, he will guide you into all truth. For he will not speak on his own accord, but will speak whatever he hears and will declare to you the things that are to come. He will glorify me, for he will take what is mine and declare it to you. All that the Father has is mine. That is why I said, 'He will take what is mine and declare it to you.'

I feel that we are evangelizing other Churches' congregations first because it is just easier to turn already saved people towards a new way of understanding. That is our self-will, not God's will. "I can tell it better, speak it better, and live it better"; all such statements are pride! Lord, forgive us for our blindness! That is the feeling about the Church-on-the-street pastors and teachers. Pay close attention:

Causing Others to Sin
(Mark 9:42-48; Luke 17:1-2)

If anyone causes one of these little ones who believe in me to sin, it would be better for him if a large millstone were hung around his neck and he were drowned at the bottom of the sea. How terrible it will be for the world because it causes people to sin! Temptations to sin are bound to happen, but how terrible it will be for that person who causes someone to sin!

Many New Church movements have confused, and in many ways brought damage to, people of God. I met thousands of people, making up their own beliefs based on where the scripture that says, "Where two or more are gathered in My Name," there is his Church! Because you are attacking Christ's Church from every direction, and that is intolerable. Thousands of Catholics are not sure if they are Christians any more in California because of open attacks on their faith! Christian children of all ages would stand around the cross and I would ask if they were all Christians and the young Christians would proudly confess their faith, praise God, however the Catholic children would look at me as if in their shame or to question their confession of faith.

This caused the Holy Spirit to rise up in me and bless all the Catholic children first. If there were not a Catholic Church, your 20 or even 500 year old Churches would not exist at all today. Over the centuries, the faithful have gone down this path! My question is, "Where is the submission in this?" New Churches launching out everywhere, new ideas and new vision, but is there greater power?

On the other hand, is it because of our inability to submit to spiritual authority? Did your home Church plant you? Or perhaps you felt that you were ready to launch yourself by some voice or power of God? Remember God has everything in order. He is the Great I am! He never changes! So where do we find the order of God in new movements if He changes not? I know God can do new things but it will be in His orderly fashion as per His word. Just as He didn't come to abrogate the law, but to fulfill it! I realize this is such a hard teaching I am not cross. However spreading division hate or projecting false witness. Well I only pray for a better unity and understanding between all of Gods faithful family. We are all God's children marching to one Lord Christ the King. Truly I tell you one Lord one teacher one word of truth. Unity in the body is Love its self.

Ask yourself why God cast Satan out of heaven. It was because of his inability to submit to God's Will and secondly, pride that cast him out of Heaven along with a third of the host of angels! Is not Satan's main tactic to sew division? Are we not doing the same thing?

Think for a moment about how the evil one would attack us. He is always attacking us in the same way, with the temptation of pride. Why do you think wives are unwilling to submit to their husbands? It is because they judge that their husbands are not righteous enough, so they feel that they should lead until the husband is ready to lead, in accordance with her mind's eye. This is Satan's playground of the unsaved. In addition, if the Church that you attend will not submit, then you must ask why there is such a problem with submission in marriage in the Church. Even if they are both Christians, Obedience is submission!

Church I beseech you to give up pride filled ambitions, and search-out our hearts for the gifting which is in every person in unity and great love using our gifts to win the lost. I have been a member of Churches where the Pastor halted the evangelization in order to support their vision over the truth of the solid message of the Gospel. They actually would stop evangelism because the new believer might attend somewhere else! Please remember the teaching of the Nicolaitans Church! In addition, God said he hates them! Pray and repent if there is any semblance of this sin in your theology or practices. Open the windows of your hearts as John the beloved writes to us.

Revelations.

Please Church, grow on in Christ, and do not worry so much about other congregations. Most of that worry is started by slander, calumny and murmuring. God says that a man that calumniates commits a serious sin!

A Letter to the Church in Smyrna

"To the messenger of the Church in Smyrna write:
The first and the last, who was dead and became alive, says: I know how you are suffering, how poor you are but you are rich. I also know that those who claim to be Jews slander you. They are the synagogue of Satan. Don't be afraid of what you are going to suffer. The devil is going to throw some of you into prison so that you may be tested. Your suffering will go on for ten days. Be faithful until death, and I will give you the crown of life.
Let the person who has ears listen to what the Spirit says to the Churches. No one who wins the victory will ever be hurt by the second death.

What does your Church look like today, i.e., overall, the majority of church members? I would have to say we are comatose. Head and not the tail, it is not about money, it never was; our children and lost souls are the true riches. We must seek deep inside ourselves to find out the truth, and then simply speak out to the Lord. Ask why are the attendance numbers declining, and why do so many float between churches, shifting in the wind with every new and improved speaker, every new mega-church? We should never forget who we are seeking, and who we are to serve. In one accord in unity and in love between one another I am speaking against disunity not any denomination or understanding. I realize it is difficult to stand in the battle. Against true evil I surrendered to carry the cross that perhaps this action might help you to stand, this is why I call out for unity and order. An Army divided against its self is not strong. And we the children of God are called to be one. It is the proper order of true love. As I was in the Navy for so many years and then the merchant fleet so after 33 years of sailing the oceans and truly digesting all the nations of our world. I attended mass and services with many of the eastern rights, Russian orthodox African Chinese, Korean, Japanese, indo china, Vietnamese churches and they are the first churches. And they are very Catholic Apostolic cessation Eucharistic adoration Priesthood. Millions suffering death and real persecution yet there church still stands firm and strong. The Catholic Church being the chair of Peter none of the first churches disagree in this truth.

14

Coming into My Native Hometown Corona Del Mar and Newport Beach

It is where I grew up. I do thank God for a great childhood and wonderful homeland, for it was at a time before the "money-god" showed up, and perverted the land and our people. I just retired from a life at sea in the Navy, and the Merchant Marines. As I said, I was born here, raised in the Catholic faith and in the tradition of that faith in Christ. God called me to see first-hand the damage created by prideful people looking for the fast way out. Today, I attend Church at Our Lady Queen of the Angels Parish with Fr. Kerry, the lead pastor there.

I vowed to protect all Christendom when I entered into the service and I will protect it today, even unto my life if God asks it of me.

In our childhood formation, we hardly ever study any farther than what others verbally teach us, and the Holy Spirit is not active in us if we cannot see the truth. Therefore, there are many truths found in history, as applied to the Bible, but a bit of hard deep study is required!

As adults, Christians are tempted to distraction by growing our churches physically, instead of spiritually. This ultimately leads some people into false teaching, because in some cases we have started to worship theologies and doctrines, and not the creator. God loves all his children; however, there is only one Christ. How many ways can we split the single word of our Lord? Therefore, we are all one in Christ! Where can we all agree? What one thread of truth can we all agree upon? I would suggest the Nicene Creed is a good start.

Nicene Creed

I believe in God, the Father Almighty, Creator of heaven and earth; and in Jesus Christ, His only Son, our Lord: Who was conceived by the Holy Spirit, born of the Virgin Mary; suffered under Pontius Pilate, was crucified, died and was buried. He descended into hell; the third day He rose again from the dead; He ascended into heaven, is seated at the right hand of God the Father Almighty; from thence He shall come to judge the living and the dead. I believe in the Holy Spirit, the Holy Catholic Church, the communion of Saints, the forgiveness of sins, the resurrection of the body, and life everlasting. Amen.

Again we are all too often deceived, and become blind in our prideful thoughts, that we must do something big for God. When we are enticed by new visions and driven by the false teachings, we are following the falsehoods spread by Islam: solely to build division and confusion within the Holy church; is it any coincidence about what has happened in Christ's church over a time period of about 805 years? That my friends, is a very long time for Satan to use all the Catholic Orthodoxy splits and reformation Church movements to separate us from Christ, and detract from the Lord's sacrifice for our sins. It has been humanity's inability to submit to the oldest Churches on earth i.e. the Catholic and Orthodox Churches—that is the enigma and problem. Therefore, study to show yourselves approved, and return to God. Repent Church, turn away from pride and return to your first Love. I am not calling us to accept all teachings and traditions, as blind sheep do, but rather, to gradually come into full agreement. We must stand for what is right and agreeable in the true teaching of

the gospels and proven long-standing traditions. These are prov-
able in world history as being of God!

Holy Spirit help us in this I humbly pray, so that all of
Christendom can stand in agreement and speak with one voice
as we should, amen! Let us praise Him louder than the angels!
I heard thousands blaming Satan and demons for their broken
lives! Satan is only here because the Body of Christ allows him.
Remember Greed, moneychangers, and pride! You let him in and
now you are crying because it is raining demons from hell. Lord
have mercy on us. Christ have mercy on us.

I say, walk anywhere with a twelve foot cross for a few days,
trust in God alone to meet your needs and you will see it for
yourself! Live it, and then the Holy Spirit will give you eyes to
see and ears to hear.

He is asking us to submit to the Rock of faith! Jesus said to
Peter, "You are Peter (which means 'Rock'), and upon this Rock,
I will build My Church, and the gates of Hell shall not prevail
against it." He is asking us to submit to this Rock of Faith. He
asks us to have high regard for great men of Love and faith, such
as Benedict XVI, for instance. I do not believe that Christ is asking us to turn all Churches over to the Catholic or Orthodox
Churches; however, I believe it is possible to deliver the true
Eucharist to every service in every Church, but we will have to
embrace some important theology. There are some false teachings, false prophets & false teachers in every Church—including the Catholic Church, Orthodox Church, and Protestant
Churches—but the whole Church is called to unity in Christ.
We are called to work together to change the wrong teaching
and dogmas. What if we submitted to each other as the body
of Christ is commanded? What if we called on angelic hosts of
heaven's armies to protect us? What if we praised God his Son
our Lord Jesus, even louder than the angels, all with one voice?
Unity is the true voice of God the Father! Unification of our
Churches, His Delight!

Well that is a big part of what I learned on this journey in the first 90 miles! Come and let us build his Kingdom together! We have the ability to stop playing Satan's game if we so choose. Let us become true sons and daughters! This is a call to holiness. This is also a call to right living in Christ!

Back to the Cross Walk.

I was Praising God for Corona Del Mar, and thanking Him as I walked past where my grandmother used to live. This is where she and my grandfather served God until they went to be with the Lord! They served at Our Lady of Mount Carmel Church, Newport Beach, California. I thanked God for the faith that they instilled in me from infancy. Did I mention that this Catholic Church used to be the only Church for miles around for generations before men invented (yes, invented) Protestantism and non-denominational Churches? Think about it. 2007 years ago, Christ died and ascended into heaven. Then came the reformation and they reinvented Christendom. I say not likely, but it did start the onslaught of revisionism and separatism throughout the body of Christ. I was living here and attending High school, when the first Calvary Church movement was starting. Where did the right of these young Churches come from? What spirit was it that has tried to overthrow or negate the Church with 2013 years of Christian history? I am not speaking poorly about such a movement and many souls and loving pastors do truly love the Lord I know this is true. It is the division that is not good fruit.

Please note that I truly love all faith-filled Churches, brothers and sisters in Christ. Since I was raised in the Church, retired from the Navy, and sent home, I found that thousands of start-up and mega-Churches had descended on my homeland. Now when I considered where to attend and serve, before I could blink, I was whisked away into a literal smorgasbord of Churches!

I found good Bible studies and the presence of the Holy Spirit in all the churches that I attended; however, the tug-of-war which ensued over whose Church I would serve was very confusing.

How does this confusion of faith affect the new believers? It is no wonder they are so scared of everything!

Christ does not have many flavors, and only One Way to serve Him, for He is God. There are many expressions of serving Him, many different kinds of service to God, but only One Way of serving God. Obedience is the only way! Be sure that it is not you "serving God" your own way. It is more likely that we ourselves are only willing to go so far to fit our comfort zone, not towards God's Will. And the way we lash out at each other! Help! Remember we are to love one another as brothers and sisters in Christ Jesus! We are all one body in Christ. Who is the body of Christ? Who is the Church? Well, of course, the Church belongs to the Lord Jesus Christ and he demands that we submit to him and each other. Therefore, we are all the Church who are the faithful in Christ Jesus and, confess his holy name!

Matthew 16

From that time on, Jesus began to show his disciples that he would have to go to Jerusalem and suffer a great deal because of the elders, the high priests, and the scribes. Then he would be killed, but on the third day, he would be raised. Peter took him aside and began to reprimand him, saying, "God be merciful to you, Lord! This must never happen to you!"

But Jesus turned around and said to Peter, "Get behind me, Satan! You are an offense to me, for you are not thinking God's thoughts but human thoughts!"

Then Jesus said to his disciples, "If anyone wants to follow me, he must deny himself, pick up his cross, and follow me continually. For whoever wants to save his life will lose it, but whoever loses his life for my sake will find it. For what profit will a person have if he gains the whole world and forfeits his life. Or what can a person give in exchange for his life.

The Son of Man is going to come with his angels in his Father's glory, and then he will repay everyone according to what he has done. Truly I tell you, some people standing here will not experience death before they see the Son of Man coming in His Kingdom."

Christ prophesied that some standing there would see the Son of man coming in His Kingdom. The apostles did witness this, and so did many others after Christ was resurrected. Our Lord returned many times to instruct his disciples. Moreover, what about the transfiguration of Christ on Mt. Tabor even before His passion for our souls? He showed us His Deity and a vision of the Godhead. Before the apostles, Jesus was transfigured and Elijah and Moses were discussing with Jesus about His coming Sacrifice and Resurrection.

The Holy Spirit revealed to me, by the word of Christ also, that Jesus will judge all sin, in this life and the next. Therefore, He is giving us, His Church, a commandment to live holy lives and to remember that He bought us at the highest price; His Passion. He shed his blood for our salvation!

So I just picked up my cross which I was called to bear, and walked up to people, asking if they would like to sign the cross. And as people came forward to sign, so often we were led to pray for our nation; but for the most part, the Holy Spirit had us pray for our families, for the peace of Christ to settle upon this Holy institution, and for its orderly structure. That is the Order of God in families, namely, God 1st, Family 2nd and Jobs 3rd. The pillars of Holy faith The pillar of holy orders, pillar of the holy family, pillar of holy children, and the pillar of holy community! Imagine the nation we could build from here. Never before seen! Could it be a lack of knowledge? Perhaps

In addition, I thanked the Holy Spirit for filling us with greater knowledge and wisdom of God's Word. I also said, "Please God, cover us in the grace of Christ, and deliver us from confusion, so that we in Orange County can enter into your rest!" That we will come to realize that You, God, have created each man and woman in your image, and have made each Christian to be a new creation in Christ, and that we are fearfully and wonderfully made. Please God, grant us peace, in Jesus's mighty name. Amen!

I received a lot of curious stares and scoffing along PCH (Pacific Coast Highway) but the children of God were refreshing to my spirit, and were simply amazing to me, rejuvenating me and encouraging me once again. What a line between believers and the deceived. There is so much work for us to do, and yet the Kingdom is at hand!

Ken and I were walking by the Newport Dunes when a news van stopped and started filming us. They asked us what we were doing. We answered "Lifting the name of Jesus Christ and being witnesses of our Lord!" Traffic was stopping to receive prayer, because we the people do not like the direction the world is heading! In addition, this was right in front of my house, so my Wife and family were all standing around and witnessing, and joining in the call of the Holy Spirit! As the camera men were filming, workers on the street and people in their cars came to receive prayer and stood as one to be a confession of faith in our Lord. We prayed together and built God's Kingdom again that day! We should all be Kingdom builders every day by living with right action in all the little things we do. If we already were, I probably would not have to carry this cross.

However I do thank our Lord for trusting me in such a wonderful way. God bless America! Moreover, grant us strength and an undivided heart, Unity to all the church. Please, Christ Jesus, I pray for unity!

Ken and I took a break and found some work dry-walling our pastor's garage. This was a time for submitting to spiritual authority, and seeking out the prayer of agreement, for the walk to serve Christ's Church! I asked my pastor about the Catholic Church due to the positive experiences we had along the journey thus far. He did not answer. I realized I had said something disagreeable to him by mentioning the Catholic Church. Soon after my question was posed? My wife tried to cast out the "demons" of

Catholicism out of me. This is where I began to realize the drastic mistakes I made in the whirlwind of the Southern California Church system. Once again after experiencing the global church I realized I was the Frog that had been dropped into the caldron of a wind fall of doctrine, men choosing faith that fits their desire? I had never experienced such a reality in all the years I had traveled the rest of the globe. This is truly new. Right or wrong I am not God my largest question is how can unity of the body come from such an event. And in such a small portion of our world, so I asked our Lord for peace between the faith of men and women!

I felt best to leave that one alone, and three weeks later, we started walking again. We walked onto Balboa Island and received a great welcome; some of the people were coming out of their homes, some with babies, and others with their children, just to witness the passionate love of Jesus our King. They were all signing the cross, rejoicing, and receiving prayer. We blessed little babies in the Lord—you can always see the light of Christ in the eyes of every child. Their Guardian Angel stands with them, from birth and through out our lives, until our death. They have different quantities and types of angels depending on their calling, and on the way, they live their lives. These angels continually are recording the events around the child or persons life to God's Kingdom.

Morning Prayer

Angle of God, my Guardian dear, to whom His love commits me here, ever this day, be at my side, to light and guard rule and to guide! Amen!

If all of us truly understood this fact better, we would love and respect our children a whole lot more than we do! God is watching over us constantly! Along with Angelic beings.

We came up to a Boy Scout troop which was on an outing. While they were waiting to board the Balboa Ferry, the young men gathered round us and let us pray with them. Witnessing the enthusiasm of our youth today brings me great pleasure! They are fed up with the whole sin thing, praise God! At least the next generation gets it. I can't help but recall when I stood on the beaches of Normandy and felt the pain of the tens of thousands of brave American soldiers, who willingly gave their lives for the deliverance of Christendom in France on its blood-drenched shores. The French were crying out, "Praise God, here come's the Christians!" Then, I compare that to what are we thinking and doing today. Was their commitment to Christ for nothing?

Let me share a story with you all about my friend James. He was 68 years old when I met him and I loved to sit and listen to his stories. I had nothing but honor and respect for James, and the events which engulfed his life in WWII. In one of his many journeys, one event in-particular stood out in my mind. He said that he was aboard the

USS Indianapolis, which was the Ship that delivered the Hiroshima bomb; He said that it was such a top-secret mission, no one knew the ship was missing out of her berth at Pearl Harbor. After the ship completed her mission and was on her return to Pearl Harbor, it was sunk by a German U boat. James would tell me of the scorching days and cold nights, as he and his crew members suffered while left adrift at Sea. With great fear, they watched sharks eating their ship mates, until a PBY spotter plane located them, and rescued the survivors some 12 days later. God, remind us of the price which was paid for the freedom to Love you in the free nations of the world.

Deliver us from the deception of false teaching, spread by our distorted institutions, especially the school system. There is so much truth to teach which isn't even offered. We as a people must begin to see and understand how our current-event mindset and socialistic assertions of political correctness are destroying the very fabric of our free society. Only pages of powerful truth can expose the undermining of history which is created by our shallow, current events-based educational guidelines. Again I thank God for granting me 33 years of world travel. Time to see and digest the facts of reality found in Geography, Science, oceanography, True History of our world learned by expositional travel all across our globe for 33 years. Today I have young students purposing their theories upon me and have never experience the expanses of reality!

With that said, we then got aboard the Balboa ferry heading to the Balboa Fun Zone, and the Newport Beach boardwalk! This is where Our Lady Mount Carmel Church is located, on 15 St. Newport Peninsula. It is the Church where my parents and the priest baptized me when I was a baby. The Bishop confirmed me at the same Church years later. When I was 12 there were many Catholics living in this area. I would ask if the people would like to sign the cross as I walked, but the Catholics would always ask what I was doing, or why I was doing it. I answered, to reinstall remembrance to Christ's Church of course, with a big smile. "Yes, but why carry a cross?" they asked. I answered, "Because I left California to serve in our Navy for all my adult life, and the California I returned to was so unholy and unchristian compared to the one I left." Therefore, I am a catechism-believing, confirmed, born-again, Bible-studying believer and true son of God the Father, in love and adoration of his holy Eucharist, the true body of Christ and as we all are who confess Christ as Lord and practice our faith. In addition, as an American Patriot, I still believe America is a nation under God of all creation but is in need of a little Churching up! The torment of our fallen sinful nature has brought me to my knees literally, and I began seeking and asking God how I could best serve His Son, our Lord, and Savior! The Crosswalk was the answer that I received, and I began a walk of obedience. After quite the beating I excepted the walk and here I am.

Once they heard my confession of faith, every one of those Americans signed and prayed with me in Jesus' mighty name! It was not a cry that the end-times were coming or some other attempt to shock people, but a witness of Christ's Love. I believe that we the body of Christ suffer a great deal because of the defective teaching of many elders, pastors, priests. Perhaps more accountable will be the modern-day scribes, meaning educators and historians, who have missed the truth and put their spin on history, systematically spreading deception, whether directly or inadvertently. I found the truth by traveling the face of the earth over 33 years! And applying God's word to the obvious, for all that is written in his word can be proven and evidenced all over the face of the earth!

James ch.5 v.3

Behold, the hire of the laborers who have reaped down your fields, which is of you kept back by fraud, crieth: and the cries of them, which have reaped, are entered into the ears of the Lord of Sabaoth. Ye have lived in pleasure on the earth, and been wanton; ye have nourished your hearts, as in a day of slaughter. Ye have condemned and killed the just; and he doth not resist you. Be patient therefore, brethren, unto the coming of the Lord. Behold, the husbandman waiteth for the precious fruit of the earth, and hath long patience for it, until he receive the early and latter rain. Be ye also patient; establish your hearts: for the coming of the Lord draweth nigh. Grudge not one against another, brethren, lest ye be condemned: behold, the judge standeth before the door. Take, my brethren, the prophets, who have spoken in the name of the Lord, for an example of suffering affliction, and of patience. Behold, we count them happy which endure. Ye have heard of the patience of Job, and have seen the end of the Lord; that the Lord is very pitiful, and of tender mercy.

Romans 1 v21-22

They knew God but did not praise and thank him for being God. Instead, their thoughts were pointless, and their misguided minds were plunged into darkness. While claiming to be wise, they became fools.

Deuteronomy 8

All the commandments, which I command thee this day, shall, ye observe to do, that ye may live, and multiply, and go in and possess the land, which the LORD swore, unto your fathers. And thou shalt remember all the way which the LORD thy God led these forty years in the wilderness, to humble thee, and to prove thee, to know what was in thine heart, whether thou wouldest keep his commandments, or not.

Therefore, as we walked, we reminded the people that Jesus taught us to Love the Father with all our hearts, minds, souls, and strength. In addition, to love each other as we love our selves. However, we have fallen so far into the deceit of Satan that it shows: we do not even love ourselves very much, in reality! Unfortunately the Church has much to blame, for reinforcing this division!

Angrily pitched against each other, each is so frightened we can no longer communicate with each other. Are church leaders in fear of losing members and their respective donations? Alternatively we are living a vision only? By our own doing we are not incorporating the teaching of the whole gospel to our disciples. Just saying we could do better. I feel we will.

Repeatedly I witnessed this problem and endured hardship after hardship when rectifying false teaching. Coming from some reformation Churches, their messages are often full of pride and deception, focused against the older Churches, each one feeling theirs is the more blessed message. Or they feel that they read the word better and understand it more. I just do not understand our pride, for this is the fallen nature of Satan! In addition, he would have us become prideful, as he is prideful!

Of course, our great hope is in Christ Jesus and he is the author and finisher of our faith, so blessed is the name of the Lord amen! However, God has to protect our nation over the deception of satanic powers due to our weak nature and willingness to sin. I say these things and reaffirm them because unity is required to fight the battle against evil forces such as abortion.

While we were walking up the Newport boardwalk heading north past 15th Street, young people came running off the beach to witness the cross and pray with us. It was a great feeling and a sight to see, so many people, young and old, loving Christ. A Catholic youth leader and his group of about 10 were all very excited to have the opportunity to share their love of Christ. In their public admiration of faith, we all joined hands and prayed for the spirit of Pentecost to fill the Church. We also prayed for stronger and more powerful disciples in the Catholic Church and the return of all lost Catholic Christians!

Men and women from many other denominations came to pray and sign the cross. There were so many that it took us 16 hours to reach Newport & Huntington Beach river jetties! People of every race, nation, and tongue signed the cross over a distance of about 12 miles. It was a wonderful and powerful day. So many young women were seeking God's protection from man's unwillingness to become good spiritual men. Practicing perfect chastity in preparation for marriage is not optional. They call it the Ten Commandments, not the Ten Suggestions! Men, do you want to understand the true desires of a woman's heart, what they really want? This is hard truth and harder to accomplish I know I am not perfect either however by digesting truth I have become far better with the protection of the holy Spirit and angelic host sent as protection for the journey. How else could a man complete such a thing? Now I am not better I suffer and bleed as any man.

But I am striving to be good as God is good which brings me closer to being Christ like each day.

Every wonderfully-true Christian woman wants a man to be their friend, to treat them with the respect due them as sisters-in-Christ, and as faithful husband, given to one woman, to lead them to a true faith in our Lord! Not an insipid Church, but a Church based on family and discipleship! In other words, Churches for full-grown Christians because babies in Christ have not yet let God prepare them for marriage! No woman is looking to divorce before her marriage even begins. Yet this is what we find all over in our Churches of today! Let alone the world outside the church. I have suffered from this reality in my life and it hurts so deeply in my soul. So really for me as well the walk is penitence

Circumstance, you may ask? Hardly so, since division begets division. Look inside your heart and ask yourself this question. "Why do we have so many Churches today?" Mainly because of pride and the unwillingness to submit to spiritual authority, and that spirit of insubordination really began back in the Arian heresy and then the reformation Church, to where we find today the spread of four square and non-denominational Churches. If we do not like something about a Church we just open our Bible, take liberties and start our own Church! I warn of this only because of the danger it can bring to the pastor's and teachers causing such things. It is because I care that I speak at all.

You know it is once again not that all reformation, Christian Churches are wrong, far from that, as some of the teaching is wonderful and very insightful. And I love the jubilance and excitement, but when it is a question as to who's Church is right or standing in battles over the bread and body of Christ, I feel sad. Winning the unsaved, that is the answer, and if you really have a chip on the shoulder about another man's Church, go with a group of elders and witnesses and have your debate or rebuttal to restore unity!

CROSSWALK

The Unity of the Body
Ephesians 4

I am in prison because I belong to the Lord. God chose you to be his people, so I urge you now to live the life to which God called you. Always be humble, gentle, and patient, accepting each other in love. You are joined together with peace through the Spirit, so make every effort to continue together in this way. There is one body and one Spirit, and God called you to have one hope. There is one Lord, one faith, and one baptism. There is one God and Father of everything. He rules everything and is everywhere and is in everything. Christ gave each one of us the special gift of grace, showing how generous he is. That is why it says in the Scriptures, "When he went up to the heights, he led a parade of captives, and he gave gifts to people." When it says, "He went up," what does it mean? It means that he first came down to the earth. So Jesus came down, and he is the same One who went up above all the sky. Christ did that to fill everything with His presence. And Christ gave gifts to people he made some to be apostles, some to be prophets, some to go and tell the Good News, and some to have the work of caring for and teaching God's people. Christ gave those gifts to prepare God's holy people for the work of serving, to make the body of Christ stronger. This work must continue until we are all joined together in the same faith and in the same knowledge of the Son of God. We must become like a mature person, growing until we become like Christ and have his perfection.

Then we will no longer be babies. We will not be tossed about like a ship that the waves carry one way then another. No new teaching we hear from people who are trying to fool us will influence us. They make plans and try any kind of trick to fool people into following the wrong path. No! Speaking the truth with love, we will grow up in every way into Christ, who is the head. The whole body depends on Christ, and all the parts of the body are joined and held together. Each part does its own work to make the whole body grow and be strong with love.

Once again, please understand. There are many wonderful Churches, putting out great effort, but too many have only partial knowledge of Christ. Perhaps they do not know Him in a personal way! This seems to be the case in the congregations I met along the path.

15

Entering into Huntington Beach

While walking the Boardwalk along the state parking lots at the Beach, I realized the answer! God's people are the answer! There were thousands of people. It was evening and everyone was at the fire pits with their families and friends. We were being heckled by only a few of the teenagers and some older people as well but for the most part; there were Christians all around us seeking prayer for their families! People are in fear for their families today. "Are the Churches not praying enough?" was my first question. Or, have we forgotten how to pray? I found that to be true of every town I entered, that constant fervent prayer is missing in California today!

I told each one that was in pain or suffering, fathers, pray for your Wives first, then your Children, aloud every day and thank the Lord for the blessing that they are to us! There were children of every race, age, color and creed on their bikes; hundreds were running to sign the cross! Truly all day long, there were new conversions, even people coming to Christ for the first time. The fields are ripe and the harvest is plentiful. If we could just leave the building behind us a little, and converse openly about our faith, the Church would grow with new believers. Instead, we have many who are fallen-away, as well as the constant shuffling of people in search of a "better" church or presenter.

The next day, there were two surf contests on the same day. The surfers were coming over to us to sign the cross, and also for prayer to do well in their contest. It was wonderful to experience the youth of today loving Jesus, and trusting in the power of prayer! However it was almost in every conversation that we had with our young Americans, which Ken and I heard over and over again: our youth have confusion about which Church was the best. The Holy Spirit had me say that the churches that taught the Holy Trinity as one being were correct. And those who, by their teaching, led the people to live by the gospels—that is where you will grow in faith. Test all things by the gospels! It was best to trust in their pastor and to always remember that the body of Christ is bigger than we can imagine. Christians from all over the world Jewish, American, Chinese, Russian, middle Eastern, African, south American, you get the picture. Also the Holy Spirit had us say to all of them that they should study their bibles daily! It is in the reading of the word of God that we build our relationship with our Lord. The word is all truth, the truth will set them free, and who the Son sets free is free indeed! Truly I say I love all the people of all the world and I find it hard to find a true enemy as long as I speak the truth in Love and compassion.

However, in order to build a stronger, more complete understanding of truth, we must not omit looking to the older Churches and the Catholic Church is the first Church. It has so much to offer in its wealth of history and that true peace is found in the Holy Eucharist the actual Body of Jesus. We can say much about the traditions of the Church, because history has substantiated these, based upon the body of Christ—made of every soul that lived before us, all the Saints!

When we reached the Huntington Beach pier, I had my guitar with me, and we sang worship songs on the pier! Walking the trail north to Seal Beach, things slowed down a little, and families once again were coming to us for prayer and hope!

CROSSWALK

Inevitably, the same story was told about the problems and struggles that the families had, just to stay together. Now including my own! There is an all out attack on our family homes today, partly brought by the Muslims and Arab Islamic nations, and communists It is one of the oldest weapons humanity has used to destroy nations long before ours They are preying on our lack of understanding of their cultures, and their insipid activities working on the destruction of our nation, and we are falling prey to their plan! Everywhere I walked, I was approached by Buddhists, Hindu, and Muslims, making insults, and even telling me soon Americans will be learning their way of living. I have visited all their countries at length over 20 years in and out of the Middle East I love the people there truly; I realize it is a test for us! Jesus said your faith will be tested! This is the test my friends! Holy War is no joking matter. This is why I am warning you of unity now. To pass this test loving thy neighbor while respecting other nations, cultures and knowing them will require more humility than we currently possess. We are all in the test together. See this affects all Americans everywhere believer and none believer solely because we put in God we trust on our money and in our national anthem. There is much to be secret in this so all I can and must do is warning for you! Turn to God, and live as holy as possible for only the penitent nation will pass. And a failing grade in this test will be devastating for the entire world. I pray we will do an abrupt about face, and become America the land of the free again!

In addition, to the ones that would listen, I explained that we are a free people here in America, an advanced society of people. They told me that the cross was a lie, and I replied, I have my faith, and you have yours. I was only walking in obedience to Christ's calling, and I typically found that was acceptable by all people of different beliefs! Even though we must respect all life, God has not called us to believe all winds of doctrine. We are Christians; Christ gave us His Word to know how to live. Reading scrip-

123

tures is required to understand the life of Christianity, whereas to accept contrary faith teaching, whether intentionally or unintentionally, is to worship false gods!

Respect, compassion, and Love for all mankind is not to form the fruit of acceptance! We as Christians must be careful to know the vile evil this is, to build a strong America again by standing in the word of God and to become a prayerful! Other faiths will respect you if you stand for what you believe standing in peace love and charity is the only path to end this 1500 year old Holy war, and they will listen when mutual respect is given! Moreover, you never know when you may win a few to the Lord by your confession! God created all humanity but those who are not in Christ are lost! Winning the Lost requires us to live a faith-filled life! In addition, they will know we are Christians by our Love! They will not know this by our fear, or by our willingness to accept everything under the sun!

2 Corinthians 10
Paul's Authority to Speak Forcefully

Now I myself, Paul, plead with you with the gentleness and kindness of Christ I who am humble when I am face-to-face with you, but forceful toward you when I am away! I beg you that when I come I will not need to be courageous by daring to oppose some people who think that we are living according to the flesh. Of course, we are living in the flesh, but we do not fight in a fleshly way. For the weapons of our warfare are not those of the flesh. Instead, they have the power of God to demolish fortresses. We tear down arguments and every proud obstacle that is raised against the knowledge of God, taking every thought captive in order to obey Christ.

Ken and I were standing in prayer for hundreds of families and children of all ages. It was a very long day. As we were walking along the board walk at Bolsa Chica State Beach, a couple of wonderful young Hispanic boys came to us. They walked with us for a couple of miles. These boys were excited to hear the message of the Love of Christ! And they were standing in their faith to be seen pushing the cross, showing their young faith without any fear!

16

Walking into Seal Beach

Ken and I were very blessed by staying at Saint Ann's and praying with the Catholic Church. The priests there were wonderful, and helped us very much. There was a visiting Priest from Ireland, and we prayed for peace in the war of the Christians. Can you imagine that Christians are fighting each other in Ireland, and Britain In 2007? When will humanity ever learn? We also prayed Ireland would remain abortion free so far God has honored this prayer. We Americans must turn from the sin of abortion not by rewriting any law. Now it is by turning from killing babies and saying no to Planned Parenthood all together!

The world has been infested with the stain of abortion long before we ever started up here. It is truly a weapon of the holy war we are currently falling too. Do to our falling lack of knowledge. The dumbing of America and the church is weakening when it needs to be stronger than ever.

Is that where the free simple reformation Church's will lead us here in California? We must ask this simple question, in order to see where and how it all began. Well the facts are established in the facts of history.

17

Long Beach

Walking the boardwalk along the harbor at the sailor's monument, we prayed with a WWII veteran and his wife. They were newlyweds, full of great stories about America in the 30's and 40's, and how sad they were to see our youth so anti-God. Why are so many of our children so angry anyway, I thought to myself.

Here in Long Beach were all the Men that lived and died, giving their very lives during WWI, WWII, Korea, Vietnam, and Iraq. How do our children and young people turn so strongly against our Lord? I struggle with that question every day. We must begin to realize that the main problem lies within our school systems. Also the Media? And our young parents are living out of a false reality such as global warming which is a lie. It is obvious that is Satanic warming not nature.

Political correctness is a bunch of fear-filled Americans with a large lack of knowledge, coupled with unwillingness to research all the facts. The so-called social and political thinkers of our system are trying to build a humanistic utopia in America. Well, did it work for Rome, Germany, France, Spain, or even Babylon?

Spiritualists approached quite often, asking about the meaning of the Earth. These people were of college age. My reply is that History has the answer; where one can find all the answers. Study and do not waste your education on parties. We shared that all the answers they are seeking could be found in the library. However, in today's reformation theology mode, that it will take quite a bit of reading and researching to uncover it! But well worth the reading because the truth is liberating and it will set you free!!!

I will never understand how our politics have become disillusioned, created by political correctness. With no real issues, no standards of right or wrong, no morality in family matters, real Americans and myself are screaming out, "Stop!

Long Beach was busy, full of people asking questions and seeking prayer for our schools. I do have great faith in our school children today. They are tired of all the deception. Our school systems are establishing seeds of faith, without Christ, and based upon false premises. Once this Generation moves out of their way, our young people will bring the nation back to health. I will give you the reason. They realize that, without morals in Family and faith in Christ, when this generation is gone, they will be lost all together! Let's face it: our children are in trouble. Too many are being raised by single parents, and are not happy. Too often, they are taking the blame on themselves for the divorce of their mothers and fathers! Some have to navigate multiple parents before coming to an age when they can step out on their own. And that is why they are mad! When I was serving aboard aircraft carriers for some 10 years, there were literally 10's of thousands of our Young men who confessed their deepest secrets to me, in order to become useful men, and women of our armed forces! I have heard enough destruction of families to last an eternity.

Raise your children parents; teach them about Christ, they are crying out to you for this. Will you humble yourselves and bless that which belongs to God, or is an immoral life so much more important? I promised all those wonderful hurting men and women that I would try to do something when my sea time was over. I am here to keep my promise to them, God bless them. Also it would appear god is holding me to my promise as well.

CROSSWALK

We stayed at the First United Methodist Church in Long Beach and spoke with the youth Leaders and children of their inner-city program. It really was wonderful to participate with their mid week youth group.

Again many of the children were from single-family homes and had no one to be with after school. The youth leaders were quite inspiring, and had such a passion for building confidence in our young people. We prayed and they all signed the cross, and we had cupcakes, and juice with the children. It was a wonderful experience. Moreover, since our host informed the children that I was a retired Navy seaman, they had many questions about what was really happening in the world around them, as I am trying to share with you as well in this text. It is not Rambo or some story out of Hollywood! No this is the way it is all over the world! Jesus is truly everywhere.

There was this one young woman there that evening from Guyana, and she was just beginning to know Jesus. We shared about her hardships when she was in Africa, and it is so touching to think about the difficulties she overcame in her youth, having to grow up in a third world country. We prayed we will never have to experience that level of deprivation here in America! She was talking about their extreme poverty and sickness in their country, and the complete Collapse of the Family unit. We here in America think that the family unit is not important. Just look at what the collapse of the family has done around the world! If we have no solid family unit here in America, then we will have no nation. If we leave our families behind, America will die, and it is happening very rapidly all around us today!

This humanism is not working on any level, and only in the last 20 years has our elite of society accepted humanism. If we do not fight off humanism, we will head to devastation like Guyana. Family is the opposite of humanism! (It doesn't take a village to raise a child, it takes a FAMILY!)

Anyway we as Americans need to ponder on this for a while.

18

Long Beach to Los Angeles

Leaving Long Beach, we entered the industrial city of Wilmington, California. We were in the middle of nowhere, when the cart broke in half. The cart was made of aluminum, so I knew it would take a special type of welder. What to do? I felt it was over at that point.

At that moment, a truck driver stopped and said there was a welding shop that could fix us up only a block away. We only had 40 dollars at the time, however, Ken and I trusted God and walked the busted cart to the shop. In addition, the truck driver was there waiting for us! He paid for the welding that needed to be done, and gave us a healthy gift offering as well!

All along this journey, God kept showing up, and it was so amazing. We received only what we needed for the time but we never were in lack. So we prayed with the driver for his family, and we grabbed a little lunch while he was fixing the cart.

Just the testimony of what had just happened got people in the restaurant excited. How amazing! God was showing us how His presence is in every action we take, and just how much He is with us, so what do we have to worry about?

This is His amazing Love, grace, and peace for his people on earth! We thanked the welders for the great job fixing the cart, and off we went. Further up the road, we reached a little corner intersection; in a part of inner city Wilington. The homeless, poor and needy all came to the cross to receive prayer. Again, Ken and I did not have anything to give, but I said that which we have I give to you. We held hands, worshipped, and thanked God. We focused on the fact that, no matter our circumstances, God always loves us! It was so powerful, there were no words to express the Love and peace we shared during our moment of communional prayer, right there on that simple street corner in front of "nobody."

These people had nothing of monetary value and neither did Ken or I. We did not even know where we would sleep that night. Yet there we were, praying a prayer of agreement of faith—in downtown Wilmington! We asked if they knew of a place where we could stay the night, and a woman said there was a Catholic Church just around the corner. We turned the corner and there before our eyes was a grand parish, St Peter and Paul's. It had a big statue of Fr. Junipero Serra on the lawn of the Parish. I walked up and thought to myself what it must have been like to walk California; in the time he walked, not knowing where he was headed or where he would rest his head, hiking through our California desert!

At that moment, Fr. Peter came out to meet us. I was able to explain what we were doing, and then Fr. Peter opened the doors and gave us a nice room to sleep in their men's Bible study room.

I had my Guitar so we played some worship music and had a little Bible study between Ken and I. Feeling so loved and so much at home at St Peters and Paul's Parish, I was at complete rest after a long day's walk and prayer!

Ken being a true Protestant and a young Christian in the faith was a little disoriented by being in a Catholic setting! Yet we stayed two days, and Fr. Peter invited us to mass, heard our confessions and bought us every meal. We were wonderfully blessed there at St Peter and St Paul's parish, once again. And Ken saw that Catholics are true Christians. I thanked the Lord for Loving Ken and I so much, He was truly guiding our steps.

I noticed that when Fr. Peter would walk out of the parish, the people and children of the community would gather around him. It was quite easy to see that his community loved him very much. And Fr. Peter was much like a parent to each one, as it should be, as a good Shepherd watching over the well-being, of the people our Lord entrusted to him! Father Peter had a prayer sanctuary added that was open 24 hours a day for his people! To pray in Eucharistic Adoration.

The next day we were heading off to Lomita. It was quiet during our walk there. Many of the people we shared with had been following us on the news and were very excited to see us. The heavily Hispanic population was quite excited to see such an event taking place, and sought out prayer for their families. The Hispanic people were excited about the message of equality, one body, and one People in the Lord Jesus. Every nation and tongue in unity with great love singing songs of praises to our Lord! And we as Christian brothers and sisters must embrace our international community, with real Christian Love and see that we are the same in everyway! What a blessing to be able to share the message of Love and Unity! Praises to God our Father forever amen!

A special intention Prayer
To Our Lady of Guadalupe

O Holy Mary Virgin Mother of God who as our Lady of Guadalupe didst aid in the conversion of Mexico from paganism In the most miraculous way, we now beseech thee to bring about in these our times the early conversion of our modern world from its present neo-paganism to return to the one Holy Catholic and Apostolic Church of the divine Son, Jesus Christ, starting in the Americas and extending throughout the entire world, so that soon there may be truly "one fold one shepherd," with all governments recognizing the reign of thy Son, Jesus Christ the King. This we ask of the Eternal Father, through Jesus Christ His Son Our Lord and by thy powerful intercession—all for the salvation of souls, the triumph of the church, and peace in the world. Amen!!!!

19

Road to Redondo Beach

We met up with a woman who had made it her life to evangelize, and she worked in hospitals helping people in need. She also served others by passing out tracts to evangelize when she was off work!

This was a real powerful woman. She had three children as well! She let us keep the cross and cart in her hotel room for a couple of days. Ken and I went back to my house to be at Church, and to rest over the weekend! We were getting too far from home and this would be the last chance I would have to return and rest! We had a strong prayer meeting, and the woman-evangelist had come down from Redondo Beach to share with us at our Church!

We talked about the events along the walk and all the wonderful miracles and new salvations. We also mentioned how the Catholic Church had blessed us! Well again, I stuck my foot in my mouth. I never realized just how divided the Church was here at home. Being from a naval background, things like this were unacceptable divisions, all of which divisions are Satanic!

I had always thought that freedom to express a love for God in our own way is very healthy, however when that same freedom brings divisions of self-righteousness and pride into Christ's church; I must oppose it while I am on watch. Being a watchman myself! Here is the testimony of the guard:

Ezekiel 33

Once again a message came to me from the Lord. He said:

"Son of dust, tell your people: 'When I bring an army against a country, and the people of that land choose a watchman, and when he sees the army coming and blows the alarm to warn them, then anyone who hears the alarm but refuses to heed it well, if he dies, the fault is his own. For he heard the warning and would not listen; the fault is his. If he had heeded the warning, he would have saved his life. But if the guard sees the enemy coming and does not sound the alarm and warn the people, he is responsible for their deaths. They will die in their sins, but I will charge the watchman with their deaths. So with you, son of dust. I have appointed you as a security guard for the people of Israel; therefore, listen to what I say and warn them for me.

When I say to the wicked, 'O wicked man, you will die!' and you do not tell him what I say, so that he does not repent, that wicked person will die in his sins, but I will hold you responsible for his death. But if you warn him to repent and he does not, he will die in his sins, and you will not be responsible.

That is the reason I feel Our Lord chose me to walk the cross. I found this out in hindsight, that I was to warn this very wicked and perverse generation unto repentance. Yes this is the Old Testament and we are not "of the Law," so here is a New Testament Truth for you who are so hard hearted! (Jesus did not abolish the law, but came to fulfill it. Old Testament stands.)

2 Corinthians 3
Ministers of the New Covenant

Are we beginning to recommend ourselves again. Unlike some people, we do not need letters of recommendation to you or from you, do we? You are our letter, written in our hearts and known and read by everyone. You are demonstrating that you are Christ's letter, produced by our service, written not with

CROSSWALK

ink but with the Spirit of the living God, not on tablets of stone but on tablets of human hearts. Such is the confidence that we have in God through Christ. By ourselves we are not qualified to claim that anything comes from us. Rather, our credentials come from God, who has also qualified us to be ministers of a new covenant, which is not written but spiritual, because what is written brings death, but the Spirit gives life. Now if the ministry of death that was inscribed in letters of stone came with such glory that the people of Israel could not gaze on Moses' face (because the glory was fading away from it), will not the Spirit's ministry have even more glory? For if the ministry of condemnation has glory, then the ministry of justification has an overwhelming glory. In fact, that which once had glory lost its glory, because the other glory surpassed it. For if that which fades away came through glory, how much more does that which is permanent have glory? Therefore, since we have such hope, we speak with great boldness, not like Moses, who kept covering his face with a veil to keep the people of Israel from gazing at the end of what was fading away. However, their minds were hardened, for to this day the same veil is still there when they read the old covenant. Only in union with Christ is that veil removed. Yet even to this day, when Moses is read, a veil covers their hearts. But whenever a person turns to the Lord, the veil is removed. Now the Lord is the Spirit, and where the Lord's Spirit is, there is freedom. As all of us reflect the glory of the Lord with unveiled faces; we are being transformed into the same image with ever-increasing glory.

Anyway, that was part of the reason for the walk. I feel it also brought continuity back to the Church! We were invited to stay in every type of Church and denomination. Over the 1100 mile journey, All Churches were praising to the same God, maybe not exactly in the same way, but not so different, with freedom in Christ Jesus! It is not freedom in all religions but only in true Christianity. All other so-called religions are trained lines of thoughts because without Christ they cannot be a religion. If you actually read the book of the Koran, it is a form of global government and not a religion at all by its own form.

If we truly study Buddha's teaching, it is philosophy not religion, because he never in all of his teaching says that he is a God. Again, it is really a lack of vocabulary and unwillingness to question outcomes found in history, which creates misinformation, and this error often times has led to war. This is how war begins! Now Hinduism is a conglomeration of stories that can have good life messages, except for the way they treat woman and subordinates. Study them side by side. Read them for yourself. Be aware of their tenets and practices before allowing these influences, whether directly intended or not, into your life. The only reason I mention this is because there is good teaching found in all that is tempting to the reader and the demonic forces would love to lock your spirit away in any form of reality anything other than truth of God's word.

20

Redondo and Hermosa

Ken and I were hassled by only a few of our Youth; it seemed to always be a small portion of our youth today that had a problem with the message of salvation. What would cause such a thing? I started to ask questions about the issue of spiritual lineage. And 100% of the time, it was an issue over a broken home. Single parenthood and the lack of time and attention available for most part was the root problem. Men, it is not so much that we cannot see the problem. Clearly we are causing our own problems with sexual immorality, demeaning sex before or without marriage. This is partly the outcome of our school system teaching Darwin's Theory, and "animal kingdom" principles. Science has disproved the Darwin theory all together due to the absence of evidence! I worked aboard many scientific and oceanographic ships over a 7-year period, which covered a great portion of the earth. I have no questions as to the origin of the earth. It has been created, and it is not very old, based upon my first-hand knowledge and experience. So men, when you follow your passions, void of self-control, and say you are "only human", ask yourself then why you are acting like "an animal."

Across the spectrum of the sciences, creation has been proven beyond a shadow of a doubt. Pride is holding up these findings. When does an apple become an apple anyway?

Matthew 18
Who Is the Greatest?

At that time the disciples came to Jesus, saying, "Who is the greatest in the Kingdom of Heaven." And calling to him a child, he put him in the midst of them and said, "Truly, I say to you, unless you turn and become like children, you will never enter the kingdom of heaven. Whoever humbles himself as this child is the greatest in the kingdom of heaven." Whoever receives one such child in my name receives me, but whoever causes one of these little ones who believe in me to sin, it would be better for him to have a great millstone fastened around his neck and to be drowned in the depth of the sea.

Let's just pause, think and pray about this quote. Here, scripture does not speak of Church, or doctrine of faith. Schoolteachers need to be quite careful what they teach and how they present it. Reading the documents of the college founding fathers, and the charters of Yale, Harvard, and Princeton, many people would be in for a shock. Most American and European schools founding charters were established first and foremost to teach scripture, creation and the Gospel, most vehemently expressing that any secular pursuit, in absence of Christian values and mores, was a waste of time. The founding fathers must be turning over in their graves at our misguided curriculum.

Children of America do not need seeds of doubt to be planted, worshipping the mind over our humanity, cultivating apostasy, and leading them away from scriptural truth into dangerous areas. All this, is accomplished at the Americans taxpayer expense. That is from the children's and parents mouths. If this continues, you may soon be looking for work!!! What will your legacy be? Does it compare with the founding fathers'? Christ is coming in his judgment in his glory, to judge the living and the dead; where will you be found on that day? Found in the love and safety of Christ Jesus I pray. I will never say when he will return for it can' not be known. It is a secret of God's timing and only he knows. It is our duty to have our hearts open and ready at all times.

Revelations 4-5

After this I looked, and lo, in heaven an open door! And the first voice, which I had heard speaking to me like a trumpet, said, "Come up hither, and lo, a throne stood in heaven, with one seated on the throne! And he who sat there appeared like jasper and carnelian, and round the throne! And he who sat looked like an emerald. Around the throne were twenty-four thrones, and seated on the thrones were twenty-four elders, clad in white garments, with golden crowns upon their heads. From the throne issue flashes of lighting, and voices and peals of thunder, and before the throne burn seven torches of fire, which are the seven spirits of God; and before the throne, there is as it were a sea of glass, like crystal. And around the throne on each side of the throne, are four living creatures fill of eyes in front and behind: the first living creature like a lion, the second living creature like an ox, the third living creature with the face of a man, and the fourth living creature like a flying eagle. And the four living creatures, each of them with six wings, are full of eyes all around and within, and day and night they never cease to sing.

Holy, holy, holy, is the Lord God Almighty, who was and is to come!" And whenever the living creatures give glory and honor and thanks to him who is seated on the throne, who lives forever and ever, The twenty-four elders fall down before him who is seated on the throne and worship him who lives forever and ever; They cast there crowns before the throne, singing, Worthy art thou, our Lord and God, to receive glory and honor and power, for thou didst create all things,

And by thy will they existed and were created." And I saw in the right hand of him who was seated on the throne a scroll written within and on the back, sealed with seven seals; and I saw a strong angel proclaiming with a loud voice, "Who is worthy to open the scroll and break the seals?" and no one on heaven or on earth or under the earth was able to open the scroll or to look into it, Then one of the elders said to me, "weep not: the Lion of the tribe of Judah, the root of David, has conquered, so that he can open the scroll and its seven seals."

And between the throne and the four living creatures and among the elders, I saw a Lamb standing as though it had been slain, with seven horns and seven eyes, which are the seven spirits of God sent out into all the earth; and we went and took the scroll from the right hand of him who was seated on the throne. And when he had taken the scroll, and when he had taken the scroll, the four living creatures and the twenty four elders fell down before the lamb each holding a harp, and with golden bowls full of incense, which are the prayers of the saints; and they sang a new song, saying,

"Worthy art thou to take the scroll and open its seals, For thou wast slain and by the blood didst random men for God and has made him a King and priest to our God, and they shall reign on earth."

Then I looked, and I heard around the throne and the living creatures and the elders the voice of many angles, numbering myriads of myriads and thousands and thousands, saying with a loud voice, "worthy is the lamb who was slain, to receive power and wealth and wisdom and might and honor and glory and blessing!" and I heard every creature in heaven and on earth and under the earth and in the sea, and all therein, saying, "to him who sits upon the throne and to the Lamb be blessing and honor and glory and might forever and ever!" and the four living creatures said, "Amen" and the elders fell down and worshiped.

This is for all that have ears to hear what the spirit is saying! This is the true spirit of prophecy that is Jesus was crucified and died on the cross to reconcile all of humanity and creation with God. Only God the father knows the time of the return of the Son who by his death and resurrection is the only one worthy to open the seal at its appointed time. It can' not be known Just be ready at all times.

21

Los Angeles

Walking through LA, this teaching came to be a more evident problem in our young people's minds. As they become older, their struggles only expand due to a weak foundation, and they suffer from abortions and lost loves. What a web of filth we've set up for our children to unravel. I pray this walk will help set us on the path of a renewal of brotherly love and compassion to all. I met a young woman who talked to me at some length, a victim of this problem.

She had been away from the Church for some time, and believed that she had to sleep with men, and take drugs to be loved. She was molested by her own father, throughout most of her childhood, and she felt that sex was the ultimate love.

My heart was dying for the right words, to bring peace to such a hurting soul. Not in some far nation like Guyana, this is Los Angeles. Total devastation of the family unit! I stared into heaven and asked the Holy Spirit for the right words and this was how I was led...

We sat down and I placed a blanket around her. I indicated that we are born into original sin and that sin brings the presence of the tempter Satan, the author of the fall of humanity. And as your father was angrily using you in such a way, he was also a sinner and in need of her forgiveness! Not only to help relieve his suffering, but rather, a place of deep inner, healing for her heart and life.

Then I shared the best relationship with her. Do you believe in one God the Father Almighty, Creator of heaven and earth? Do you believe in Jesus Christ, God's only Son, and that He is our Lord, Who was conceived by the Holy Spirit, born of the Virgin Mary, that our Lord suffered under Pontius Pilate, was crucified, died and was buried? Do you believe that on the third day He arose from the dead and that he ascended into heaven, and is seated at the right hand of the Father? She said yes and I asked that God would receive her prayer of forgiveness, and to set her feet back on the path of righteousness! She began to weep and it gave my heart such joy to see, The Power of the Holy Spirit blessing yet another lost soul. Then we shared that Christ is her husbandman.

James 5

> Ye have lived in pleasure on the earth, and been wanton; ye have nourished your hearts, as in a day of slaughter. Ye have condemned and killed the just; and he doth not resist you. Be patient therefore, brethren, unto the coming of the Lord. Behold, the husbandman waiteth for the precious fruit of the earth, and hath long patience for it, until he receive the early and latter rain.

I humbly explained by the power of the Holy Spirit that she and all people who love the Lord are his precious fruit. By her confession, she would start to be dressed by the vinedresser, which was the Holy Spirit, our helper. She had to return to living out her faith, within the true Church, serving the Lord Jesus, which is true Love. Then she asked me how she could live such a life after all of her past.

Relationship is a strong word; she had many relations with men, and I likened them to envelopes in our memories. And in

CROSSWALK

the naturalistic life, all people are seeking joy, safety, love, and happiness through sinful lusts and passion, and that she was not alone. We all struggle with this temptation to find that euphoric feeling! So as relationships form, we tend to store imaginations of the perfect lover or that one true relationship! Each person is quickly filed into an envelope to judge the next person by, then faster and faster we disqualify each relationship. And our case file grows which acts to deepen our inner convictions and wrongdoing against ourselves. This besets us with constant worrying: Will I get pregnant? Will I need another abortion? It is a battle all the way around! And just then, Christ comes and by his amazing grace, we are forgiven! Then He connects us with a Church family, where deep healing begins to transform our lives. He delivers us out of the envelope lifestyle; then we begin to fall in love with the creator of all things. We start to become useful to the kingdom and Jesus authors our footsteps. And if marriage is his will for our lives, he will prepare us for a spouse which he will bring alongside at his timing, and for his purpose.

We can all see the true key of wisdom here, that is to take action, get out and surrender all to Christ, confess each envelope hidden in our past, become free from our burdens of sin and death. Moreover, it allows us to start building new envelops of good works in Christ, to begin to store our treasure in heaven where we will spend eternity, and to build a relationship once again with the Father. Once He has washed and cleansed everything, pray for that relationship to be strong, because God has the very best in which He has prepared for you!

I told her that I felt that God had someone very special just waiting for her, but first she must learn to trust in God, to meet and know His Son. I also told her that Queen Mary, and all of heaven's armies would rejoice for the return of her precious soul! And that first she must build a relationship of love in Christ Jesus where nothing else mattered. Because no husband or wife can fill the need of the Love of the Trinity and the Kingdom of

Heaven holds for all humanity. Amen! And when Christ does bring someone for us we must always keep Christ as the husbandman, so we do not fall at each other's shortcomings but help strengthen each other in our time of need.

Ephesians 3

For this cause I bow my knees unto the Father, from whom every family in heaven and on earth is named, that he would grant you, according to the riches of his glory, that ye may be strengthened with power through his Spirit in the inward man; that Christ may dwell in your hearts through faith; to the end that ye, being rooted and grounded in love, may be strong to apprehend with all the saints what is the breadth and length and height and depth, and to know the love of Christ which passes knowledge, that ye may be filled unto all the fullness of God.

We then shared that the battle raged every day and to defeat the wiles of the devil we must read the word of God and understand the full Armor of God. Ephesians 6 explains the true life in Christ and the protection from the devil!

Ephesians 6

Children, obey your parents in the Lord: for this is right. Honor thy father and mother (which is the first commandment with promise), that it may be well with thee, and thou mayest live long on the earth. And, ye fathers, provoke not your children to wrath: but nurture them in the chastening and admonition of the Lord.

I shared with her that many people get hung up on this teaching. In her case, her father was not living in the Lord and that her true Father was the Father of all orphans and widows. This was God in the form of Christ Jesus, and to stand fast in the knowledge of the Love Christ has for us all!

I must say in my own life I have been married three time's mostly the US Navy is a hard life for a wife to fallow too hard for my love alone was not enough. However when I was at home from deployment to Bosnia, Darfur, and two Iraq wars, well my sons, and I would lay in their bedroom together and I would tell them of my deployments, and the need for all they had to suffer. I said I had a hard time finding an enemy as all people in every country; race and creed all need Love, of family food, and shelter from the storms of life. I thanked God for my family's safety here at home. That they did not have to suffer the petulance of Genocide So I shared with them the hard truth's found in our world that is was a peace of me that brought me to walk the cross because we would read scripture together and I would place prayers under there pillow's to let them know how much God, and I loved them. Today they are men raising their own children. Children that share and look to God for the same hope's. God knows I pray for them still seeking that he would bless and watch over them all, and keep them from harm. I am alone today can't say I understand I will have to ask our Lord when I arrive to atone for my own short comings.

> *Servants, be obedient unto them that according to the flesh are your masters, with fear and trembling, in singleness of your heart, as unto Christ; not in the way of eye service, as men-pleasers; but as servants of Christ, doing the will of God from the heart; with good will doing service, as unto the Lord, and not unto men: knowing that whatsoever good thing each one doeth, the same shall he receive again from the Lord, whether he be bond or free. And, ye masters, do the same things unto them, and forbear threatening: knowing that he who is both their Master and yours is in heaven, and there is no respecter of persons with him.*

Also, this was good news that God chose her as his own, and he looks not upon our sin; but we were to work, and serve all that we do as unto the Lord God. That was why she must submit

herself to spiritual authority in a Christ—centered Church! So
if god has you doing his good work and you are suffering hardship well we know there is a battle and I still do not fully know
why I am here today with our lords cross all I know is I am here
and it is happening! So all you sowers of good works let's stand
together in the Unity of Love and forgiveness. So our children of
the whole world can be relieved of the pain of genocide. This is
the fruit of church unity world peace. I know we can do it. The
world has suffered enough. Let's stand together now and ask God
for reconciliation. And by our, Love and Unity we pray let there
be Peace on earth.

Continuing EPH 6

*Finally be strong in the Lord, and in the strength of his might.
Put on the whole armor of God that ye may be able to stand
against the wiles of the devil. For our wrestling is not against
flesh and blood, but against the principalities, against the
powers, against the world-rulers of this darkness, against the
spiritual hosts of wickedness in the heavenly places. Wherefore
take up the whole armor of God that ye may be able to withstand
in the evil day, and, having done all, to stand. Stand therefore,
having girded your loins with truth, and having put on the
breastplate of righteousness, and having shod your feet with the
preparation of the gospel of peace; with taking up the shield of
faith, wherewith ye shall be able to quench all the fiery darts of
the evil one. And take the helmet of salvation, and the sword
of the Spirit, which is the word of God: with all prayer and
supplication praying at all seasons in the Spirit, and watching
thereunto in all perseverance and supplication for all the
saints, and on my behalf, that utterance may be given unto
me in opening my mouth, to make known with boldness the
mystery of the gospel, for which I am an ambassador in chains;
that in it I may speak boldly, as I ought to speak.*

The deep healing that she would need to receive would come
from reading the word of God for herself. Is I had to seek for

myself. All Christians need to build a commanding power from praying the scriptures themselves! That the armor was all about scripture knowledge, producing wisdom that would ultimately deliver her from her pain and suffering! And to practice the armor daily this would make her strong in faith and that God would prepare a husband for her! And it will be the right husband for her and he will possess the same level of faith! A true man of God will practice the wisdom of armor in intercessory prayer (speaking daily scriptural prayers of blessing) over their families and the wife in submission to the husband, protecting the husband's back with her shield of faith. This is a part of the mystery of the union of marriage!

So again, we can see there is so much to learn about true marriage in the scriptures. What if we began to study and teach these principles in our schools and Churches? What power we are overlooking! Far more powerful than all the armies of the world combined, if you really want peace, that my beloved, is the path to world peace, and peace of mind heart and soul. Then to my new sister in Christ I said my peace I give to you. I have nothing else to offer but what I have been freely given. I also therefore give unto you. I walked away with her, and her tears dried up, and with greater wisdom and understanding of what the world is all about. Truly, I say that the Kingdom of heaven is upon us!

Walking Further into LA, we came to Venice Beach where we were inundated with thousands of people! More than ever, persecution was on people's lips, saying that the cross was a lie and irrelevant. The most interesting truth of the whole walk was that not once did mockers try to defend their stand! Other than a cuss word here or there, it was only a remark, and off they ran. The devil has weak foot soldiers. I found this was true every time I had an opportunity to engage in conversation for the 1100 miles, we travled, so what are we so afraid of? Since we are Christians, God calls us to speak boldly about the truth of Christ our Savior.

John 3

"There is no judgment awaiting those who trust him. But those who do not trust him have already been judged for not believing in the only Son of God. Their judgment is based on this fact: The light from heaven came into the world, but they loved the darkness more than the light, for their actions were evil. They hate the light because they want to sin in the darkness. They stay away from the light for fear their sins will be exposed and they will be punished. But those who do what is right come to the light gladly, so everyone can see that they are doing what God wants."

Pope Benedict XVI Teaches about Civil Right of Religious freedom

I quote: the Church's diplomatic relations from a part of her mission of service to the international community. Her *engagement with civil society is anchored in the conviction that the task of guiding a more just world must acknowledge and consider man's supernatural vocation.*

The Holy See strives therefore to promote an understanding of the human person who receives from God his essential dignity and with it the capacity to transcend every social order to move towards truth and goodness. From this foundation, the Church applies the universal values, which safeguard the dignity of every person and serve the common good to the vast array of cultures and nations that constitute our world ...

It is to faith communities that political and civic authorities can turn for a determined commitment to shaping the social order in accordance with the common good. Such community be sanctioned as a fundamental civil right and afforded protection by robust framework of juridical norms, which respect the laws and duties proper to religious communities. Such practical support of religious freedom by political leaders becomes a sure means for authentic social progress and peace.

Again unity in progress is by far and away the largest single body of Christians on earth! Do we all have to become Catholics and leave our Churches? No, according to our Pope Benedict XVI better yet we are already Catholics, Big C being the fullest teaching authority on earth little c being the rest of Christian religious so we are already on the way in accordance to the definition of the Greek word meaning universal Church, or whole Church to the degree that we live the Catholic faith! Much of what Protestants term 'fundamental Christianity' is nothing but Catholic doctrine. Of course, Catholics have the full embodiment of the faith, whereas Protestants only have a part of it. For instance, "You are justified by faith, without the deeds of the Law."

The law is part of Catholic doctrine, but a lot of Protestants will claim that it is not, and thus deceive lukewarm Catholics. We are all one in Christ, the sooner we understand the truth the better off the whole world will be in Christ!

It is my understanding of the universal Christian Church that Pope Benedict is saying stand in truth, live as a true witness of faith and have reverence and respect for all humanity!

For they will all know you are Christians by your Love! And it is my prayer that we can see this remarkable work of God. This work which we discovered while on this walk, there have been healings, deliverances, acts of loving kindness, not originating from Ken or anything of myself, because we in ourselves are nothing; these miracles were of the Trinity of Christ, and his witness by God in His Son's crucifixion! In so many ways, Ken and I just had a front row seat to watch the work from his mighty hand and even as I spoke I know it was the Holy Spirit which blessed my lips to be able to meet the needs of the ocean of hurting humanity that Ken I encountered all along the trek! I wish I could bring into view the sea of human hearts that are not mentioned but the book would become valiums long. And so as I was reaching out to one, Ken touched five more.

22

Walking Up to Ocean Beach Pier

A "wise" man, with a science background, stopped us by his laughter. He could not believe his own eyes. He began questioning us about the Cross. He said. "Don't you realize that cross is a fairytale?" I asked. "Just what do you mean by a fairytale?"

With his wisest answer he rebutted, "Humanity has reproduced creation by genetics, and can make a human with just a sample of any man's DNA, and the egg of the woman." Of course, I agreed completely, answering him yes, sir, that is true. Then he went on about tetra-reformation of the moon and Mars and all we do in outer space, and going deeply into modern medical science and all of our technological advances. The list went on and on. He seemed quite intelligent and very well informed.

I believe he was a professor at UCLA with all the degrees that higher education can offer. Ken and I quietly listened intently, clinging to every word, as we learned of his educational background. Now, in bringing his argument to a grand finish in somewhat of a rage, stated, "See? There is no God!" I then rebutted his statements. All you have said is true—we have uncovered and molecularly reconstructed all things, which are created. He smiled smugly, and then I said humans are without question, the greatest puzzle builders of the known universe.

Then I asked, "Could you Please, Sir, answer this puzzling truth for me." I walked over to the sidewalk and plucked a blade of grass, which had pushed its way through the cracks in our concrete to survive.

"Civilization," I said; as I plucked the straggly blade of grass and held it up firm in my hand. Then I said "Sir, I will put down my cross, and agree with all of your evidence, if you can do one thing for me." I gave him my card with my contact info. "Here is my challenge and my question:"

Use every piece of technology available in the entire world and create this blade of grass from nothing at all! This little blade of grass pushed up through man's concrete jungle! We cannot kill creation, and we need it to exist. Creation itself proclaims the truth of God. And that He is the designer as well.

He looked at me very bewildered and, with a strange, puzzled look, this wise man sadly walked away! It was so easy to see that he was deeply hurt and angry with God, separating himself from the all too obvious truth. Perhaps a loss of a loved one, I could only guess but it made me quite sad. All too often we carry burdens that we were never meant to carry, and we become bewildered to the wonderful Joy that life is to all of us.

God, there is true joy in serving you! Why can't we just surrender?

All along this walk, I received such blessings and great sorrows at the same time! We see this wonderful truth of what we just shared in this portion of God's Word.

Romans 1

For the wrath of God is revealed from heaven against all ungodliness and unrighteousness of men, who hinder the truth by unrighteousness; because that which is known of God is manifest in them, for God manifested it unto them. For the invisible things of him since the creation of the world are clearly seen, being perceived through the things that are made, even his everlasting power and divinity; that they may be without excuse: because that, knowing God, they glorified him not as

*God, neither gave thanks; but became vain in their reasoning,
and their senseless heart was darkened. Professing themselves
to be wise, they became fools, and changed the glory of the
incorruptible God for the likeness of an image of corruptible
man, and of birds, and four-footed beasts, and creeping things.*

So this poor professor of great human knowledge and intellect
was actually very foolish in his thoughts, in refusing to give God
the Glory due his divinity! Higher education itself is a wonderful
and most important blessing from God!

As per the writing of Pope John Paul II, our minds are our
souls. Found in the Companion's teaching and it is our hearts of
his chosen in which Christ resides, and bringing us into complete
unity with the oneness of the spirit and with great Faith and
Love for all of creation and our fellow man!

Blessed Charles De Foucauld

Warned France and their culture, to live Holy lives, to call for
national—and international repentance or the Islamic and the
Moorsmen would invade.

History records that in less then 40 years after his warning, Hitler overran France; then after their liberation by the
American and allied forces, France still would not repent, and
turn to God. Now today, France is overrun with Muslims that are
burning their towns and communities. No dis respect to Islam or
Muslims no rather I respect their power for the test they bring to
us. No I respect and Love them very much. Although I retain my
Catholic roots. And call them my friends. For I know firsthand
their struggles, and pain.

My message to America is in a similar situation; America must
repent or fall to the same demise. "Is it God's will?" many people
ask me this question. I say no! Devastation and pestilence comes
because of our unwillingness to serve God, turn from our sin, and

read His Word! Complete repentance is completely required for God to heal our land!

Charles De Foucauld Meditation on Psalm 1

You tell me I shall be happy, filled with the happiness of true blessedness, on the last day that even in my present wretchedness, I am a Palm tree planted beside living waters, the living waters of God will, love, and grace and that I shall bring forth fruit in its proper season. You take the trouble to console me; I feel I am without fruit, without good works. I tell myself: It is eleven years since I converted, and what have I done? What are my good works compared to those of the saints? I see myself with hands empty of anything good. Yet you take the trouble to console me, saying you will bear in your proper season. But what season is that. The proper season for us, all is the Day of Judgment. You promise that poor as I am if I persevere in the good fight with a good will I shall bear fruit at that last hour. And you add; you will be a fine tree with leaves eternally green, and all your works will prosper in the end; they will all bear fruit in eternity. O God, how good you are!

How divinely consoling is the Heart of Jesus! It is as though you had dictated these first words in the Book of Psalms to tell us what you once said by the Sea of Galilee! My yoke is sweet and my burden is light. I thank you, My God, for the consolation you give us, consolation of which our hearts stand in such great need!

I quoted this portion because that is the true nature of a repentant heart seeking God. If you are a businessman, teacher, government official, military, father, mother, sick or healthy person, give praise to the One worthy of all our praise who is Christ Jesus!

23

Santa Monica Heading to Malibu PCH (Pacific Coast Highway)

Walking along the 27 miles of coastal homes, the sight of the cross was very well received. So many people were cheering and waving with their hands hanging out of their car windows. Yet still again some were angry. And still others were very afraid of Christ's return; I would have to guess for good reason!

I had to share with them the presence of God, just softly mentioning the reason why Christ has not already returned. It is because of his great understanding of our human frailties and weaknesses. God is not so angry with us that his grace and forgiveness cannot blot out our sins. We must remember Christ paid the price for all sin but only some would accept it, and claim Christ as Lord. Much rather, it is His great pleasure to forgive our sins, and to lead us unto repentance so we may receive greater Joy! If we would only repent and turn our hearts toward Him, God will bless us and heal our families, and our lands will be restored, Amen! However if not the Great trembling and tribulation, of which you are all are so apparently afraid of; will come by your own hard-heartedness. Sounds a lot like Ramses, Pharaoh of Egypt, remember?

By his own words and actions, God destroyed the great nation of Egypt. Now remember, Pharaoh brought the killing of every first born of Egypt upon himself. All I can say to the hard hearts of today found right here in our once great, American nation is good luck with your stand against God! And if God should allow you to decimate our culture, by the blood stain brought by abortion and all manner of heinous sinful nature what will you name the new regime? The fourth order of the fourth right well there you are. Running furlong into Hitler's trap, Beware not so easily dismissed.

In addition, I pray that this sinful generation be removed from power, moreover that the true Americans will stand up and vote now for the God fearing leaders to rule so the people can rejoice! Once again!

Which brings to mind another Kingdom, which possessed very Great Power, and it was full of humanistic wisdom, mindsets, and ideals, with the full intent of taking an anti-Christian stand. This man was quite well-educated by man's standards, and a powerful humanistic leader, and in many ways the people's choice. His name was Joseph Stalin, USSR.

There is a great statue which shows Joseph shaking his fist at heaven declaring that there is no God! At the time, Russia was very, very strong. Yet today their once mighty empire is fallen, because of Lenin and Stalin's stand for communism, and their hard-hearted murderous ways. They turned their power against God, and all of God's people within their own borders, Stalin then rattled the sabers of war against his own people where he ordered the murdering of millions. Some-were around 52 million Christian and Jewish Russians were murdered in Russia's own genocide. As I said ex-Navy retired so with true for knowledge America was never truly at war with the Russian people but we were standing against the Russian order of genocide. Don't believe me read Russian history. Blessed John Paul II and Ronal Reagan and Mikhail S Gorbachev worked together to bring an end to the slater when the East German wall came down. It ended

If you can imagine such a horrific event, the Russian martyrs were mainly Christians and Jews, Russian Orthodox, the smaller population of Roman Catholics, and any fundamental group that stood against Stalin's pride and arrogance.

While flexing his atheistic Anti Christian powers, they used all their humanistic leadership skills to become a world superpower as well. So it came to pass, that it took less than 40 years for the once powerful nation to crumble.

Today Russia only exists in devastation! Soon the good people of Russia will get back on her feet, thanks be to God, because their entire nation is repenting and turning back to God, and strangely enough you my fellow Americans and running directly in the same temptation and will suffer the same genocide and dumb anguish as they have the past 60 years. Not ling to suffer so much. Now mostly due to the loving support, that is coming from Holy churches around the globe. It is the same body of Christ that Stalin tried so hard to destroy in his puny lifetime. They are reaching out to our many Russian families, our brothers, and sisters in the Lord. However they are still in terrible and need our love and support America buck it up n today. What if we really showed Russia our best side, in this their hour of need, and do the same in Iraq? Still Russia is a true national testimony of the faithfulness of Our All Mighty Lord's willingness to forgive sin on an entire nation.

Why? God is love and he is pleasant and kind!

A nation cannot mock God and survive! Good luck, libertarians here in America today, who takes a Stalin-type, stand.

It's still not too late to repent, and you will be saving your children's lives from this same misfortune. All of these things take time, and the price of your selfishness will be paid by your children who will have to fight a much greater war for what you deem as popular or political correctness.

God is certainly saying to us—turn away from sin and choose life!

Walking along the Malibu cliffs the weather was wonderful in the month of June and the waves were great. Ken and I decided to take a swim and do some surfing around the Malibu pier; it was great fun sharing some of events of the crosswalk with my brethren-surfers. And people sunning on the beach as they got up, came over to sign the Cross! Truly I say to you that there is great hope for our nation, if we can soften our minds a little, and love each other a whole lot more. Just forget about ourselves a little, and begin loving one another as Americans from the heart. Not "sexually"—that is lust. One Nation under God—it kind of has a nice ring to it, I think. It was a very long walk that day, ending with a great swim.

Ken and I camped out by the Ventura county line, and played guitar, and reminisced about all the days we had walked, and the wonderful people we had met along the way. I had a cell phone, so people were calling for prayer and giving testimony of answered prayers. A man we had prayed with a little earlier called me. He had bought us all a nice dinner to share. He came into the camp and fellowshipped with us. He was a funny type, and had great life stories. We sat around the campfire for a while playing worship songs when he said he had to go, but he thanked us from his heart for the prayers, and he took off. Our new friend came back from time to time, over the next couple of days, until we walked too far away. What a great Guy! God I miss all the wonderful smiles and conversations of the normal American people. Praise God forever.

24

Malibu to Point Mugu Naval Station

The walk started moving a little faster as we were along the winding waterfront. Still many people would pull over into turnouts and receive prayer for everything from family needs to intercessory prayer for our state and nation. I am by far not the only one concerned about the turn toward evil here in California. Oh, yah, we Christians still out-number the atheist activists—we are just not as organized. Check me if I am wrong, but just perhaps, unity of the Church is what God is requiring here.

We came around Point Dome where a very excited man and his son stopped, took pictures of the event and received prayer. This man would bless us many times during our journey! We arrived at Point Mugu at about 3pm. We had a little problem with the civilian gate guard about the cross coming on the base once again. With my military ID and the Officer of the Day's permission, we walked across the base and to the Pacific Beach camping area, where we pitched our tents and stayed for three very nice quiet days. Now Ken and I had walked our first 250 miles per the bike route along the Californian coastline! Our feet were sore, and we needed a much needed rest, praise God!

During our stay, many people on base asked questions about the Holy cross, and what we were doing. We sang and played Guitar around the campfire, and swam and surfed during the days but the water was very cold! Still Ken and I were having a great time. The next day, my friends from Laguna and their sons met us in their nice, comfortable motor home; the whole family was heading up the coast for a vacation. It was great to see them again and, the boys were having a great time camping. See—that is the message of it all: Enjoy what God has given us, and be happy at whatever it is we are given to do, and it will be the best life for each person.

Romans 9

Who are you, a mere human being, to criticize God? Should the thing that was created say to the one who made it, "Why have you made me like this?" When a potter makes jars out of clay; doesn't he have a right to use the same lump of clay to make one jar for decoration and another to throw garbage into? God has every right to exercise his judgment and his power, but he also has the right to be very patient with those who are the objects of his judgment and are fit only for destruction. He also has the right to pour out the riches of his glory upon those he prepared to be the objects of his mercy even upon us, whom he selected, both from the Jews and from the Gentiles.

I know that I am not saying or preaching anything new but that is because this is a true statement and there is nothing new under the sun!

Lately I have been hearing that God is doing a new thing, rattling through the pulpits of America's pastoral staff. I just questioned within myself, and I know that I am not sure of everything, because I can live in the Holy Spirit but who can truly understand God? However, is it not the same God that said he changes not? I am Who am. I can believe better that we have been greatly duped by the enemy!

Yep, in order to better divide and separate the Church, and judging the results from the twenty years I was away, I must say there is something very wrong. We have thousands of crosses on top of buildings and more Christians than ever yet, all hell has broken loose on the Church because divided, we are not strong.

I believe that it was America's motto not long ago, stating that united we stand, divided we fall. It was a song as well.

After three days of resting, Ken and I broke camp, then started walking the 5 miles to get off the base.

The Naval-base Chaplain came to me and told me that the Chaplaincy had become so politically correct that everything written for Mass or services had to be edited by ethicist entities from all the armed forces! I said what a difference 7 years made; I had retired in 1996 and was working in the Merchant Marines over the last 7 years in the Middle East and North Korea! This Chaplin knew something was "stinking in the woodpile!" We agreed and prayed that God would help us in America! I believe we can see another noticeable Prophecy that is taking place today!

Revelation 13

And there was given to him a mouth speaking great things and blasphemies; and there was given to him authority to continue forty and two months. And he opened his mouth for blasphemies against God, to blaspheme his name, and his tabernacle, even them that dwell in the heaven. And it was given unto him to make war with the saints, and to overcome them: and there was given to him authority over every tribe and people and tongue and nation. And all that dwell on the earth shall worship him, every one whose name hath not been written from the foundation of the world in the book of life of the Lamb that hath been slain. If any man hath an ear, let him hear. If any man is for captivity, into captivity he goeth: if any man shall kill with the sword; with the sword must he be killed. Here is the patience and the faith of the saints.

I can't help but see this as Mohammad's Islam and Muslims; after all, who has been fighting the saints over the past 1100 years? And been given authority to do so? And they have literally murdered 100's of millions of people, all over the earth, and in their own borders as well. The murdering has not stopped even until today. How lucky we are to be Americans—for now? Tic, tic, tic

Well then, turning from God at times of spiritual warfare is a very wrong move! Now more than ever, prayer is required of us all, Protestants, and all other denominations come boldly before the throne room of grace! Catholics and all Orthodoxy, pray the scriptural rosary and all manner of prayer!

With all our hearts, let us sing by our faith singing out a glorious song of praise that will ring out thundersly with a great sound of beauty before the throne room of God. For a season, let humanity praise God louder than the angel's above. Amen!

Praying and Singing songs of deliverance, and praise to the Holy one!" Holy, holy, holy Is the Lord God Almighty. Worthy is the Lamb!

Yes Lord Jesus Let there be peace on earth and good will to all mankind. All Praise Honor and glory to you the Father of all creation. Amen!

25

Walking from Point Mugu to Oxnard

Walking through the farm lands located just south of Oxnard was great. All the strawberries were in season and Ken and I ate our fill at the pick-them-yourself fruit stands. It must have been our season because again God "wielded His sword" and we were "bearing great fruit" in the strawberry patches!

The Hispanic farm workers were very kind, and we prayed with many of the farmers! And again, so many families were hurting, seeking prayer and signing the cross. The cross at this time had so many signatures that it had to be flipped repeatedly, and we still had 1000 miles of walking! That night we stayed at a small motel just before coming into Oxnard and after a Bible study and a little Mexican food, we slept very well!

26

Walking from Oxnard to Summerland

From Oxnard to Summerland was a very long walk and although we did pray with many people, the time went fast, and it was nice. It was beautiful walking along the coast, and just praying over the land until we reached the little town of Calabasas, where a landslide had covered three homes, just the winter before. It is a very small town and the people there had mixed opinions about our walk. Some called us to pray over the area; others were angry with God for the lost lives of their dear friends. We did pray over the land where once families lived. My heart went out to the poor people that were faint of heart. Some still asked me why God allowed such a thing to take event. I had no answer but that their hearts would not be so unforgiving that some day they will see them again! Many of the people agreed and signed the cross of his mercy and Love. I can only suppose that God allows hardship in our lives in order to strengthen or test our faith.

Obviously, God does not see death of the body as we do. I likened it to the changing of the butterfly, the caterpillar spins its cocoon and some how a metamorphosis takes place, and out of the cocoon comes forth this wonderfully splendid butterfly! I imagine death through God's eyes is a bit like that, and when I think about it in that light, I also feel a bit less afraid of the one thing all humanity must face.

Then with a weary good bye, we walked away and into Summerland We walked 29 miles that day and it was getting dark. God hadn't blessed us with any offerings yet, so we were just going to find a place along the roadside to camp for the night. I said Lord we are so tired and it has been a long day, and only a couple of minutes passed when my cell rang. It was the Man and his Son that we prayed with back at Point Dume. He blessed us and paid for a nice hotel, dinner, plus a little offering to help on our way in the morning. We did stay in contact for the next 100 miles or so, but then it faded in the past as the road ahead grew longer and longer!

27

Summerland to Santa Barbara

The road to Santa Barbara was beautiful and Ken and I talked with quite a few People. when the phone rang, it was my brother. He indicated that my mother had flown down from Oregon to see me and Ken, just to check up on us.

It had been some time since we had seen anyone from home, so I was very excited to get to spend the day with them! We went to the Santa Barbara Mission and it was a wonderful time. My family is 9th generation Californian, and a lot of our heritage was in the support and building of the old missions throughout Alta California. As I have mentioned before, my only intent to share my ancestry is to emphasize how stifled faith of our time has become, in the hope that we can rebuild it to a whole new glory. One People One Church Standing United as one all nations' raises creeds and tong's seeking and finding the love of Christ Jesus in there heart.

Walking into the mission was inspiring, even though I had been there many times. However, this time I really prayed and sought Christ on the history and events of the growth of the mission. The early Friars were wonderful and endearing to the native Californian Indians. And they brought Aztec and Incan Indians who were now Catholic Christian's {by their own choice} along with them, as interpreters. The friars brought food and cattle. They taught the Californian Indians how to farm and build bright vibrant communities which sprang up all around the missions. The Friars evangelized Alta California with the power of building splendid communities of faithful followers of Christ.

Gold was not the issue at this time, that is still obvious by the way they lived trading California bank notes {in other words, "bear hides"} for goods to passing trader ships. This historical fact can be found today by visiting the old mission structures, and grounds which stretch the length of the coast of California. They brought water to the once-empty wastelands of southern California. Some of the old mission aqueducts are in use today! I believe if we can imitate community building in the way the Friars taught the early Indians, that we would be much better off today.

If People today stopped having their grand visions, and missionaries stopped traveling to distant places and worked out in our local communities, as the Friars did, we could recapture our nation and the heart of America. The beauty and sanctuary of these historic Spanish missions are important for us to grasp, because they show the passionate love which the converted Aztec, Incan, and Alta California Indians all shared for Christ, before the USA existed. I visited Don Juan Cabrillo gravesite, the first officially-recorded citizen of California and explorer. The legacy of the missions is a monumental treasure to the Christian Californian Indians. And to us all thank God!

Afterwards; we went and shared a very nice lunch. My Brother Steve bought Ken and myself a couple of blow up camping mats.

They turned out to be great, thanks to Steve and thanks be to God! We placed the cross in a hotel room and enjoyed the streets of Santa Barbara with my family for the day!

I heard that my wife was upset that I had witnessed to so many people and walked so far. I ask my brother to remind her of the times Heaven almost took me home, and that it was her prayer of agreement that sent me at the time I left. I also asked

Steve to remind her of the thousands of miracles that were taking place daily.

Ken was a witness, and had become quite a prayerful man himself! People were coming to faith, and being healed. So much was happening I still do not fully understand all that God had intended for this walk—just that I had to finish it.

This walk was the Potter telling the clay what it must do! Personally speaking, working at sea the trade that I love and sitting at home at my house, living a normal life, would have been my first choice. The walk was not my idea anyway. I was only a sailor, fresh off the ship, little prepared for such an adventure as this. Being obedient to the call was costing me absolutely everything, yet I had no choice. I suppose that is reckless abandon in Christ. I am not sure why things were happening the way they were.

I just put my head to the plow and trusted in the Lord and Ken and I were off the next morning, and with new mattresses in tow. We pressed on to Santa Barbara with the cross!

We walked through the Hispanic section of town almost all morning, praying and loving our Hispanic brothers and sisters in Christ! It really was wonderful. Ken brought out tracts in Spanish and some of the young local boys helped us pass them out, while others were dancing and playing in the streets. They helped us push the cross up and down the foothills of Santa Barbara.

It was just about noon when we met a large group of homeless people and who were all saying they were very hungry. There was a hamburger stand across the street, so I gave all we had left to Ken to buy hamburgers for them. It was great fun passing out the hot burgers and fries to the people. They ate and asked questions, and then we prayed for all of them at their request. Wow, it was a wonderful and powerful time speaking with and helping people in need.

After that, we walked down toward the boardwalk. A man came over to us, relaying a horrible story of a life in alcohol and drugs. Interestingly enough, he was in an AA program and our Lord was seeking him. He was broken and weeping as we shared about our Lord's amazing grace! At 52 years old he had never met Christ and he gave his heart to the Lord that moment. Tears of deliverance flowed down his face. Simultaneously, it touched another man who had witnessed the event; the Holy Spirit placed it on his heart to give us a wonderful offering, and we were very blessed. I don't have the words and can't possibly recount just how much God was watching over us! I came to realize that every meeting was authored and appointed of God. Ken and I was only the vehicle he had chosen. What a privilege to witness the loving and enduring work of Christ Jesus! His Love is so amazing, his creation uncountable Joy to all who believe!

Walking down to the pier, we met with some French foreign exchange students. The young people shared with us that in France, such a walk would be impossible. France was a strong Catholic Christian country and I was just there some 4 years before. The youth shared with me how fast the hammer came down on their ability to express their faith. Moreover, twenty young French men, and women signed the cross and could not wait to show their pictures and witness to their families and friends back in France!

Credence Clearwater Revival once sang a song and some of the lyrics went something like this: Take a glass of water, make it against the law. See how good the water tastes, when you can't have any more.

The French youth, explained that when the Muslims moved into their country, they swayed their government. Now, people from another culture run "rough-shod" over what was once Christendom France. (Is anyone paying attention to the lessons here?)

Well once at the pier, we had a clever conversation with a woman who believed that all gods lead to heaven, and all paths lead to heaven. (Pantheism) This is the scripture we shared together.

John 1

In the beginning was the Word and the Word was with God, and the Word was God. The same was in the beginning with God. All things were made through him; and without him was not anything made that hath been made. In him was life; and the life was the light of men. And the light shineth in the darkness; and the darkness apprehended it not. There came a man, sent from God, whose name was John. The same came for witness, that he might bear witness of the light, that all might believe through him. He was not the light, but came that he might bear witness of the light. There was the true light, even the light that lighteth every man, coming into the world. He was in the world, and the world was made through him, and the world knew him not. He came unto his own people, and they that were his own received him not. But as many as received him, to them gave he the right to become children of God, even to them that believe on his name: who were born, not of blood, nor of the will of the flesh, nor of the will of man, but of God. And the Word became flesh, and dwelt among us (and we beheld his glory, glory as of the only begotten from the Father), full of grace and truth. John beareth witness of him, and crieth, saying, this was he of whom I said, He that cometh after me is become before me: for he was before me. For of his fullness we all received, and grace for grace. For the law was given through Moses; grace and truth came through Jesus Christ.

So I went to the letters of 1 John and started the normal evangelistic scriptures. We went round and round in a wonderful, peaceful conversation that drew a rather large crowd. We discussed questions on both sides of the issue of Christ versus humanism. It was a very calm and exhilarating conversation, never getting over-heated or too excited. It was rather fun to be in apologetics with so many at one time!

No one broke down and declared Christ as Lord; however, many seeds were planted that day. There was a wonderful Catholic man in attendance, who enjoyed the opportunity to share with us. He lived just across the street and told us how refreshing it was to share his faith—out in the open! He said sadly enough that Santa Barbara's coastal area was filled with demonic activity!

We shared with him what we experienced walking through town and that there were still many Christians in the area. Although this faithfulness was found holding true through the Hispanic neighborhoods, we surely experienced the demonic around the beach boardwalk!! He blessed us by letting us sleep at his home.

Our new-found friend fired up his barbeque and we had a great meal as he shared with us about his faith. Then we worshipped together in song and prayer. He shared some of his life's stories, and we really enjoyed this precious man's hospitality! The next morning, we had breakfast at Sambo's Restaurant on the beach and then moved on walking ever northward.

28

Santa Barbara headed to Gaviota State Park

This day's journey was mostly along the freeway and uneventful except for the excited truck drivers that would blow their horns from time to time, going by at 80 miles per hour.

But when we entered the state park, we met a family that had been living out of a tent for weeks and the man could not find a job anywhere. He was an automotive mechanic. It was disheartening to see him and his American children homeless, living out of a tent. So we built a nice campfire and prayed for work for this man and his family. That night the young family was sharing that they were raised in the Mormon Church and how he left the Church, and became a Christian. He indicated that the Mormon church was teaching people false doctrines of faith, about national take-over and making money!

Imagine that? I do not understand the powerful motivation factor of greedy people! I am sure there are so fine Mormons as well, as we had some nice young Mormons sign the cross along the path we traveled. We had a great time together and we decided to rest another day there. The campers all gathered round and we had a great time talking about how blessed we were, especially here in California.

There came another group of people from a community church in Santa Cruz. They were surfing "the ranch", which is a surf spot near there. So we talked about how important it is for us to be the best examples we can, for our children and families, and if we are going to keep Church in our country, we had better start living it.

George Washington, in his inaugural speech, said that in order for us to maintain in true freedom as a democracy here in America, the Church must lead and the government should support the Church. These are the words of our beloved first leader, and we still have not reached the reality that he understood so well. And again, President Reagan stated to the American people, that the way back to healing our land, was that we the people must become an ownership society. Once again, affirming the sentiments of our first leader. Will we give Christ's Church the position it demands or are we going to fall apart into dilapidation? They agreed and come the next morning, we were off once again. And they went and caught some great waves I am sure! I would have loved to join them Very much!

29

Gaviota State Park to Lompoc

Another day and a difficult walk, with the mountain rising from Gaviota, was very long and steep, but once at the top it was all down hill from there. There weren't many people in the area, just a lot of ranch lands! I was happy to have such a friend as Ken with me, sharing life's stories and the gospel; being that he was from the Chicago area it made sharing life's tales interesting for both of us! He had never seen California and I could learn all about Illinois from Ken. He was a great storyteller and wonderful company on such a long journey up the coast!

Well about 7 miles outside of town a man stopped his car and ran over to us yelling, "You two, you have to stay at my house in town when you arrive." He gave us his address, we thanked him and said it would take us a couple of hours to get there

So Again Ken and I had walked through some beautiful Californian hill country. I had driven it before, and it is quite beautiful, but walking somehow was so much more surreal, looking at all the valleys, hills and mountains in every direction. It was much like life was standing sentry all around us. I am looking forward to the Kingdom of Heaven for it will be even more beautiful.

By that time, Ken and I arrived at this man's family house in Lompoc. He had everything all set up for us: hot shower and a wonderful dinner prepared by his wife for him and his very large family. One daughter was ill, and so we prayed for her healing, for their whole family while we all shared the love of Christ our Savior, and it was a fabulous evening in their home. God richly bless their charity, humility, and love, I pray God through Christ the son would answer the prayer of healing. They were of a different faith so what I have witnessed is that we are all softly unified. In that we all are seeking God's love and salvation of Jesus in the same body which is Christ our Lord. Also at some level we are all connected in the same love hope and charity. Perhaps unity is only that we open our doors to our hearts and invite all people we encounter with open hearts and using Faith hope and charity along with a strong love of Christ our Lord to be our guide. All of us Gods children Standing together to fight against the works of the satanic powers. Such as pride, covetousness, Lust, anger, gluttony, envy, and sloth! It is hard and we all suffer these temptations yes I suffer as well I am only a sailor even now, however by standing united in faith each in his or her own church however connected by our Lord in heaven we can tear down the walls of satanic strongholds and the temptations will lessen. Marriage will remain intact, and babies will live in a better Land. Even bringing an end to abortion.

That morning, Ken and I got off to an early start. We walked through the city of Lompoc. We met another young man who confessed to be overdosing on chemicals. He looked really bad off, so we prayed for him and helped him until we could see he was feeling better.

We stopped our walk and spent a couple of hours with the young man, and finally got a number to reach his mom. She reserved a hotel room in Lompoc, and bought us our meals in the motel that night. Some of the local Churches heard about the walk on the radio and came over to the motel. They were truly excited to meet us.

Lompoc is a bit of an isolated area from the average California city, and the children were wondering if they were the only Christians left in California!

No Catholic or Christian broadcasting was available up there! We talked with many different Christians that came to the motel just to speak with us. The next day the young people all wanted to walk to Guadalupe with us, and so at about 9am ten of them showed up to our room and off we went. It was on a beautiful Saturday morning!

We stopped in a little café and had breakfast there. It was fun speaking with the young people. They were having a great time. After breakfast, we began our 22-mile walk. The young people were amazed at how many people loved our Lord, and his passion of the Cross!

Walking a little farther, we ran into some gang members who asked if we were, "like, Jesus Guys." I said I go to Church if that is what you are asking. Then I asked if he had ever been to Church? The young man replied as he shook his head, stumbled, and sheepishly said, "No." I then asked if he would like to walk with us for a while, but they refused, and I was saddened when he walked away!

Not long after that, we walked across another young man's path who was carrying his guitar with him. He asked if he could walk a while with us and we welcomed him. He played well and actually knew some Christian songs. All the young people were enjoying getting signatures on the cross. They had no idea there were so many Christians right in their hometown.

It hit home in my heart at that point! This is what so many Church plantings tend to cause, encouraging all the division in the Church today. Even back home in Newport, this is evident truth. If Christ's people are called to make an impact, we aren't making very much of one. When I witnessed the numbers of believers all along the coast, yet we make little impact. How can this be? We compartmentalize ourselves, which is the problem. It is so simple for Satan to keep us separated and remove the power of the Church, and so we can be our own worst enemy at times.

Walking out of Lompoc and heading to Guadalupe was open farmland. Many of the field workers would wave and come to sign the cross. It was great for the kids, and they were hanging in there right to the very end.

About a mile before Guadalupe, a truck stopped and out hopped the formerly-addicted young man we had prayed for back in Lompoc!!

He said that the prayers brought such revelation to him that everything was looking better in his life. He asked if we would spend time with him and his mom, because she was so happy. I said, "We have the cross and cart. What will we do with them?"

As it turned out, his mom was a member of Calvary Chapel Guadalupe, and the Church was just down the road where we could store it. We walked the cross to Calvary Chapel and the young woman working there was very excited to speak with us. It was wonderful to see so many people excited about our Lord and his passion! About a hundred people signed the cross that night. There were new converts to salvation and people recommitting their souls to God. It was great to share the love of Christ! The parents of the children came to pick them up, Ken, and I along with our new friend's went back to Lompoc, and couldn't help but wonder when we would be able to go forward.

Ronda my wife called and said she would meet me in Pismo Beach, and that made me very happy! So we stayed in Lompoc for three days and prayed with our new friends in Christ our Lord. Then on Saturday, we walked into Pismo Beach. Once again walking through Oceana and Pismo Beach, we met many people and prayed with lots of families around noon. We stopped and had some lunch at a little taco stand. The Hispanic woman who served us was so interested in our Crosswalk event. We started talking with her and found out the cross meant so much to her because her brother was killed in a drunken driving accident, along with many of her friends. She had a pink, blue, and white bandana with all the names of the people that were involved in the fatal accident and we prayed for their souls in heaven. We agreed in prayer, and asked God through Christ our Lord to have mercy by healing the plague of alcoholism and drug addictions from our land. Were so much damage has come to so many lives, Then the young woman tied her bandana around the left arm of the cross and gave the mourning of her brother and friends unto our Lord, as we prayed for God's peace for her family.

A peace of my own testimony would fit here. My father had a terrible time with alcoholism. In my house while growing up alcohol had been a huge part of my childhood and there was a lot of violence in my home, when alcohol was involved. Quite abusive! However there was my Mother who was a staunch religious Catholic and we attended the Mass as good families do. Other than my father was never there. He felt the church would fall down if he entered the parish! Still the sin of my father visited me during my teens and I had a real fight with it. Until I joined the Navy because in my sea bag was a little Gideon's bible and it was the only book we could read through-out Boot camp. Well over a couple of years of prayer and trusting in the promises of God I was delivered from alcoholism. Being at sea for up to 10 months at a time helped me see clearer. And by witnessing the pain and devastation that genocide brought so many others well it made it much easier to forgive myself of my past and all that I believed I had suffered. Also individually praying for and forgiving all persons that I felt had hurt me in life. The little Gideon's bible was the path out for me. For it started me down the path of knowledge reading the bible and true history while sailing the seven seas. And also having the opportunity to walk in Iraq, Israel, Turkey, France, Spain, Italy, Bosnia, Portugal, Africa, China, Korea and so many other islands and Nations. Some people call me Gulliver as in Gulliver's Travels. Well I was set free at 22 years old and set free in deed. Life has not been easy yet I have enjoyed the ride with Jesus my Captain my King. I have seen firsthand the beauty of humanity. The greatness of international reality Gods creation! As I read I could check history within the passage of sailing for 33 years and fighting for freedom for all humanity not only Americas self-image of interests. Most of the time I was fighting of the dignity of which ever humanity, fighting to overcome hunger, poverty, and genocide wherever it is found. My fellow Americans please pay attention. We can be a light for the whole world to see as we are made up of every nationality of the world every race nationality creed and religion. Freedom is for all Love is the fruit of peace and freedom. Stand in great Love and acceptance. You can learn a lot from your Neighbors. Or you can teach and share your love of God with as many as will listen!

She thanked us and we went on our way walking into Pismo Beach. I saw Ronda for the first time in a month. It was July 4th weekend and Pismo Beach was packed out. I felt that all the hotels would be full and there would be "no place at the inn" for us, so to speak. Just then we met a wonderful older couple who spoke to us about the cross, and how her husband had been a Gideon for some 60 years, God bless him. I shared with him how much his service to God's calling had changed my life for the better and the little Gideon's bible wielded my path to the all-powerful knowledge of God and his creation. He said he knew seeing the underlying connection of Jesus in all of god's family! Moreover, they opened their home to all of us and we stayed the whole July 4th weekend fellowshipping with them, and having a great time there at Pismo Beach!!!

It was a bit of nostalgia for me because my father would take the whole family camping there. When I was a young boy, we would go clamming and mom would make great giant pots of Pismo clam chowder. We also would ride motorcycles and drive 4x4 trucks all over the dunes in the early 60's. You could do stuff like that in those days.

Well I could see that Ronda had mixed emotions about the walk, and, understandably, wanted me to come home. We argued too much for the little time we had together. I do not know how to explain the power that drove me on to complete the journey I was sure it was in part due to the walk itself, as a couple we were coming under attack from spiritual warfare. And I had been gone from home for many days by this point. Loneliness is powerful. I realized I was serving and walking for something much larger. My Gideon friend saw the problems we were suffering, as well and reminded me to complete the walk, and to trust in God so I pushed on.

I would ask and pray for peace. I still had 700 miles to go, and I could not get her to understand the blessing that the walk truly was, nor about all the hurting people in California. Who could blame her—since she hadn't experienced what we'd seen. I reminded her of the hospitalization I had suffered and the calling of the walk. Ronda knew long before our marriage that I might have to walk, and she had consented to it. We had been only 2 ½ years into our marriage at the time, so it was a difficult separation. For the both of us! Oddly enough, it had been Ronda herself who started me out in the first place. This occurred after I was in the hospital—for the third time.

Anyway, she stayed and walked with me for about a week. We walked to San Luis Obispo which is mostly ranches and vineyard lands. Once in San Luis Obispo there were many young adults seeking prayer. There was a bit of witchcraft being practiced in the area—we know this because they were rather open about chanting some kind of incantations and blasphemies of the cross our direction, but those people practicing such things are deceived and in great pain so we prayed for them in the silence of our hearts.

Once again I blame today's school system for a lot of the problem with our youth today. Perhaps the Catholics have a valid point in Communal prayers, in seeking Saintly role models over earthly ones. When we stumble, we cause others to stumble as well. See this is what our Bible teaches us.

Matthew 22
Discussion about Resurrection

That same day some Sadducees stepped forward a group of Jews who say there is no resurrection after death. They posed this question: "Teacher," Moses said, "If a man dies without children, his brother should marry the widow and have a child. The woman's husband died, so she got married again. That husband died, all the way to the seventh husband who later died. In the resurrection, to whom shall she belong to? Who will be the brother's heir? Well, there were seven brothers. The oldest married then died without children, so the second brother married the widow. This brother also died without children, and the wife was married to the next brother, and so on until she had been the wife of each of them. Then she also died. So tell us, whose wife will she be in the resurrection. For she was the wife of all seven of them!" Jesus replied, "Your problem is that you don't know the Scriptures, and you don't know the power of God. For when the dead rise, they won't be married. They will be like the angels in heaven. But now, as to whether there will be a resurrection of the dead, haven't you ever read about this in the Scriptures? Long after Abraham, Isaac, and Jacob had died, God said, 'I am the God of Abraham, the God of Isaac, and the God of Jacob.' So He is the God of the living, not the dead."

Now the way I see and understand this scripture verse; it is about understanding the very heart of worship. All the angels and all of humanity are created to be in a constant living worship unto the Lord our God! As we see in the transfiguration on the mountain, our blessed Jesus took Peter, James, and John the beloved, with him to pray. There his appearance became dazzling white and Elijah and Moses stood at his side proclaiming Jesus as the Son of the Living God. The apex of faith in our own resurrection and everyone that went before us is in living resurrected bodies, right as we breathe our next breath. As we pray in one accord in great faith that the word of God is in fact all true, then all of creation is in constant communal worship before the throne room of God. With just a little understanding, we can believe by faith when we come to the throne of grace, there is a presence of a Living Kingdom filled with saints. It is by the witness of their lives that can comfort us and help in guiding us into eternity. Let us look at Pope John Paul's II communal prayer with our blessed mother and Mary is communing with our now-resurrected pontiff. And I quote:

> *Mary says to us today: I am the servant of the Lord. Let it be done to me as you say (Lk 1:38). And with those words, she expresses what was the fundamental attitude of her life: Her Faith! Mary believed! She trusted in God's promises and was faithful to his will. When the angel Gabriel announced that she was chosen to be the mother of the most high, she gave her fiat humbly and with full freedom, "Let it be done to me as you say".*
>
> *Perhaps the best description of Mary and at the same time greatest tribute to her, was the greeting of her cousin Elizabeth, Blessed is she who trusted that the Lord's words to her would be fulfilled (Lk:45). For it was that continual trust in the "providence" of God, which most characterized Blessed Mother Mary's faith.*

Here is the point I am making: if our brothers, husbands, and wives could catch the faith of Mary and once again realize that we are all joint-heirs of the Kingdom of God, a full return to holiness and piety will be the lasting result. For example, what if Mary had an abortion during her seemingly unfortunate circumstances?! She could have been stoned to death for this pregnancy out of wedlock! Now open your hearts and listen to our pontiff's next statement.

> *All her earthly life was a "pilgrimage of faith." For like us, she walked in shadows and hoped for things unseen. She knew the contradictions of our earthly life. She was promised that*

her Son would have King David's Throne, but at his birth. There was no room even at the inn. Mary still believed the angel, who said that her Son would be the Son of God: But she would see him slandered, betrayed, condemned, and left to die as a thief on the cross! Even still Mary "trusted that the Lord's words to her would be fulfilled (Lk: 37)

This woman of great faith, Mary of Nazareth, the Mother of God has been given to us as a model of faith. To further explain Our Blessed Mother Mary has been given to us as a model of the walk of faith pilgrimage for every Person. We ask, Queen Mary, to help lead us into Holy lives, surrendering our will over to God's will, in all things with great faith! We ask, Mother Most Holy, with the peace of God in our consciences, with our hearts free of malice and hate, that we shall be able to bring true joy and peace to all, which come from Your Son, Our Lord Jesus Christ, Who lives and reigns with the Father and the Holy Spirit forever and ever. Amen! Most of my European Naval service was during John Paul's II's papacy. And I was connected in spirit then as I am today. Perhaps this was a piece of the new evangelization movement. Not so much my own thing but joined in the harmony of unity of Jesus and his church. I see it as a gift for the deliverance I have enjoyed in my own life. Truly I say it is a very small price to pay. Also I can see how much it is helping multitudes of thousands and thousands to start down the path of the same freedom! All the generations before us used saintly lives to try to emulate holy walks before the Lord, as for today, our role models are anything but saintly. Satan is in, and Heaven is out. We can't effectively teach heaven without lifting up the Body of Christ, which is every person that ever served in the body, every person, saint, angel, cherubim & seraphim, and every living creator on earth. All of these are giving God praise and glory every minute of every day. That is what it is like in the throne room of our risen Lord. We call all of humanity into perfect harmony with the plan of God's perfect will. That all may be saved in Christ Jesus!

30

San Luis Obispo to Morro Bay

This stretch became a time of reflection. Ronda told me that she was finished and going home. Once again we had to say our good-byes and south she went. It made me quite sad, but I didn't have the words for my own wife's sorrow. However, Ken was there and he helped me by saying she really could not understand that somehow she was blinded to the whole blessing that the walk was for so many people. Never a dull moment, about 15 miles down the road a woman stopped for prayer. Her husband left her, and stole all her possessions. She and her child were living out of her car and that she couldn't find a job anywhere.

I was praying that Ronda was still there for this woman because Ronda had much the same experiences in her life. The poor woman was in great tears, and in God's amazing grace, Ronda pulled up at that moment to share some last thoughts and concerns. She had driven almost to Santa Barbara and the Holy Spirit had her turn around and come back to us. Moreover, I asked her to hear this woman's suffering and to pray for her. Ronda went to pray with her, while I spoke to the Kids in the van.

After hearing the testimony and a long time in prayer, Ronda finally conceded and understood. She stayed with us in Morro Bay campground, and things calmed down quite a bit. I thanked the Lord for peace in my marriage and friendship with Ronda. It was quiet in Morro Bay, it was very nice to have a rescue vehicle along with us, and it was quite wonderful to share some of the walk with Ronda and our children, my foster and adopted daughter who was 12 at this time in great joy!

Our nephew Steven was with Ronda. He was 15 and loved walking the cross, so walking from Morro Bay to San Simeon we split the walk. Ken and Steven walked from the campsite to Cambria, and Ronda and I drove ahead in the Van to Cambria where we enjoyed a very pleasant breakfast together.

Then we drove up to San Simeon to find the place we would stay for the night. We found a nice Best Western and stayed there. The next day we drove back to Cambria and my foster daughter, young Erika and I walked the cross into San Simeon. From the Best Western we made 30 miles that day and prayed with so many people both in Harmony and Cambria, and all along the route on PCH of central California. We had a great night's rest at the Best Western that night, and all the people working at the hotel were very excited to hear all about the walk.

We took the day off to see Hearst Castle and it was a wonderful and relaxing day at the little San Simeon Village. With Ronda, the kids and Ken my companion, I enjoyed it so very much! Praise God for rest and peace.

The next day we got an early start and walked from San Simeon to Gordo Beach. It was an uneventful day, walking, praying, and meditating on the beauty of the central coast. It was the first time Ronda, Ken, and the Kids ever saw elephant seals in the wild and they were having a wonderful time watching them.

We stayed the night in Gordo Beach. Ken was having thoughts about going back to his family, so he called his friend in Lompoc, who came and picked him up. Ronda, Ken and I prayed together and felt it was time. I thanked him for being such a wonderful friend, and he was gone that evening. The next day brought Big Sur. I had been praying about Big Sur most of the trip, because I was concerned about the narrow roads there. Since Ronda was there with the van, I decided we would lash the cross to the top of the van and drive to Carmel Highlands to restart. As the narrow roads we could have caused an accident there. For safety for all concerned. Ken had left, however; young Steven was interested in taking the job.

So Ken moved on with his life. I prayed that "God would richly bless him". Much to my joy and surprise, God supplied young Steven. I missed Ken very much; however, Steven brought a new aspect to the walk. Being a young man of 15 without a real home, discipling Steven while on a real pilgrimage would be good for my soul, and Steven's.

He would walk 300 miles of the trip with me. As we will share, it was a Walk of Love and healing for me, for Steven and many others that the Lord would touch along this part of the adventure with me.

31

Carmel Highlands to Monterey

It was quite eventful walking on the bike path. We met up with many poor, hurting, lost, and down hearted people. We prayed with them all, and tried to build their hope as we walked throughout the winding streets of the tri-cities area and prayed for many families in need. There were people with sick babies and relatives for the most part. When we arrived in Monterey we went to the Mission and there was a wedding in the chapel. So we walked around the grounds and enjoyed studying about the lives of the transformed Californian Indians. Our History books have certainly been changed in a big way; why can't they express what it's really like: the feeling of His presence, the walking on Holy Ground, the legacy of years of powerful faith? It is history and it is real!

Humanism is a scientifically proven lie, and it is infesting our world at an alarming rate. Without scientific or Historical backing how can it stand?

There are so many absolute truths found in nature itself—a flower is a flower after all, is it not? There is a huge problem with the whole concept of political correctness. What is that anyway? Anti-Christ is what that is! The systematic elimination of God's Name and the beauty of the Christian faith is deliberate revisionist history. There just isn't any proof to support the stand of natural selection among humans (There is evidence of adaptation among plants, animals and even insects—minor color changes, etc.) or evolution after actually traveling the entire planet. And being a sailor for 33 years I have seen the real thing:' God's word is all-true and that Peters Catholic Church is the largest Church on earth! Christianity: 2.1 billion, including Mormons Islam: 1.5 billion (2005) http://www.adherents.com/Religions_By_ Adherents.html

2006 *Annuario Pontificio,* the official Vatican yearbook, 1,098,000,000 Catholics in the world. http://www.catholiccul-ture.org/news/features/index.cfm?recnum=42515

There are less Muslims, than Buddhism, then Hindu. And a host of others to the best I could see on earth. Not that numbers matter so much God does not draw such hard lines and I don't believe he is keep score this information is only to help us to see we are all Gods people funny how we draw such dividing lines, let's have a lager look at the whole and reconstruct some peace in our lives.

Well a little later on we had dinner on the "Fisherman's Wharf", which I have always loved. After I graduated from high school, I moved to Santa Cruz, and we would often drive down to Monterrey. We surfed and after an arousing day of fun and surfing we all ate on the Wharf, which in the mid-Seventies, of course, was a bit different then! The next morning, Ronda, my wife, left us, staying in contact by phone almost every day. Young Steven and I started out on our journey, walking ever northward and once again having to fully trust in God to meet our daily needs. In Monterey, we met up with a newscaster and were back on the news, reaching CNN national television. I asked our Lord about his intentions for the walk and I still do not fully understand his purposes. I suppose I never will until the day I meet Him, on that glorious Day when my life's pilgrimage is ended.

While walking through the artichoke fields and farmlands, making our way to Seaside, we ran into an all Christian Bicycling Club that was heading south. We prayed together, asking our Lord to heal our lands and protect our families from the brutal satanic onslaught being waged against them. About two miles after that, "coincidentally", out in the middle of farmland, our front tire blew out. At the same time, "God-incidentally", another group from the same club rode by, with all the equipment we needed to fix the flat. We thanked them, and I thought to myself how great it was to meet good, strong, American young men—who love the Lord and were willing to lend a helping hand. Along the trek, up the central and northern California coast Bicycling Clubs would be a source of great companionship for news and friendship.

The walk was going out via the "banana telegraph" way ahead of us and the people and bicycle clubs were watching out for us, along the Northern road.

32

Seaside to Marina City

After fixing the flat and leaving Seaside, we were again walking along a side road, which ran parallel? to PCH. A man heading to Santa Cruz stopped and gave us a nice offering that we really needed because we were running on empty.

As he shared with us that he was deeply hurting and crying for a sick family member, we prayed for healing and thanked the Lord for his willingness to help us! He said he felt much better. The one main thread, which was becoming all too obvious, was the separation of the body of Christ. We are everywhere but we are standing in the storms all too often alone. It has become so obvious this is due to the battles over silly doctrinal differences that no one can really make a good argument over, given that there is no support for division in the Bible.

No doctrinal differences can be allowed to usurp God's call for unity. We are all one body in Christ! Faith in Father, Son, and Holy Spirit is all that is required! We are called to grow and become Christians from the transformation of each Life in Christ. From the first day with my new disciple Steven, we experienced God's loving miracles all around us. It was wonderful because Steven was so excited to see that God is real and works out all the little details throughout our adventure in faith.

By this point, it truly was a faith journey, because, from here on out, the cities were farther and farther apart, and God would show up assisting us in marvelous and miraculous ways every day it was the oddest reality I have ever experience. And most of the time, He would show himself at the very last moment.

From the words of Pope Benedict XVI:

> *Finding the Face of God, the western world is weary of its own culture. It is a world that has reached the time when there seems to be no longer any evidence of the need for God, let alone Christ, and when it therefore seems that human's could build themselves on their own. In this atmosphere of rationalism, closing in on itself and that regards the model of science as the only model of knowledge, everything else is subjective. Christian life too, of course, becomes a choice that is subjective, hence, arbitrary and no longer the path of life. It therefore naturally becomes difficult to believe, and if it is difficult to believe, it is even more difficult to offer one's life to the Lord to be his servant.*

That is exactly what I experienced along the entire walk. We are a spiritually broken people due to our personal differences, even though as I found most people of all ethnicities confess to have faith in God. Even more often, the cause of these problems is Christians standing alone in the world, because we splintered ourselves by pride, creating division. Self-evaluation, reunification and solid Bible teaching is what is required in this mostly Christian nation and world of ours.

Much like young Steven and myself, I was placed in Steven's life to give him a chance to meet God in this fashion he meet him face to face at 15 and to become an disciple into the body at such a young age. Wow what a blessing that is! My only wished I had walked the cross at Steven's age and watched God move in the way he does, because now Steven understands at 15 how much God is in everything we do. My journey home was much more painful a very long testimony in deed! Guiding our new brothers and sisters in faith is what discipling is all about. Making

Converts is good, but discipling them means teaching them who God, Christ and the Holy Spirit are.

From what I can see, due to the walk and input from all the people polled, the largest problem with the Church body today is that we have focused on internal business practices, using marketing tactics to drive a vision or agenda. This type of action caused much of the present division in Christ's Church. All too often we are making converts not true Christian disciples and we push them all off into the wind with little or no understanding of faith installed into them. Which lead to humanistic understanding instead of spiritual reality? And we the whole body of Christ are called to act as one body unto discipleship not simple conversion alone.

Discipleship is desperately needed in order to stand the coming testing and trials each life will experience. What hinders discipleship? This is mainly due to poor leadership and inability to interpret scripture with the eyes of true servant hood. Effective discipling programs need to reinforce morality and Christ centered values into our young people and new converts as well. The Catholic Church calls it RCIA—a one year program that must be performed before any baptism can occur. I am the first to agree that the program can be far better. However it does allow the human soul time and reflection to learn and find if the way of Christ is truly for them. Perhaps later however a strong seed is laded and the case for Jesus is established. Patient loving discipleship is the wright path.

This was the most evident truth of the walk. Christ spent *3 years* teaching the 12 apostles and it was not until the day of Pentecost that they truly understood and were sent out to make disciples except for a shot while when they were sent to share the message of love with the Jews first. So all too often, we spend little time truly teaching converts how to live Godly lives. In addition, we emphasize "head knowledge," which is great but we need to engage their "heart knowledge," in faith, just as the

Apostles could hardly do anything without the Holy Spirit. Our Church schools are a good example of proliferation of error, too. I observed so many strange, personal interpretations of the Holy Spirit; I had to question whether it was more deceptive than holy. By this time, I had talked with tens of thousands of different believers and atheists, many Islamic, a few Buddhists and an occasional Hindu; I found they were easily preying upon our simple, passive and even reprobate American mind. All the true out lined by the Vatican bi C little c Christian denominations did share some things in common—an inability to explain the impact of faith in the global arena. They were only making converts as well; it has become the battle of conversion versus discipleship. If this were not true, the Churches would already be unified in spirit and in truth. We the citizens of America cannot rely on the authorities, political or religious, to show us the truth.

When I think about what a shallow society we are building, it reminds me of the house "built on sand." Some Christians, perhaps in the interest of scriptural stewardship and "saving the earth," are even able to believe that a tree is not a tree, but some type of spiritual being (an imported idea from Japanese "Animistic" beliefs). They should be more concerned with the scriptural roots of their faith and spiritual health of their family tree. Perhaps the reason why it is so obvious to me is because, being in the Military so long, I was sheltered from the subtle distortions creeping into our members' everyday lives. Here is what Paul taught us about some of the new Church movements cropping up

1 Corinthians 1

But did I, Paul, die for your sins. Were any of you baptized in my name? I am so thankful now that I didn't baptize any of you except Crispus and Gaius. For now no one can think that I have been trying to start something new, beginning a "Church

of Paul." Oh, yes, and I baptized the family of Stephanas. I don't remember ever baptizing anyone else. For Christ didn't send me to baptize, but to preach the Gospel; and even my preaching sounds poor, for I do not fill my sermons with profound words and high-sounding ideas, for fear of diluting the mighty power there is in the simple message of the cross of Christ.

I know very well how foolish it sounds to those who are lost, when they hear that Jesus died to save them. But we who are saved recognize this message as the very power of God. For God says, "I will destroy all human plans of salvation no matter how wise they seem to be, and ignore the best ideas of men, even the most brilliant of them."

Walking through Moss Landing, we had another cart problem. The whole side of the front bike tire was worn out and the tube popped out. We looked over into the Moss Landing slue, and lo and behold, right next to us in the middle of nowhere was a tire on a rusted rim, exactly right size. What were the chances of that happening? There wasn't a bike shop within 35 miles in any direction. And there was that tire. In fair condition to, God was in absolutely everything, everywhere we went. So we put the tire on the cart and it remains there today.

I suppose that one thing rang clear after having walked 800 miles it is that obviously, there is a God and all of heaven is real. That being said, then we must know that there is a devil and hell is quite real, too. How can people believe in angels and goodness and light, and omit the uncomfortable realization that we have an enemy? How can people sincerely praise the works of God, while "writing-off" the works of darkness, as just bad luck? I know it is God's perfect will that no person will ever go to hell, but that all people will come to the full knowledge of Jesus the Lord which is the narrow gate to heaven. First we must acknowledge the battle, then we must equip ourselves, and finally we must train others— all for the glory of God.

Along the way to the city of Marina, we walked through many farmlands and fields on the winding bike path. It is there that we met a wonderful man. He worked as an overseer on the large farm, and he had such a wonderful love for people, especially for his farmhands mostly Hispanic. He drove up, and gave Steven and me a great sandwich and talked with us about how the owner built a farmhouse for his workers and the little community was formed. His heart was wonderful, he truly was a caring man, and he followed us in his truck for a while.

We were just talking about the great day it was, with all of God's creation! With the farm to our right and the ocean views to our left, the pathway was so beautiful. At about 1 pm his lunch break was over, so he said 'God bless' and 'good-bye', and returned to work.

At the entrance to Marina at about 4pm, we came across a very little Christian Church, which helped us out, letting us set our tents in their schoolyard for the night. There was a little restaurant nearby, named the Great Artichoke, where we had the specialty artichoke enchiladas, chips, salsa, rice, and beans. It was wonderful, a great little Mexican restaurant, filled with fine people.

Early the next morning, we were off once again, heading up to Sunset State Beach. We were truly trusting in God for the weather to hold up, and for just about everything else. Farmers and workers often asked us to pray over the land for a healthy and plentiful crop, and a good season in general, so we did. Steven, being a young man, loved the nature aspect of the walk. I shared with him how perfectly God designed and spoke all things into existence, and that everything in its own way serves a great purpose in God's wondrous plan. Also that, in one way or another, everything that he created is a testimony of living worship, and very pleasing unto our Father. Steven and I soon stopped walking just for a moment and sat down along the side of the road on some rocks, sharing some of life's US Navy experiences together.

Roman's 8 vs. 18-30
God's Spirit Helps Us

For I consider that the sufferings of this present time are not worth comparing with the glory that will be revealed to us. For the creation is eagerly waiting for God to reveal his children, because the creation was subjected to frustration, though not by its own choice. The one who subjected it did so in the hope that the creation itself would also be set free from slavery to decay in order to share the glorious freedom of God's children. For we know that all creation has been groaning with the pains of childbirth right up to the present time. However, not only creation groans, but we, who have the first fruits of the Spirit also groan inwardly as we eagerly wait for our adoption, the redemption of our bodies. For we were saved with this hope in mind. Now hope that is seen is not really hope, for who hopes for what can be seen. But if we hope for what we do not see, we eagerly wait for it with patience.

In the same way, the Spirit also helps us in our weakness, for we do not know how to pray as we should. But the Spirit himself intercedes with groans too deep for words, and the one who searches our hearts knows the mind of the Spirit, for the Spirit intercedes for the saints according to God's will. And we know that he works all things together for the good of those who love God who are called according to his purpose. For those whom he foreknew, He also predestined to be conformed to the image of his Son, in order that he might be the firstborn among many brothers. And those whom he predestined, he also called; and those whom he called, he also justified; and those whom he justified, he also glorified.

I must say that I truly enjoyed young Steven walking with me. He was from a broken family and had suffered much loneliness and despair from not having a father to raise him into manhood. In constant, silent prayer, I hoped with God's help to supernaturally fill those needs in young Steven's life. No young boy or girl deserves to be without a father, and today it seems we don't even care about proper parenting, whether as single parents or in intact marriages. I prayed in silence, saying, "God, what an honor it is to share some time, walking with Christ, to glean from the fervent love this young man had for you already in his heart!"

And not by me but by the might of the Holy Spirit, Steven learned how to open up his kind heart, and pray for the needs of others. Steven became the mighty "prayer warrior!" I never asked him where he learned to pray like that but I imagine it was from all his painful lonely times of need, even at the tender age of 15! What we have done to ourselves here in America, I could only wonder...

I would remember the innumerable times Christ had me praying for all types of things around the world. Then Steven asked me what I felt my "greatest moment" was in the Navy.

Pondering his question, I picked a blade of straw from the ground I remember the sweetness of it, as I started chewing on the end the length of it hung from my lips. Then, as we walked quietly through the farmland I began to share with Steven about a gift God sent me while we were talking about creation.

I was the coxswain of an oceanographic side scan boat, operating just off the coast of Ra Duam, a sand point in the far northern Indian Ocean. At certain times of the year, thousands of whales would come to their baby rockeries, and at times, the whales would come and play with us. They would come so close, yet the huge creatures never hit us, sometimes getting near enough to pet them.

After serving years and years at sea, I just thanked the Lord for such a deep relationship with his creation. Some days I would swim to shore on my lunch break, and go for a run on their sand-blown Middle Eastern beaches, with giant crabs all around, and not a person in sight. Then one day as I had to stop the boat, I was standing on the back deck. Just then, a whale raised his head up out of the water! He was magnificent, raising his huge body slowly out of the water only inches from the boat!

I remember he had a pinkish beard, with his giant eye staring down at me. I don't know why, however he seemed gentle enough. The engine was off and we weren't going anywhere, so I just stuck my arms out like a big cross and bowed, and said hello to the giant whale's face peering down at me. Where was I going to go anyway, with the boat stopped?!!! He stayed there for a matter of minutes, no fear, just a wonderful quiet moment with this monstrous, most special creature. He went back down, I started the boat, and that was that. And I was thanking the Lord for such a wonderful moment. I truly love the ocean and all of God's creation; little did I know but I was about to have an encounter with creation just up the road…

I think Steven truly loved my whale's tale, almost as much as I loved spinning it.

Off again, we soon met up with a great Christian Californian Park Ranger. He talked with us for quite some time and offered us a sandwich. We had walked some distance, so we accepted. We prayed again because he was also having family problems and he didn't have any answers. We could just tell he was deeply hurting.

We did not get deep into it so we just prayed a little prayer and he was thankful. It is just so amazing to me how easy it is to care for people and their feelings if we could just get by ourselves. We started walking and soon we reached Sunset State Beach Park, where we camped for the night. It was crowded, and Steve and I built a nice campfire, played guitar and sang many Christian worship and campfire songs And some sea chantey's music just for fun. The campers shared their family stories and it was such a wonderful time, we stayed two days.

After that Steven went surfing and I stayed at the camp, answering questions about our Lord and faith in general. We have had the word of God for some time now, and yet, there are so many unanswered questions, different understandings and interpretations of the same Word. Being near Santa Cruz, marijuana abuse had to be at the very core of some of the wild thoughts about our Lord and his creation. I knew we were in pot country for the rest of the journey, and I must say that I was a bit concerned about what effect this north-central culture would cause Steven. But he told me about all the boyfriends his Mom had down south, and he personally was over the whole pot and drug thing. As a 15 year old man, Steven went on to say that no good thing can come out of alcohol or any drug! This young man never ceased to amaze me, by the depth of his wisdom, at 15. Well so, I stopped worrying. But I still watched out for him because words are all too often just that, words, that is.

33

Off to Aptos

To my Uncle and Aunt's house. we didn't have far to walk
that day, only about 8 miles. That morning, coming into
Aptos I looked over to my left and much to my surprise, there
was my Aunt Beverly. She had pulled over and was staring at me.
She asked what I was doing, endearingly supporting the biggest
smile God knows I love her had not seen each other in 33 years
price of freedom comes at a heavy cost. Calling me a "knuckle-
head," or something like that. Well, I said what can I say? I felt
the Lord had called me to the walk and that he must have wanted
to give things a little "Churching up" around the Fine State of
California. And it was a "nice day for a 1000 mile walk," anyway.
My Uncle Paul and Aunt Beverly are also Catholics and original
Californians, this being a Catholic Christian state longer than
the USA has been a nation. Our nation is not getting any better, in these modern times. So I went on a little "journey." Bev
asked us to stay with them and we did. My relatives and I reminisced about old family stories, as Steven listened. And I caught
up on all the things I missed over the past 33 years. I also had the
chance to share some of the naval adventures of stormy seas and
foreign lands.

My uncle Paul had been a merchant marine as well—he has
always been a mentor of my manhood. Of course, Aunt Bev
reminded me of what a "pickle" I was as a youngster. I said yes, I

was not exactly an angel and I'm still not! How God can use an old washed-out 90 lb bag of sea salt sailor like me was somewhat of a mystery. But we had always been "shipmates," Jesus and me, and I shared another "whale of a tale" because I had not seen them for some so many years during my Navel service. What a funny way to meet once again after so long

Then Paul asked for a true story about my life at sea. It was in the far North Atlantic and the seas were 125 feet high—real mountains of water rolling by the hull of the USS Forrestal. The once-busy massive vessel was like a ghost ship, everything was "baton down the hatches." Most were sea sick in bed and I was out walking on the bulkheads. It is impossible to explain the beating a ship can withstand! It was midday and sunbeams broke through the darkened, hell's-angered ocean. I wanted to see more, so I wandered up to "Vulture's Row," some ten stories above the flight deck. (This was before Lieutenant Dan, from Forrest Gump???) winter of 1982 I took some chain and tightened myself to the railing. I could see the entire "ocean theater" surrounding me, and giant ships were being swallowed up some entirely by the monstrous waves.

And the waves were crashing down on the deck of the USS Forrestal, some 50 to 75 feet of blue water, crashing over the bow and rolling down the flight deck, all the way to the center Island. It was a bit frightening, and then my friend the Lord reminded me of this one verse in the Bible. I could here is voice ever so softly hidden in the gale force winds.

Mathew 8

Then he got into a boat and started across the lake with his disciples. Suddenly a terrible storm came up, with waves higher than the boat. But Jesus was asleep.

The disciples went to him and wakened him, shouting, and "Lord, save us!" We're sinking!"

Being a sailor, reading the Bible was my life, having no social life to speak of. Sometimes verses would just "pop out" at times like this, and just then, it was as though the Lord Himself was right beside me. He'd tell me how much he Loved me, that he created all of the oceans, and loved the majesty of it. He reassured me that all would be fine and to enjoy it because it was a gift few will ever see or come to understand! All of a sudden, the temperature became balmy warm, and the hard-blowing wind did not bother me any more. My fears had been removed, as me and my Savior spent time together riding the storm out. Storm surfing on board an air craft carrier is something I will never forget.

I have made many new converts, which I was able to disciple at sea, with that sailor's yarn! Ever since then, the Lord and I have been "shipmates," and I do love Him with all my heart. I will challenge any man about their "salt" or worth, because if there is no Love of the Lord in a man, he is still a boy. Remember 4000 other men were mostly sick. This was in 1982 and after that time, I would ride many a stormy sea, just me and my beloved mate. Jesus King of all!

My Uncle and Aunt loved the old story and we sat around the kitchen table talking it up, catching up on old family stories I had missed, just laughing and having a splendid time together. That is what I have been talking about, just like the storm, how much more precious is the interwoven Love of a family.

I could just imagine that Jesus was there at that same table, laughing and having quite a time with all of us. Christ our Lord is truly present. What is he sharing with you in your life? Foot prints in the sand, perhaps.

One night a man had a dream. He dreamed he was walking along the beach with the LORD. Across the sky flashed scenes from his life. For each scene, he noticed two sets of footprints in the sand: one belonging to him, and the other to the LORD. When the last scene of his life flashed before him, he looked back at the footprints in the sand. He noticed that many times

*along the path of his life there was only one set of footprints.
He also noticed that it happened at the very lowest and saddest
times in his life. This really bothered him and he questioned the
LORD about it: "LORD, you said that once I decided to follow
you, you'd walk with me all the way. But I have noticed that
during the most troublesome times in my life, there is only one
set of footprints. I don't understand why when I needed you
most you would leave me." The LORD replied:*

*"My son, my precious child, I love you and I would never
leave you. During your times of trial and suffering, when you
see only one set of footprints, it was then that I carried you."*

Well wiping the tiers from my own eyes. An old salt like me crying. Only the Lord can make me cry like that.

The next day we spent getting together with cousins and old friends, driving to Santa Cruz and Felton, reuniting with all the people I love after being gone so long. It was touching, and Steven and I had a great time seeing the massive Felton Redwood groves; reflecting upon these surroundings drummed up memories of when I used to surf up and down the coast as a teenager. At one time, so long ago, I used to live in Felton and other coastal places back in the 70's. No matter where we move to or how long we've been gone, we still yearn for the place of our youth, which is entrenched in our psyche; as well, no matter how far we go, or how long we are away from it, according to Proverbs, when we are trained in faith as a youth, even if we depart from it, we will not turn from it, for it is entrenched in our souls. After a nice hot shower and sleeping in a bed once again, it was fantastic. Rejuvenated physically and emotionally, it felt great the next morning; we would be off to walk to Santa Cruz this time.

34

Walking to Santa Cruz

We were back in a well-populated area, with lots of questions and prayer requests, and we saw for the first time in a while the underlining hatred of some Americans for the Church. While Santa Cruz was a tad "wild" in the 70's, it was far from atheistic, as so many have become. It has to be an education problem. Ignorance is not bliss; it is the road to perdition.

The beauty of God's creation has been used to despoil the faith of a nation. And the mind, originally to be used for God's gift of knowledge, has become the devil's playground. With this two prong attack, the enemy has made inroads into our culture to shake the foundations of our faith so discretely, rationally and strategically that no one even felt the tremors prior to the quake.

It is apparent that over the course of this past century, people with supposedly "good intentions" (and we all know where this leads), under the guise of scientific inquiry or social progress, used science to confuse the truth of the word of God. Leaving science behind, their task grew to disprove creation. After all, negating the wonder of our Creator would elevate one's pride through world-wide fame and success. In spite of their efforts at achieving new wisdom and discovery, science has overwhelming substantiated the truth of scripture! The Bible's authenticity has been affirmed in concurrent secular-historical writings. Research has documented the fact of the Great Flood, based upon clay sediment deposits found worldwide during the same time period. There's the Shroud of Turin's image, documented as "inexplicable and unrepeatable" by NASA scientists, including atheists who have converted after their experience. There's the mantle of Our Lady of Guadalupe, in which a picture has been found within the reflection of the eye, including ocular properties. And what about the "incorruptibility's?" There is so much more that science cannot explain, and none of this can be found in school curriculums. Along with all that the Bible does say, scientists have found to be true by using science itself. However refusing to see the very scope of their findings.

I had many young people telling me about their studies during 7 years of higher learning, and I was not impressed. Most of them could not even have a deep conversation because they only study current events, as described in current textbooks, approved by the state in which one lives for high schools, and written by the professor of the moment in collegiate offerings. A deeper study would at least require research from some original source material, which does happen at some colleges, and ideally some travel overseas. I know there are self motivated individuals that push and strive for a real education, but they are so few. But it is a rare thing that an American receives a real education. If education was taught without even mentioning Christ He will show up in all the truth, found in every aspect of life as we know it today. Woe to the false teachers in our schools today.

A Warning Against False Teachers

When I was on my way to Macedonia, I urged you to stay in Ephesus so that you might instruct certain people to stop teaching false doctrine and occupying themselves with myths and endless genealogies. These things promote controversies rather than God's ongoing purpose, which involves faith. Now the goal of this instruction is love that flows from a pure heart, from a clear conscience, and from a sincere faith. Some people

*have left these qualities behind and have turned to fruitless
discussion. They want to be teachers of the Law, yet they do not
understand either what they are talking about or the things
about which they speak so confidently.*

Supreme Court Cases: 1948, banning religious instruction in
public schools 1962, banning teacher-led prayer from public
schools 1963, banning Bible-reading and the recital of the Lord's
Prayer in public schools

This is in reference to our teachers today. Many know the
truth after 2000 years of Christianity, yet we make an immoral
stand, deliberately teaching lies and spreading ambiguities to
our children. Some will attend Church on Sunday and teach lies
on Monday morning. When our country was strong we would
teach the Bible in our schools until 1964, we made a huge mis-
take and removed Bible instruction from our schools. The very
people that are fighting to separate Church, and state are all
too often uninformed, and the powerfully using miss information to obtain a chosen governmental position. Just know that
moreover, however covertly a very small Muslim constituency
quite militantly swayed the law to remove such teaching from
our schools. Biblically much of this is a secret. So I can speak on
such a teaching. Other than it is a test of American faith in God!
It is on our money even I God we trust so I can warn you all that
your faith is being tested in this way. You are so warned! It was
not worked out on any level! God is sending his Son back very
soon but until then we, as Christians, must defend the faith and
our rights. What have we let happen, even with crosses on every
street corner and even with Churches full on Sunday? Where is
our strength in numbers?

Mathew 10

*"Woe upon the world for all its evils. Temptation to do wrong
is inevitable, but woe to the man who does the tempting. So*

if your hand or foot causes you to sin cut it off and throw it away. Better to enter heaven crippled than to be in hell with both of your hands and feet. And if your eye causes you to sin, gouge it out and throw it away. Better to enter heaven with one eye than to be in hell with two. "Beware that you don't look down upon even one of these little children. For I tell you that in heaven their angels have constant access to my Father. And I, the Messiah, came to save the lost." If a man has a hundred sheep, and one wanders away and is lost, what will he do. Won't he leave the ninety-nine others and go out into the hills to search for the lost one. And if he finds it, he will rejoice over it more than over the ninety-nine others safe at home! Just so, it is not my Fathers will that even one of these little ones should perish.

We also met so many wonderful Christians walking into Soquel, it was truly uplifting. We were in front of a gas station, the cart fell apart, and Steve and I felt that the walk was over. Yet again, just at the same time, a man saw our dilemma and said he could help us. He was a hermit and lived only a block away at the Soquel Lutheran Church. The Church sat on about 3 acres of land, which was open to the area hermits, and they had in turn built a used bicycle shop on the grounds. About 15 hermits resided in this 60's-fashioned commune there on the property, and they helped us rebuild the crosswalk cart. They gave us a great place to pitch our tents and opened the doors to their humble homes to bless our hearts. We stayed the weekend together. At night we would build a great campfire and share with them all the wonderful stores about all the people we had met over the past 800 miles. Walking is not as straight a line as driving.

Steven and I attended Sunday morning services there, and enjoyed it very much. After walking so far, and having so many faith experiences, the divisions are so apparently artificial. I see the bride of our Lord as a single body, blowing like fine wheat in a field, but being violently thrashed by a combine, separated into neat, baled little stacks. This wheat harvest does little good to the community, stored away in buildings. Outside, there's a fierce storm of torment, blowing everywhere just outside the doors of our Churches, causing famine. As scripture says, unless a grain of wheat falls to the ground and dies, it remains just a single grain, without harvest. Will we take a stand in faith that testifies to the believer? Remember, He who is in each of us is greater than he which is in the world Amen!

On Monday, we spent most the day welding and shaping the new cart and it took a completely new shape. Our friends even made us a wooden bumper, which had the crosswalk name engraved upon it, much improved!! As in life, each trap the devil lays for us, God uses for good! Tuesday morning we left our friends, waved good bye and headed ever northward.

35

Soquel to Santa Cruz

Again, many people were curious about the crosswalk. They sought prayer and helped us out in our journey. It was fun for me to once again walk the streets of Capitola, Santa Cruz, and out to Natural Bridges State Park where I had surfed hundreds of times and working construction, before entering the armed forces. We were often approached by many spiritualists of every type, creed, and occult form. Fortunately, it offered us the opportunity to share Jesus with people who otherwise may not have heard of our prince of peace, King Jesus. There were people with spikes, multi-colored hair and tongue rings. Being away for so long, I asked if that was the appearance, they were going for, and what it was all about. Most said it was what was happening and just wanted to fit in with their peers. We looked past their appearances and underneath there were our American children, hurting and lonely, I found none of them to be wicked to the core. All too often afraid of their future or if they had one at all thanks to a lying tale of 2012 and thousands of end of the world stories.

The problem was not their appearance; that was only the symptom of something far more tragic. We the people of America just stopped caring for our children and Fathers' have dropped the ball altogether. Far too many never met their fathers, acting out in a fashion of an unloved and forgotten generation of our

American youth. At this point, I was pretty worn out just trying to grasp the denominational wars of our Churches, when we are all called to reach the lost and destitute. That in this country all too often have been created by us. Pick up a 12 foot cross and walk a 1000 miles and you will see what I am sharing with you all. My fellow American's!!!

The Great Commission

Then the eleven disciples left for Galilee, going to the mountain where Jesus had told them to go. When they saw him, they worshiped him, but some of them still doubted!

Jesus came and told his disciples, "I have been given complete authority in heaven and on earth. Therefore, go and make disciples of all the nations, baptizing them in the name of the Father and the Son and the Holy Spirit. Teach these new disciples to obey all the commands I have given you. And be sure of this: I am with you always, even to the end of the age."

Love, Honor and a clear vision to our parental duties has been abdicated, and this has torn our American fabric straight down the middle. Where are the real hands-on parenting and teaching which society requires? It is not a "spectator sport" or for the faint of heart. As the Families go, so goes the Churches, and culture altogether. God help us I pray and please grant us a clear new vision to reach our lost generation of American children and our world! Jesus please grant us a clear vision, and a hope for their futures! And all Mighty God do we ever need to seek your blessing upon America as never before!

Remember this old tune, "God bless America land that I Love, stand beside her, and guide her with the light that shines from above!" How many voted to remove this standard from our American schools in 1964 shame on all of you, just what were you thinking. Your improper thinking has literally decimated about 3 generations of our families and children. (Can't find any evidence of this being banned from schools…Help?)

May God raise a holy standard before our nation and raise up true sons and daughters, I pray in Jesus' mighty name Amen!

America as a whole needs to turn from sin and become the work force that seeks to bless these our youth, our lost generation, with much love and compassion. To rebuild our American workforce and become the best we can be once again! America I know we hold within our God Given constitution and the true American spirit the ability to live free and be a true light of faith love and neighborly brotherhood to all we encounter.

36

Walking from Santa Cruz to Ano Nuevo Beach

This was mainly open land, and we were able to make good time. At about 10am we reached Davenport and had a great breakfast. People were gathering around the cross all over again, and we could see all of their wonderful faces from the restaurant. Having left pens by the cross, we could see the people signing, taking pictures and smiling, especially the little children. It was a special sight again to see our Lord ministering himself in such a quiet witness of his passion for us his people.

"Preach the gospel with any means possible and if necessary use words." Saint Francis was right. The witness of the cross, and the tens of thousands of names that were written on it, bore witness to the awesome power of his name. After breakfast, we started to walk northward once again and the central coastline was both a constant reminder of the splendor of God's creation.

By walking, we could smell the wild flowers and cypress trees as well as the splendid salt air softly blown from the ocean. Driving by at ninety miles an hour, how can one take the time to appreciate the surrounding blessings of God; His gift to us all? Such a wonderful land, I often pondered on what it will become. What will we do with our stewardship?

Colossians 1

Here is the image of the invisible God, the first-born of all creation; for in him all things were created, in heaven and on earth, visible and invisible, whether thrones or dominions or principalities or authorities all things were created through him and for him. He is before all things, and in him, all things hold together. He is the head of the body, the Church; he is the beginning, the first-born from the dead, that in everything he might be pre-eminent. For in him all the fullness of God was pleased to dwell, and through him to reconcile to himself all things, whether on earth or in heaven, making peace by the blood of his cross.

Everything bears witness to Christ our risen Lord. All things are His and all living creation is His to command. And by His wonderful grace, we are given stewardship of all. What a splendid truth. What would be accomplished if we could only see the creation as a gift instead of belief? All too often people along the walk would say that they do not believe that there is any truth. Isn't a rose a rose any more, or when does an apple become real? When it is on the tree or when you taste of its wonderful flavor. Has drug usage, sexual immorality and sin destroyed the reality of life?

Drugs aren't necessary, just take a walk, and glean from God's gift to us in nature. Oh, yah!

Feel His presence in the silence and natural majesty. In Jesus' time, people eagerly gathered round to be close to Him. What if we sought to touch His robe, seeking health and wholeness?

Some people inquired about the cross and requested prayer. For the most part, it was a peaceful soldering up the coast. Young Steven was having a wonderful time, as we shared biblical stories and truth, and on the lighter side, old surf stories, and military life on a global scale when I was about his age.

Prior to this trip, I had surfed with young Steven from time to time, when his mom would bring him over some weekends.

I really admire Steven for his fortitude. I know his life; and he had it tough. His presence was a continual blessing and daily reminder of the innocence of young manhood! And I am confident he is going to become a fine man and great father someday.

When we arrived at Ano Nuevo, there were no camping grounds. We tried to reach the nearby youth hostel. The sunset was spectacular, and as it was about dark, we just hid in the brush along the road, admiring the very starry night. Ano Nuevo is an elephant seal rookery. All night we heard the seals whaling their love calls, "OR, OR, OR", they said. It was rather relaxing actually to an old sailor like myself. My brother Steve, cousins Greg and Paul and I would drive up to the reserve, and surf out here fairly often. From time to time the huge seals would stick their giant heads up out of the water right next to us as if to say, "Hi". I slept well on that thought. The next day we would walk into Half Moon Bay and we needed our rest after all.

37

Ano Nuevo Beach to Half Moon Bay

The next morning brought wide-open land, offering lots of time to reflect on life, seek God's wisdom and inner peace. I truly feel that we are all too often missing God's best because of our inability to meditate on His presence in absolutely everything. Steve and I had nothing and were given only our day's provision as we served. Never lacking any good thing, just enough to live and be happy. Money is fine, life in itself is a blessing, and I know not everyone can experience this type of faith walk. This is due to the individual's tendency toward anguish and anxiety, as well as our culture's move from a global economic healthy capitalistic system and moving toward the third right's style imperialistic values. What do I mean?

Revelation 18
The Fall of Babylon

After this I saw another angel coming down from heaven, having great authority, and the earth was made bright with his glory. And he called out with a mighty voice,
"Fallen, fallen is Babylon the Great! She has become a dwelling place for demons, a haunt for every unclean spirit, a haunt for every unclean bird, a haunt for every unclean and detestable beast.

> *For all nations have drunk the wine of the passion of her sexual immorality, and the kings of the earth have committed immorality with her, and the merchants of the earth have grown rich from the power of her luxurious living."*
>   *Then I heard another voice from heaven saying, "Come out of her, my people, lest you take part in her sins, lest you share in her plagues; for her sins are heaped high as heaven, and God has remembered her iniquities.*

In many ways, it could be said that the weapon of the Middle East is sexual immorality, greed, and lust. OPEC is the wine that the nations are "in bed" with and the rest runs down hill from there. They tempt the Christians all over the world but we are supposed to know better and decline their temptations. That is why we are experiencing so much trouble here at home. We have the same curses in so many cases i.e. witchcraft, palm readers, tarot cards, and astrology. The outcome may be fun and exciting, at least initially, until the bondage sets in, and we become captive to these activities, unable to stop our lusts. And the farther north I traveled, the more witchcraft we would encounter and it is ugly. There was a young wiccan occult follower that wanted out of his debauchery, asking for prayer and telling me of some of the atrocities in that culture. Witchcraft never leads down a bright path. Satan lives there. We live in these truly different days. They must stop at all costs, or there will be no good place to live. Most of this was generated by the 60's-80's drug culture. As the Church, this is an all out war. It is time to start praying and taking right action, so we don't lose anymore ground. If you are afraid, think of the legacy you will leave your children. This will take Church and State collaboration, as many police forces have learned and developed task forces to address it; it is more about the children, and setting right priorities for the future. However both can benefit life if reality is reflected upon overall out come to the betterment of the whole family and greater community.

Coming into Half Moon Bay, we came by a great farmers' market. Many people came to sign the cross, brought us fresh fruit, and helped us with financial support. We were able to sleep at a Best Western Half Moon Bay that night and the hotel matched the rate, so we stayed two nights. It was a much-needed rest and we had some great Bible studies. Steven and I meditated on the word of God. On a spiritual journey such as this, the revelations of what it was like to truly trust God occurred as He met our every need, on a daily basis. I just had to question where the boundary is, where God's abundance stops and our interpretation of blessing begins. Humanity has wrestled with this question forever. I suppose it is all a matter of consciousness and awareness. It will be a matter to ask in the day of his splendor looking forward to the words, "Welcome my good and faithful servant," and all of this will have been but a fleeting moment.

38

Half Moon Bay to San Francisco

We were back in the population again and we once again shared with a great number of people.

I for one truly loved Half moon bay as a local surf spot in 1977 and I build many homes here in those days. Having spent hours walking the coastline watching and surfing enormous waves every day was a simple pleasure. Half Moon Bay was a very small crab fishing, and farming community in those days. So I shared with Steven about all the fun we use to have. I remember having warm hot cakes, in the morning, and Dungeness crab delights and fresh fish and abalone of every kind. Man where have all the good times gone? It is a much darker reality Today. Something called gothic culture. I won't speak on it as I truly have now Idea of what it is trying to say??? All I can see is it has some disturbed attributes just saying. Still once again once pasted the appearance of the persona the one's I spoke with just wanted to know what was true. I suppose this is why I am taking time between shipping out to write this Book to all of you! For in its self it is something to digest and ponder on for it is real and I did walk and this is what happened. But to find real truth I must suggest you seek out and read the History of the Catholic Church. The Catholic Catechism and find a great mentor to help figure out what is real and what is not. I leave this with you for my Love of the half moon Bay I left to serve in the Navy. Where I did see the world peace be with you all the little children and parents and grandparents there. I realize without question that people in general in one way or another are just the most wonderful reality. I have enjoyed all the conversation and people I have spoken with so very much. It has been the greatest experience to meet so many people. Different and diverse in every aspect, wow I must say people are great all over what a wonderful reality.

39

El Granada, Moss Beach, and into Montara

Once there, we stopped in a little coffee shop and had some coffee and pastry on a bright shining morning. We had problems with the cross message causing the conviction of hearts. Persecution in itself is not a bad thing. It is one of The Holy Spirit's tools which is supposed to lead us unto repentance. It is our conscience's warning mechanism that He uses, to show us of what we are to repair and repent.

The good news is this persecution works the same for all people. When we sin, our consciences feel persecution and we go to Church, and repent—simple. This is much like car maintenance. If you do not change the oil, the car breaks down. Steve and I were able to share this message with some of the wait staff and people outside by the cross. Some came to repentance while others were still angry at the sight of the cross. For me the sight of the cross has become this miss understood stark contrast between darkness and light, which causes people to stumble so often. When a person feels the calling of the truth of God's love, the darkness immediately begins to persecute back at that person. Sometimes it comes from people, in the form of peer pressure; other sources may be an authority figure, loved one or family member. Such influences will all too often discourage an individual from change; keep you in fear and in the dark. The darkness is the lie of the false reality mostly derived by some point of conjecture, theological false teaching, or unproven theories such as Global warming; the lie has become familiar place, so we tent to stay in the haze even though you may be suffering greatly by it. As the saying goes, "misery loves company." And sometimes it's just our own mind, mulling things over, repeating the old tapes of inadequacy, which is not really natural to us but the enemy's tool. Some tactics used will discredit the goodness of God, in the form of attacking the church, focusing on the imperfections of church leaders or members, or dismissing the need for rules in exchange for indulgent "fun"—suggesting church is for the "weak" or those needing a "crutch." Far from it, since being a Christian requires strength and endurance to "run the race". There is no shortage of distractions and diversions from God's goodness, though all fall short. I am guilty as charged however son of dust another messenger only crying out in the wilderness.

Tools to break free from the lies of demonic attack remember for every conviction, the enemy tries to wield his lie, to shortchange us from the glory of God. Do not fall into despair fore that is where satanic forces would love to place us Quit and locked in fear. Call on some friends or better seek out spiritual council from the Christian church's big C little c I would suggest the Catholic Church. Only because they have been at it the longest in dealing with satanic depression, and temptations! May I suggest you call your friends and go out and have some fun? Go work out Surfing take a walk or a drive, whatever makes you happy and get your joy back as quickly as possible. Most of all stay in church and fight the good fight.

Next up was Rock-Away Beach. It was mid-morning, and an absolutely picture-perfect day. The sun was out and the shore was packed with surfers and beach people. We were walking the coastline of Montara, California. We had many people signing the cross, and questions and answers time with so many. It took about 4 hours to walk 2 miles. Well this is what we were doing so wow what a great sunny day and such great fellow Californians. Mite I say the surf was really good that day as well. See the way out of depressing is to challenge it and go have some fun in the Lords creation.

Staying on the path to Pacifica from Montara, it was rough going over the Devil's Slide area, which is PCH's nickname for this portion of highway. It was very steep up and down with very narrow winding roads, offering us very little shoulder in which to walk. But the road traffic was light and very kind, helpful, and forgiving as well. I must thank them at this time. Many had been following the crosswalk on the news. Some of them came up to us in their convertibles to thank Steve and I. So again there is a lot of light but too much darkness in America today as well, and if we are going to overturn the darkness of the lost generation, we must unify the body of light. Amen brothers and sisters?! What does darkness have to do with the light anyway? Unite! Set your heart on God, turn from the ways of the world, and bless the people all around us with the Love, which comes from Christ!

Walking up the steep mountainside Steven started singing in his deep, gravelly voice, out loud:

"Jesus loves the little children, all the children of the world; red or yellow, black, or white they are precious in His sight; Jesus loves the little children of the world."

Up and down the Devil's Slide, we sang that little tune at the top of our lungs and it felt great! God was using Steven's lyrical intervention to break strongholds in the area. When praise enters, darkness has to flee! Of course, we will never know the full impact of our acts of obedience. But it was fun after all, singing and walking down the back side of the mountain, through the tree line, singing and blessing the area! Give praise to him! Our Lord and savior heal our land and recover our lost generation! Father reconcile America back to yourself, I pray. Amen!

Walking over the mountain, we lost our cellular phone. The very first strip mall we came to had a Cingular wireless phone outlet. I only had 100 dollars left. Steve and I pushed the big cross up to the door and the manager, who was a Christian, said she had a used phone we could purchase. We were back on the wireless with internet and everything for less than 50 dollars! Thank you Pacifica wireless and all thanks be unto God!

We were able to go over to Denny's and have lunch. Once again, the witness of the cross was doing its own thing and people were taking pictures and singing their names to it. We could see in their faces that God was blessing, healing and mending them, both hearts and minds of the people, as only the trinity can do amen! The sight of it touched the people so much that the people in the restaurant paid for our lunch and blessed us with many offerings. Once again God blessed us and we could move forward, and Steven was happy because he could get on the internet and play games on our new phone.

I would like to expound on the people's statement regarding the entire walk. It was people of every ethnicity; Chinese, Japanese, and all Asians, Greeks, Hispanics, black, white, Jewish, Lebanese, Iraqis, and all middle eastern people that confess Christ.

Christians of every race, creed, language, and tongue, touched by the witness of the cross, blessed us, and helped us on our journey. God is color blind, and his family is everywhere around the globe, the blessed community of all God's children! And I figure we are all going to be friends in Heaven on that day of his calling, so I will shed the cloak of indifference, and separatism right now and fall in love with everyone that loves Christ Jesus, or not for there is kindness in all humanity. Sometimes we just have to look harder. We the people, isn't that what our forefathers were trying to achieve?

We can never accept anything—outside of Christ—as truth. Not all lines of the spoken word or thought are truth. All too often, we let our whimsical imaginations deceive us. God requires us to Love all people. God requires understanding, patience, and long-suffering from us as Christians, whether Catholic, Anglican, or Evangelical. He requires us to believe in the Father, Son, and Holy Spirit before we can enter the body! Anything diametrically opposed to this would be treason! This is spelled out by our independence and bill of rights! These were written to preserve freedom to seek God, Christ and the power of the Holy Spirit, not freedom to worship all gods. It is clear on that point. Unfortunately America is racing down an idolatrous path that is already devastating lives in its wake.

40

Pacifica to San Francisco

There were many children and youth who loved to share and pray with Steven. He was always so gentle and willing to listen to the needs of people. He made friends easily. He is such a fine young man to accept such an assignment every day. Day in and day out, he never wavered in his faith, and kindness. I wondered what would happen if we could raise our children to be so remove from fear and to open their hearts of faith like Steven. God was using Steven in every way; I could just stand back and watch His anointing at work. In addition, I thought we were encapsulating our greatest resource in our Church building process; our youth.

We have become locked in fear by life's daunting demands, which we created ourselves by the way! But our youth can cross boundaries that I could never begin to approach, a "generation gap"! This is installed through our thoughts which show up in our actions and our words. What If we could learn to embrace each other in Christ? By observing young Steven's faith, it renewed my joy, inspiring me all over again in Christ! What can we do, what must we do, to recover a lost generation of beloved compatriots? I cannot tell you the answer but I do know where it can be found! It is found in your conscience and forms softness in your heart and gentleness of Spirit. Take time to self evaluate, and learn to truly find Christ in others around you; which is the fundamental building blocks of community!

41

Walking through Daily City

In this rural area, while walking past homes and communities, people of all ages would come to their windows with faces of amazement, or confusion, as the cross came walking by! Again, every race, color, tongue, and people came out to ask for God's healing and blessing over their children and communities! We prayed for the shroud of indifference to be destroyed and that Martin Luther King's vision would come true. His "I have a dream" speech was his cry. Are we ready to fulfill his vision in Christ? It is certainly overdue in coming. I humbly prayed that Christ would lead us unto repentance and guide us with His light, which guides us from above in each community. On the bike path, we came to a mountainous hill seeming to go straight up, when a man came out in his truck. We tightened a hitch strap to his bumper and he pulled us up that hill. He was not a Christian but he desired to learn more about the kingdom and had a real interest in what we were saying. So we stayed and shared with him a while. His girl friend arrived, a Christian who had been sharing her love of Christ with him. Coincidence perhaps, but I think not! We discussed the principles of dating and building a God-based relationship founded on mutual respect and great Love, how it was all important to remain chaste, and to seek God together hand in hand. He would bless them if they could "wait" for marriage. And just to do the very best they could to treat one another with an excellence of spirit.

See I began to explain Jesus loves each of you so set your hearts on him. Then see each other as a son or daughter of Jesus in that person next to you, well you would not hurt Jesus no of course not. Then as you go to church together seek a lifelong marriage and for the endurance to always be together thick and thin come what may.

The man stated that he was willing, so the young couple let us pray for them, for God's guidance and protection from temptation. They were so moved that they helped us find a motel for the night, just before entering San Francisco. After sleeping in our tents, the hotel was a real blessing, and Steven and I went straight to sleep (after a quick Bible study of-course). I thought about the next day where we would enter San Francisco and the Bay area. I must say that Steve was excited, and as was I, for the salvation of souls but mostly at this point we were more driven to see what excitement and opportunities Christ though the Holy Spirit would bring our way. After speaking with Ronda, I knew to expect Brother Daryl to meet up with us in the morning. I had met him once before and was excited to see him again. The Lord had done so many miracles for him and his wife over the past couple of years, and I looked forward to catching up on the praise report.

The next morning, Steve and I got the cross ready and started walking northward up 41st Ave. in San Francisco. There were many hotels and people arrived with their loaded down cars while on vacation. Many were already excited to visit the wonderful sights the bay area has to offer, but were not expecting to see a cross slowly moving among them! Americans from all over were seeking prayer and telling us, no matter what the day would bring, we were the highlight of their day.

Many of them had seen us on CNN news. Steve and I wondered how many people were being touched by the witness of the cross, all across America. Some of them were testifying that they had seen us on the news as far as North Carolina. Wow! Jesus is so powerful, which was all I could think, because the whole walk was about The Triune Godhead, which deployed the mission in the first place. After undertaking a divine beating! Well god was right I enjoyed the whole experience!

42

Entering San Francisco

Turning left onto Lincoln Way, Steve and I walked along Golden Gate Park where there were many homeless, and those in need of prayer. I felt that the Crosswalk brought love and hope to people who were in great need. Often they are found around the Church; we as a nation just refuse to do the hard work of winning the lost and downhearted. Over time I have found that most of them are looking for acceptance, and a true caring touch of God's Love, shown unto them, given to them by us, God's people. So Steve and I gave what we had, and prayed for all who asked. Reaching the Great Highway, we headed north once again. Steven was excited because his Uncle was coming to walk with us for the day through San Francisco. It was exciting for me as well. Having only met Dwaine once before this, I thought this would be a great time of sharing and getting to know my new brother in law.

It was at that moment when a woman pulled over to ask for prayer. Her family had fallen apart after her husband had left them, and she was living in their car, raising a teenage man alone. The pain it caused them was horrific to see. Her son was with her in the car, and had given up on God. He could not understand why his father would leave them in poverty and suffering.

His father actually was fighting them, his own family, not willing to give them any support. In the US court system of

243

today, this behavior with a good lawyer may be allowed, but not in God's court!

Again, by the grace of God the Father, I had the ability to share with the young man about the problems in America, of shattered families. I explained that God was his true Father, and that he would watch after him and his mother. That Jesus had a great plan and a purpose for his life, no matter the present circumstances he was facing today. Then Steven started to share his situation to the young man, and it was better than any words I could think of. So I spent time praying with the mother, then Steve's Uncle Dwayne walked up, and he started helping this little family to grab onto faith.

They were away from Church and so we led them back to a prayer of agreement, and hope in Christ Jesus. It was easy to see the Holy Spirit was working and healing their hearts. In writing these events about people's lives, it is so difficult to explain the instant transforming power of God. His Love is everlasting, His Word is true and He's faithful all the time.

The young man was much happier and wanted to get involved in a youth ministry in order to make good life chooses. Moreover, the Mother was quite grateful and loving in our prayer of agreement. She was going to build a better relationship with God and her extended family and seemed much more focused. The hard part was accepting the truth that we could never know the outcome of our prayers.

But in faith, we kept moving forward to serve the Lord in the best way we can! And trusted the Lord would bless all the people we touched.

Now it was Dwayne, Steve and I walking together. Turning on Cabrillo St., we started walking into downtown San Francisco! It was awesome, people were once again waving, and we could see the glow of happy children's faces pressed tightly against windows in order to see the cross walk by their homes. Resembling a parade of holiness walking down the streets, we marched to the hymn, "Onward Christian Soldiers," as the silent anthem played in our thoughts.

The wonderful glowing face of a child is indescribable. What do we do about so many broken families? How do we pray for them? Lord Jesus what prayers must we pray? The Lord answered me in time, and for me it was silent meditational evaluation of the needs of a curtain area coupled with a silent praying of the rosary. Along with many other meditation and prayer. Mostly praying to bring an end to abortion all together fighting the good fight for life! I often remembered my dear friends way off in the Philippines.

They are a beautiful and very Catholic and spiritual people. I was also moved into the True Life in God devotional prayers (http://www.unitypublishing.com/Apparitions/VASSULA-%20 Mark.htm) as the Lord was answering this exact prayer. In peace and truth what is the reason for such anger in all the division found here in our free America, I could only wonder? What have we done here at home? Where one is suffering and another is blessed? I know in many cases stewardship is to blame, but all too often it is our willingness to take the easy way out; to not stick to the path of righteousness. Our society itself then becomes the problem.

Then we turned north on to 27th and down to the Presidio and Lincoln Blvd. Once we reached Presidio Park, we were nearing the Golden Gate Bridge. I began wondering what would start happening once we got there, being that it was August, and visitors from all over the world were vacationing there. We immediately were approached by many people in the Presidio Park. Heading up the hill we finally reached the Golden Gate Bridge, and the bridge superintendent told us we could not walk across the bridge with the cross, he was afraid there could cause an accident, since the bridge's walkway was narrow, but he offered to have a state vehicle take us across. I could surely understand his point and this scripture came to mind:

Obey Your Government

Every person must be subject to the governing authorities, for no authority exists except by God's permission. The existing authorities have been established by God, so that whoever resists the authorities opposes what God has established, and those who resist will bring judgment on themselves. For the authorities are not a terror to good conduct, but to bad. Would you like to live without being afraid of the authorities? Then do what is right, and you will receive their approval. For they are God's servants working for your good. But if you do what is wrong, you should be afraid, for it is not without reason that they bear the sword. Indeed, they are God's servants to execute wrath on anyone who does wrong. Therefore, it is necessary for you to be subject, not only because of God's wrath but also because of your own conscience. This is also why you pay taxes. For rulers are God's servants faithfully devoting themselves to this. Pay everyone whatever you owe, taxes to whom taxes are due, tolls to whom tolls are due, respect to whom respect is due, honor to whom honor is due.

With this understanding, we accepted his kind offer and rode across the great bridge where we were able to restart the journey in Sausalito on East Rd. And quickly we were on our way heading ever northward once again.

43

Sausalito

It is a quiet town nestled just to the North of the Golden Gate. There are many little restaurants and shops in this small yet not-so-sleepy bay front village. There were many people coming for prayer and to hear about our journey, some of whom were following us on television. The distance we had come was becoming a tool that would draw some to hear about our Lord, and his passion for all of our hearts, and Christ's willingness to clean our souls! The Holy Trinity loves us so much! There are no words to describe the Love of the Godhead, Father Son, & Holy Spirit!

We had quite a group around us when all of a sudden, at a stoplight, an Italian man came running to greet us. He ran across the street, and grabbed a hold of me and would not let go, speaking ninety miles per hour in Italian. I could understand his enthusiasm I could understand some of what he was saying, as I lived in Italy off and on over a ten year period while deployed overseas in the navy. He said he was quite excited to see what we were doing. Soon his wife and whole family were around us, and she began translating. I felt that this was a wonderful witness of the global corporate love of Jesus, supporting the message on the diversity of the Body of Christ, and that people of every race, nation, and tongue were already in love with Jesus.

In so many ways, the new global evangelization started in Italy after Vatican II and is now worked its way here. Of course

It reached California's coast some 600 years ago, with the establishment of the first missions in Florida and, 380 years here in Californian missions. After all my time in the Navy as a sailor, I saw that the Church was everywhere—though we have "universally" fallen asleep. I often wondered how people could travel the world in the mission field and not notice the same thing. The Church is everywhere; we only need to come out of our own self-righteous visions, open our eyes and see the Church as a whole and not splintered as it is today. Heading North Dwayne had to head home to San Rafael and family, after having a great day of sharing and evangelizing the bay area.

Steve and I moved forward through Corte Madera, Kentfield, San Anselmo, and into Fairfax were we stayed the night. So many people blessed us that day with their Love and true generosity, giving us financial gifts & meals. Just before reaching Fairfax, we met a pastor and his wife. We shared the walk, and all the wonderful people we had met along the way. They were so moved that they paid to have us stay in the local Best Western. It was very nice to have a hot tub to soak my tired body in. We had walked another 300 miles since Santa Barbara and all of our clothes and shoes were holding up great! I knew God was watching over us each and every day, blessing after blessing, day after wonderful day. Steve and I had nothing really monetarily to speak of and God's blessing was just enough for each and every day. Life lived this way for me had become an all consuming fire of the Father Son and the Holy Spirit! Now I am sitting in my room, missing the experiences and people we encountered along our pilgrimage. Where would all of this lead? I could only wonder. Steve and I got in a Bible study and prayed for all the people that had signed the cross along the Distance of California's coast, of which we had shared together the last 300 miles. We prayed that God would bless them and heal our land.

The next morning, Dwayne called and asked if we would like to take a break and stay with him and his wife for a week. We accepted the offer and he picked us up in his truck. It was great to get to know Dwayne and his family. What would happen with Steve his nephew, being only 15, was discussed. Since summer was coming to a close school time rapidly approaching.

Dwayne offered to give Steven a home, a place to go to school and a real life. I thought that was wonderful but I could see Steve had some reservations about the whole thing. And after all it was still summer vacation, and I believed God would work things out in the way he does. So we stayed and fellowshipped with Dwayne and his family and friends for a week. It was a wonderful rest and I would need it as it would turn out. The following Friday came around, we drove the cross over to Bodega Bay and started north once again. Dwayne, Steve and I started walking and Dwayne's son followed in their car. We were making good time through the open countryside now that we were entering Northern California. We walked to Jenner. People were stopping in their cars for prayer and taking many pictures. I am not sure at this point, how many people had been saved or helped by the witness of the cross, but it had changed my life forever.

We stopped in Fort Ross and got some lunch. A Lady that worked there was a Christian, but in such fear for the demonic powers that were tormenting people in the area. We prayed with her that the powers would be broken and destroyed by the Blood of the Lamb and that her whole family would be saved and protected. After lunch, we started for Salt Point campsite where we planned to spend the night. We prayed over the land and for the deliverance of all the demonic powers that were operating there. Reaching the campground it was full of people and families, camping and playing volley ball and all types of outdoor games. We had a great blazing campfire, Dwayne Steven and I had a Bible study, and we prayed for all the people of the day. Dwayne and I had a wonderful brother-to-brother talk about his life, and there we had a real heart-felt time. Life's brokenness and interruptions brought by our own dictions. We had much different lives. The both of us living our life's to different ends yet ending at the door of Jesus. Each seeking our Lord to fond our own healing, that only the Lord can give.

44

Salt Point to Anchor Bay

The next morning, Dwayne had to head home and back to his life.

Steven and I headed out once again, the countryside was beautiful and we were making good time through the little towns found along the Northern coast. Reaching Sea Ranch, a resort area along the central Californian coast, a couple came running over that Ken and I had prayed with all the way back in Los Angeles. They were amazed to see how far we had come! They had a group with them, and it was great to share with people that had been following us in the newspapers and on television.

I said thank you for reaffirming the impact this little act of obedience can have on the earth. They blessed us with wonderful offering and off we went walking ever northward not ever really knowing what lie before us.

45

Gualala

We stayed at a campsite nestled in a monstrous Redwood grove along a beautiful emerald river. It was during the week, and we had the site mostly to ourselves. We played guitar and sang worship songs of joy—with all of creation which stood majestically as silent witness. It was humbling to be engulfed by the mighty forest of ferns and all manner of vegetation and standing sentry over us all were the mighty redwood tree's, and all that God had created.

Job Chapter 40 verse [6]Then the Lord spoke to Job again from the whirlwind:

> *Overflow against the proud. Humiliate the haughty with a glance; tread down the wicked where they stand. Knock them into the dust, stone-faced in death. If you can do that, then I'll agree with you that your own strength can save you.*
>
> *"look at the hippopotamus! I made him, too, just as I made you! He eats grass like an ox. See his powerful loins and the muscles of his belly. His tail is as straight as a cedar. The sinews of his thighs are tightly knit together. His vertebrae lie straight as a tube of brass. His ribs are like iron bars. How ferocious he is among all of God's creation, so let whoever hopes to master him bring a sharp sword! The mountains offer their best food to him, the other wild animals on which he preys. He lies down under the lotus plants, hidden by the reeds, covered by their*

shade among the willows there beside the stream. He is not disturbed by raging rivers, not even when the swelling Jordan rushes down upon him. No one can catch him off guard or put a ring in his nose and lead him away.

Know that I was not doing this under my own strength or for my own goals, or reward but rather, so that God would turn his wrath from us, bless the people and heal our land. For He is the only one who can! It was a bit eerie as night fell in the mist and dewy dampness of our silent witness of the giant redwoods. I just remembered how many were healed and brought into the kingdom all along our path, praise God forever amen! And we slept well.

The next morning, leaving out of Gualala, it was a short walk to Anchor Bay, only about eleven miles, but we found a great site to stay. The people were so friendly, a camper beside us paid for a two-day stay and we welcomed the rest as we had walked quite a distance from Bodega Bay. Steve went surfing and had a lot of fun. The water was much colder so far north but it was a fun day together. That night Dwayne's wife came into the camp and said she was searching everywhere for us. She'd been arguing with Dwayne about Steve going back to school. I said there was nothing to argue about. Steve had to get ready for school but after witnessing the abilities of Steven, and knowing his heart, I said Steven was a man now and could make his own decisions.

So everything calmed down and we prayed. Steve said he wanted to get a great education, and do something with his life. I silently reflected on the shattered young boy that started walking with me some 400 miles ago a little rebellious, due to his extended families personal problems. However by the call of god his willingness to see that His life was his to Guide by Christ's light love, and wisdom was fully with him now Steven could move with the light and Knowledge of Christ to better navigate his life. I replied that he had made a very wonderful decision, and

I prayed that God would guide him from now on in life also to always remember that God was his Father.

Steve said he knew now what to do when life gets a little tough—that he would trust God in all things. And off they went straight away. I would never see them ever again. I missed Steve immediately but he had made the right choice to get a good Solid education. Not just of the value of Knowledge in its self is folly! Wisdom and direction for anyone's life must also be applied. In order to seek and fulfill the destiny God has for every one of us the path is found within the reality of true higher learning, for it is there solid truth revels itself, All will find who truly study and thirst, and seek the power of truth! Truth is absolutely real and can never be bent or distorted and it will be a blessing for our lives if we seek out the truth and refuse the lie. For seeking the truth in all things is wisdom. And a firm rock to stand upon reasoning is a true gift from God the creator. And the sword of wisdom is the gift of truth; and from separating the lies from the truth is how a person receives the crown of Knowledge!

Steven called me not so long ago, and he had joined the United States Marines Corps. He is in Iraq today. I pray that God will protect him, and guide him in all of his ways, and that he will watch over Steven in times of peril, as Jesus watched over me in my times of need! He is in steadfast faith, and dedication to God and country. We can all learn a lesson from the faith of young Steven—may God richly bless Him!

Well the next day I found myself alone for the first time during the whole walk. I made myself some breakfast and prayed God would strengthen me and bless the next 300 miles I had left to accomplish. Then I walked up to town, did my laundry and picked up some supplies for the road.

46

Anchor Bay to Manchester

Well the next morning, I loaded the cart and off I went. It was a bit different being alone, and living the life of a hermit much like the Apostles of old. It was a time where I was to enter into deep uninterrupted prayer and reflection on the walk, without the need to entertain company. I came to enjoy the prayerful solitude, and deep sessions of intercessory prayer with the Lord, although I did at times become quite lonely. Still many people stopped, shared, and walked short distances with me, as they sought out all types of prayer.

47

Point Arena

I was keenly aware that I was stepping into hill country, and that I was heading towards the mountains. Looking up the steep road heading through Point Arena is where one of the world's greatest point breaks exists. Surfers understand the meaning of this. I had a nice lunch and a great conversation with a cyclist heading to San Diego. He warded me of the mountains ahead, but that the cycle clubs of America had heard of my pilgrimage, and were looking out for me along the path. I thanked him, and off I went. Mountains—I wished I had Steve or Ken with me now. But I just trusted God and pushed forward.

48

Walking into Manchester

I stayed at Manchester State Beach where I met another man cycling all around the world. He had started some where in Northern Alaska and headed to Argentina. "...For what reason?" I asked. No particular reason—was his reply. He was retired, and just wanted to do it. I admired his fortitude, and we talked and shared adventures I had lived out while in the Navy discoveries found in our world wow all the great food and places cultures and people that I had met along the crosswalk and truly all over the world that night. He was a bit like me in that he could not understand all the need for divisions in the Church. Being a traveler like myself, traveling all over the world on his bicycle you go to Church where you can and all the Churches are saying pretty much the same thing. It is crazy when you see divisionism for what it is. We just decided to agree that "it is what it is," and love people anyway. And we agreed that this was the best way to live life! Having personal respect for all Gods people!

49

Manchester to Elk

This was open land for the most part and I was continually moving, except for the occasional cyclist heading south stopping to pray or take a picture. I was coming to love the cycle clubs and they enjoyed the conversations and prayer along their ride. Coming into Elk was nothing but switchbacks; up and down again I went, through the wonderful tree lines, and back into the mountains with majestic views of the northern coast there. Some of the road was so steep; it was hard to keep my feet from slipping. Logger trucks were showing up on the road that was steep and dangerously narrow, yet the Lord showed me that He was so much into the little things, and would have me in a turnout or safe shoulder whenever a logger would pass by. It became so obvious when time after time he proved it to me. It had to be God. Finally, I arrived in Elk, a very small town along the ocean, but there was a little Lutheran Church which I approached to see if I could stay the night. A woman behind me asked what I was doing. I shared with her about the walk and the love of Christ. She admired what I was doing and helped me get a hold of the pastor. He gave approval to set the tent up in the back yard. The woman then told me her story—since she was to be my next-door neighbor for the night. She had lost her faith in God, but she liked my kindness and willingness to serve. She said her thoughts were turned away by the Churches over all the hypocrisy, questioning the divisions. She said "we can't even agree on anything" and the overall confusion was more than she could bear, so she stopped going.

But the spirit in me discerned that she was reaching out fore the truth of Christ. So I softly explained. She was right, the Church had many problems mainly due to the sin problem of man. That I was also a sinner, I shared that the Church was a wreck because we are in it, in other words there are no perfect people and so we do the best we can. However, Church gives us a place to find goodness, fellowship and peace forgiveness teaching and strength from God for each person that attends. And that the message helps us to get to know God and to learn how to live this life the best we can. That faith comes from the hearing of God's word, and then this portion of scripture came to me for her.

Romans 1

> *For I am not ashamed of the gospel: it is the power of God for salvation to every one who has faith, to the Jew first and to the Greek. For in it the righteousness of God is revealed through faith for faith; as it is written, "He who through faith is righteous shall live."*

She thanked me for speaking with her, the woman replied she would think about what we had discussed. And I went across the street and got something to eat. Then I sat and prayed in my tent for my new next-door neighbor for a while which lead into a personal Bible reflection. I asked what the walk was all about and this was the verse He gave me.

1 Corinthians 12

> *But now God has set the members, each one of them in the body, according as it has pleased Him. But if all were one member, where would the body be?*

Therefore, I took it, as it was not for me to know, only to joyfully accept the call and to finish it. The next morning, I was packing up. The Lady came out and gave me some provisions to eat, and breaking into tears, gave her heart once again to Jesus. How great and awesome is He our Lord shows such compassion for us when we turn away he is always vigilant, and awaiting our call to repentance waiting, and waiting what a wonderful truth— I had not spoken a word that morning. Christ had touched her heart in such a wonderful way. She became a Christian by the witness in her heart, amen, not by any words of mine! I said if she were the only person I reached during the whole walk, it was worth all the walking and suffering, just to reach her alone! I silently thanked the Lord and off I went once again.

50

Elk to Mendocino

First thing in the morning, I was off singing the song, "Our God is an awesome God,. He reigns from heaven above, with wisdom power and Love, our God is an awesome God!" I was praying in the spirit, lifting up the name of Jesus Christ our Lord, right there in the presence of some of his greatest masterpieces, the Great Californian Redwoods. However, this was just a foretaste of his wondrous creation because this was a small grove, and I quickly walked out of the wonderful trees. Now once I reached the cliffs that stand before the little town of Albion, I saw the beginning of the beautiful Mendocino coast. For the first time in years, I would come here quite often as a young man. Before entering the USN, Just then a young man pulled up in his van and offered to put me up at an all-Christian retreat. I was pressed to make it to the northern border now, and passed on the invitation. Still he said he and his followers were watching, had been tracking the walk on Television, and it was fun sharing with some of the youth and young men and woman that were there from there retreat. They were located some 20 miles inland from Albion, California. I grabbed a little lunch and headed north just before reaching Little River.

51

Little River

A family pulled over, having followed the crosswalk for weeks now, and were excited to witness the obedience of faith. I prayed with them and they said that the times were evil, and that they were constantly tormented and harassed for their faith. I said it is only for a while and exactly as it should be, but not to fear the torments for He is greater within us than he that is in the world. And blessed be the name of the King of Kings Jesus! It was time for the bride to stand in holiness in the spirit of truth and righteousness. An army divided against its self was not strong! And we prayed for greater strength and unity.

Then I asked if the Van Damme Beach Campground was close and they said it was only 3 miles ahead. I pressed on up the road to Little River. I was going uphill all the way. When I reached the park, I walked in and a state trooper conveyed to me his concern about the mountain road ahead. Once again for mine safety and the safety of others along the narrow road. I told him I was going to stay in the park for a couple of days, and would figure it out, although I had no way of knowing how that would happen.

So I pulled into Little River Park and made camp, and the peaceful surroundings were soothing to my spirit. Families were signing the cross and singing worship songs with me at the campsite, while hundreds of others watched and listened as we worshipped.

I had another cyclist camping next to me and we shared and laughed about the people who persecuted Christians; he was also a great traveler and realized that these types of people were Al to often afraid not realizing what a wonderful world we actually live in. And we'll all too often they are living in a community bubble, lost and afraid of the unknown themselves.

People without faith are lost and hurting, disappointed with life, and devoting themselves to the quest for more grief, by feeding into the lie of a world that truly does not exist, seeking satisfaction with personal "stuff" baggage of the past, often caused by family problems. It is just so empty expulsion of energy.

It's wonderful to have stuff, please understand. It is the quest for things, a stuffy lifestyle that can never satisfy. Only Christ can fill that hole in our hearts. We continued sharing about Jesus, with our camping travels that night around the campfire. Soon it was bedtime and the next day was Sunday. I would attend Church in Mendocino.

The next morning, I was packing up the cart and getting ready to attend Church. The family that stopped just the afternoon before said they were looking for me, and had remembered I was going to stay in the park. They were dressed and ready to go to Church and invited me and my new friend to attend with them. My friend would ride his bike and I road in the car with the family. We attended the local Presbyterian Church.

I remember the message was on Church unity and the joy of a life in Christ. Of course, I enjoyed it very much. After the service, the mother of the family introduced me to the pastor. He had heard of the crosswalk. I mentioned my need for a ride to the top of the mountain and a member of the congregation gave me a lift to the top. The Lord provided a way through, and I was able to comply with the state trooper's commands. On the way up I saw his concern, the road was extremely windy and filled with narrow switchbacks and I could see how easily I have caused an accident. Well I was dropped off at the town of Leggett and now officially in the outskirts of Redwood country.

52

Leggett to Garberville

Just outside of Leggett, heading North you will find Standish Hickey State Park. I chose to stay there and press on early in the morning. After I set up camp in a wonderful grove of tall Redwoods, a man and his wife walked up to inquire about the mission I was on.

I answered their question explaining it was not a mission, but rather, a calling and a walk of obedience. As for myself, I found it a revelation of the state of affairs I had returned home to after 33 years shipping all over the world, along the path. The husband replied saying, "You see, that is what is wrong with America. There is no God, and if you people would just stop, the nation would get better." And they quickly walked away.

I figured that the Redwoods would bring out a darker side of people because there has been a lot of witchcraft practiced in that area. But I never would have guessed the power of the demonic in some parts of the Redwoods and southern Humboldt County.

I slept well that night. The next morning, I packed up the cross, and off I went walking up and down winding hills, in and out of small patches of great Redwood groves. It was beautiful hiking through the northern Californian hill country in early September, because the forest was empty of vacation traffic. This allowed me time to just connect with nature and I began to see and feel the community of life's connection with nature. With all the business found in life such as conversations, cellphones, video games, work, we could go on and on about this. However it was by walking so far in perfect silent adoration of nature that found is found all around us constantly. It was here I realized what modern society was missing out on, inner peace found in meditation and deep endless silence. Eureka! There it was God called me to walk because he could speak so easily through me because I was disconnected from all we would call comforting. Now I was plugged into absolute reality. Well I connected with the Holy Spirit through the beauty and connection with nature its self.

What I am saying is I can recreate what it was like before cities and business of man's endeavors, and drive for greater achievement. Along with the need to be busy all the time well we separate our communion with quite nature which is all around us.

Our four fathers know of this reality of soft quietness and the greatness of our nation was established by the quietness of still waters and soft green pastures. Tree's and all things living. Yes this is the connection I truly understood having sailed the seven seas in secluded serene panoramic views of the horizon ever moving before me! My true friends were the clouds of the sky, and the fish and every kind of the sea creature, as nature unfurled before my presents. The congested lifestyles we have built for ourselves block our communion with reality, and reality of nature our connection with it is so absolutely blocked that we fail to rejoice in its spender and beauty. And if you can be still enough nature its self has a voice it is the voice of reality of Gods Glory soft, and very pleasant. Our American Indians, pioneers and early settlers knew of what I am sharing with you now. It is found in early writing from every nationality, and culture, all over the world, it still exists today. We will have to truly slow down, and quite or souls if we are to ever find it again. This very reality of God's greatest love is now the cause of our greatest fear! Such as the Hoax of Global warming and a dying planet created jargon? Created by people who seldom travel in any real since of the word, try sailing the seven seas for 33 years before you spout off and scare people half out of their wits for no good reason. I would be the first to say we can be better Stewarts of our world. But the world at large is just fine. Just thought I would share with you but that is another book all together! Rod's Travels un-plugged, the path from fear!

53

Smithe Redwood Reserve

There was a small restaurant market, which are typically found in the area. It was about 9 am and I had been walking for about three hours. So I went over to get a cup of coffee and some breakfast. Abruptly as I entered, about twenty people immediately said they did not want me on their land and asked me to leave. I said good morning, and their reply was "don't talk, turn around, and keep walking." And I did what they asked, it had been the first time I had felt that type of opposition. It only made me sad to think we Christians are on our way making the same wrong decisions as so many other nations have in the past.

This type of hard-line rejection can lead to much greater separation, a hardening of borders, and the waging of wars over such border encroachments.

If you only study history, the same thing has happened all across the globe repeatedly. I prayed to seek God's understanding on the subject of the difference in demonic activity and hatred of the cross in this area.

The understanding I got back was very interesting. Solano, California happened to be the end of the linked chain of missions; in some ways, it sought to and established holy ground for centuries. And that seemed to ring true, the further North I walked. So as to would seem I was now departing from a more spiritually-protected area.

Moving on, I came across another, Christian-owned outpost and they were quite interested in the walk. They never saw such a thing and we talked for some time. They were afraid in that part of California there could be trouble for me. Well I said God got me this far I will continue to trust in him. But I enjoyed talking with them as well as a little coffee and breakfast which was great. I thanked them and off I went. At this point, it was not the people or demons; I was more concerned about hungry mountain lions or something like that. Then the Lord gave me this scripture to comfort me.

Luk 10:1

After these things the Lord appointed other seventy also, and sent them two and two before his face into every city and place, whither he himself would come. Therefore said he unto them, The harvest truly [is] great, but the labourers [are] few: pray ye therefore the Lord of the harvest, that he would send forth labourers into his harvest. Go your ways: behold, I send you forth as lambs among wolves. Carry neither purse, nor scrip, nor shoes: and salute no man by the way. And into whatsoever house ye enter, first say, Peace be to this house. And if the son of peace be there, your peace shall rest upon it: if not, it shall turn to you again.

And in the same house remain, eating and drinking such things as they give: for the labourer is worthy of his hire. Go not from house to house. And into whatsoever city ye enter, and they receive you, eat such things as are set before you: And heal the sick that are therein, and say unto them, The kingdom of God is come nigh unto you. But into whatsoever city ye enter, and they receive you not, go your ways out into the streets of the same, and say, Even the very dust of your city, which cleaveth on us, we do wipe off against you: notwithstanding be ye sure of this, that the kingdom of God is come nigh unto you. But I say unto you, that it shall be more tolerable in that day for Sodom, than for that city. Woe unto thee, Chorazin! woe unto thee, Bethsaida! for if the mighty works had been done in Tyre and

Sidon, which have been done in you, they had a great while ago repented, sitting in sackcloth and ashes. But it shall be more tolerable for Tyre and Sidon at the judgment, than for you. And thou, Capernaum, which art exalted to heaven, shalt be thrust down to hell. He that heareth you heareth me; and he that despiseth you despiseth me; and he that despiseth me despiseth him that sent me. And the seventy returned again with joy, saying, Lord, even the devils are subject unto us through thy name. And he said unto them, I beheld Satan as lightning fall from heaven. Behold, I give unto you power to tread on serpents and scorpions, and over all the power of the enemy: and nothing shall by any means hurt you. Notwithstanding in this rejoice not, that the spirits are subject unto you; but rather rejoice, because your names are written in heaven. In that hour Jesus rejoiced in spirit, and said, I thank thee, O Father, Lord of heaven and earth, that thou hast hid these things from the wise and prudent, and hast revealed them unto babes: even so, Father; for so it seemed good in thy sight.

I will trust the word of God. I decided not to fear, but to continue knowing Lord would protect me in the rest of the walk as he has already shown to me over the past seemingly endless miles!

For the most part walking the next 9 miles into the small town of Piercy was beautiful but uneventful as well. The state highway ran along the outskirts of the small town and I just walked on by in order to reach Richardson Grove State Park. By night fall so it was a day walking with God and nature again.

54

Richardson Grove State Park

It was twilight when I arrived. The sky was so beautiful, filled with fiery red and orange clouds floating in a marine blue sky, seeming to grow out of the forested mountainside. It was breathtaking. In many ways the walk was a reminder of the, magnificence of God's great creation, I was comforted realizing the theater I was abased in, there in seeing God's face and handy work in even the simplest of things. The walk for me was a slow, wonderful, peaceful journey through Christ's creation,—made for us! We can take better care of it if we see creation for what it is. Please know there is nothing to fear the world is fine we only need be better Stewarts where we live around us.

55

Richardson Grove

I must say, is a beautiful Park, although it was about dark by the time I set my tent. It was a long walk that day and I just climbed into my tent, while reading my Bible, I had a wonderful conversation with the Lord among His trees. I even played a little Guitar worship, and slowly went to sleep. The next morning, feeling quite refreshed, pressing ever northward on I went. It was about an 8-mile walk into Benbow, another 6 into Garberville, and there would be many steep hills to cross. The Highway was good, wide road now with a great shoulder to walk on. But once I reach Benbow, there was a very steep and long grade to overcome, and it was a warm day, so I just took it in sections. There were some trees every so often, where I could find shade and comfort. I was on US 101 walking through Trinity National Forest. Now, where do we think the name trinity came from anyway? So far so quickly we have fallen!! When I stopped for my rest, there were wonderful panoramic views, which were more and more revealing the higher I got. I was able to see clearly over the foothills. When I got to the top, I could see Garberville in the far distance but it was all down hill from there.

Once I reached Garberville it was about 4pm. I was walking into town when a homeless man came running over to me. He was younger and very excited about the cross. He was dressed in a tie-die shirt and jeans, with big black eyes. He said he was half-Indian.

He was hurting and did not know where to go with his life. Well, I said a good place to start would be in Church and to make good decisions—one day at a time. Then, try to get working in a good company, or within the church would be a great start; then, all things can get better from there. We prayed for God's intervention in his life and he received it. He said he would try to get started right away. And off he went.

He had mentioned that the hippy day's festival started that day, meaning Saturday. And the whole place felt like I had stepped back into the 60's, it was amazing really. I wondered where they found all of the clothes for such an event—and the hair!!! I really felt a little Arthur Blessed nostalgia going through there, in the place he must have walked at some time during that period of the sixties.

Ironically, I did have some people ask if I was there for that purpose. I said no. It was just God's timing once again. And I was able to witness to lots of people. Stepping into a little café for dinner, many young waiters and servers were quite intrigued with the cross. The fact that I had walked there from San Diego baffled their minds. We shared that it was a calling because it could have never happened under my own power—so all the glory be to God amen!

The waitress had a serious problem with her husband. She was seeking advice from me. I finished my dinner, stepped out of the café, and read my Bible on the woman's behalf. As she was being physically abused by her husband, Seeking God's wisdom in His Word, I quietly to myself prayed scripture to determine how to answer a person in such torment. Many people came up to sign the cross. Husbands, wives, and their families so many were coming to the cross in this small town. All of them were asking for a prayer, for God's protection for their families! By their own statements were so much under demonic attack. One Grandmother was deathly worried about her unbaptized grandson. There is so much pain in the American homes today, I thought to myself. It was by far the number one sought after prayer, along the entire journey. Then the waitress stepped out—she had ended her shift and was walking down the main street with me a little while. Then the Lord gave me a word of wisdom just for her.

James 5

Ye have lived in pleasure on the earth, and been wanton; ye have nourished your hearts, as in a day of slaughter. Ye have condemned and killed the just; and he doth not resist you. Be patient therefore, brethren, unto the coming of the Lord. Behold, the husbandman waiteth for the precious fruit of the earth, and hath long patience for it, until he receive the early and latter rain. Be ye also patient; establish your hearts: for the coming of the Lord draweth nigh. Grudge not one against another, brethren, lest ye be condemned: behold, the judge standeth before the door. Take, my brethren, the prophets, who have spoken in the name of the Lord, for an example of suffering affliction, and of patience. Behold, we count them happy which endure. Ye have heard of the patience of Job, and have seen the end of the Lord; that the Lord is very pitiful, and of tender mercy.

You see, I began to share with her that it is now the time of the "latter rain" & all the Churches seem to agree on this point. The separation of the wheat from the chaff has begun. And today's families are being ripped apart in this process all over the world. Her husband was divorcing her. She went on to say that he was quite abusive as well. Yet she found great pleasure with him when he was sober. I mentioned that she must pray for him, because that is the wife's position as the helpmate; she must return to Church, seek out living a Godly life, and learn to love God with all her heart, because Christ Jesus was her husband, the husbandman of all of his chosen people. True undefiled Love and Joy, is only found in a life seeking Christ our Lord. And the best way to get started was to enter a woman's prayer group that would help her find Christ's answers to her troubles. There is no other way to find peace of heart that will last for eternity. Meaning in this life or the next! She said she would seek a way back to Church, and she recommitted to her faith just then.

Walking down the street, I talked with so many people. They were all dressed up in 60's garb and when I finally got to the other end, getting a room at the Best Western, found the woman behind the counter was on the fence about faith. I believe she was truly touched by our sharing. Many people were now coming out of their offices to share with me their faith. One older man of WWII vintage was in deep distress about the misinformation found in our media and schools, and the agendas hidden behind our false social service programs in America today. But he had great faith and I very much enjoyed listening to his knowledge. Our youth think they know everything when we can glean so much from our elders!

After the sharing, I walked back out to the cart and there was a young man about 20 years old, telling me how he hated the American flag and that he felt our nation has nothing to do with Christ.

I explained the meaning of the flag: red stripe represented the blood of Christ, white Holy Spirit, Blue Field River of life—cleanses the nation and stars represent that we are citizens of light in the kingdom of heaven. And he fought, and fought, and fought—no matter the apologetic statement I offered. At twenty he had it all figured out. At least he had no problem with the cross, and salvation. He confessed to be a believer; he just hated the flag, and our nation! Why all the hatred against America from our children? What could have caused such a thing? He was maybe the sixth person that had a real problem with the flag and the cross together, so we parted to agree on the greater fact that Jesus was all that mattered. We live in a free nation, and we have the right to our beliefs, but Christ is Lord and the Trinity is real and that is not a freedom for those of us that believe, according to Christians within Christ's body.

It had been a very long day indeed so I got a room at the out skirts of town going into my room I got some rest. The 60's festival was really rolling outside, and people were on party time, Sounded like they were having a lot of fun. My room became louder and louder, when the phone rang at about 2am. One of the partygoers lit the flag on fire, which burned some of the cross. It was blackened but not damaged. Even the soft parts of the cart burned to the ground. The whole thing was engulfed in flames. Yet the cross itself was mostly unharmed just a little blackened. There is no explaining it away; it was a real miracle, defying the laws of physics. The next morning, the town sheriff came out and told me he belonged to the Baptist Church in Redway.

Pastor David came out, along with the entire city of Garberville, to help fix the cross. They donated everything that I needed to get back underway. The cart got a new paint job behind the little Redway Church. It was a real blessing. Pastor Dave opened the Church for every type of help needed and became a real friend. It took about a week to get everything together, and to meet the people of Redway and Garberville. It is a great little town. However, there was a lot of demonic activity outside the Church in parts of the little city, you could feel it.

I attended services on Sunday and spent the day thanking God the Father, Son, and Holy Spirit and all the people in Pastor David's congregation. He is a faithful pastor with great biblical knowledge and a real heart for the lost!

And Monday morning, I was off, walking once again. The week of rest had been wonderful but it felt great to get moving once again. The new cart was an improvement, with a better flag. It was an immediate improvement all around what a blessing. So what Satan intended for evil God turned it for his glory!

56

Garberville to Stafford

Reaching Miranda, I got off US 101 and entered The Avenue of the Giants. The walk became so enriched by God's natural beauty that it actually felt that all of creation was silently rejoicing in a wonderful harmony. It can only be experienced when you can first believe, and then stop take some time from your busy life to connect with creation for once you can join into creation its self the next connection is to enter yourself before the throne room of God! In mind and spirit of course.

God's Spirit Helps Us

For I consider that the sufferings of this present time are not worth comparing with the glory that will be revealed to us. For creation is eagerly waiting for God to reveal his children, because the creation was subjected to frustration, though not by its own choice. The one who subjected it did so in the hope that the creation itself would also be set free from slavery to decay in order to share the glorious freedom of God's children. For we know that all creation has been groaning with the pains of childbirth right up to the present time. However, not only creation groans, but we, who have the first fruits of the Spirit also groan inwardly as we eagerly wait for our adoption, the redemption of our bodies. For we were saved with this hope in mind. Now hope that is seen is not really hope, for who hopes for what can be seen. But if we hope for what we do not see, we eagerly wait for it with patience.

This is a truth but as we walk through Life, we have such a problem with its understanding because we are not seeking God and or his Kingdom. We as a people have become so self-involved with our needs; we have separated ourselves from the connection. With Gods Kingdom that is all of creation every living thing on earth.

With his throne room

"Our ancestors had the Tent of Testimony in the wilderness constructed, just as the one who spoke to Moses directed him to make it according to the pattern he had seen. Our ancestors brought it here with Joshua when they replaced the nations that God drove out before our ancestors, and it was here until the time of David. He found favor with God and asked to design a dwelling for the house of Jacob, but it was Solomon who built a house for him. However, the Most High does not live in buildings made by human hands. As the prophet says,

"Heaven is my throne, and the earth is my footstool. What kind of house can you build for me,' says the Lord, or what place is there in which I can rest?

It was my hand that made all these things, wasn't it?. "You stubborn people with uncircumcised hearts and ears! You are always opposing the Holy Spirit, just as your ancestors used to do. Which of the prophets did your ancestors fail to persecute? They killed those who predicted the coming of the Righteous One, and now you have become his betrayers and murderers. You received the Law as ordained by angels, and yet you didn't obey it!"

His kingdom can be found where ever we are. When I was younger and surfed all the time, I would call on the Lord and we would surf together! Often as an man at work at sea I would silently thank god for my Job and all the people I was in charge of, also for my strength, and protection See, he wants to share everything provide everything we have, and become involved in all that we do, every detail. This is our relationship with Christ and we can live better lives if we see Christ as a friend.

Just about 5 miles south is a wonderful grove campsite, where there is a visitor center. I decided to camp their so I set up camp and started playing my guitar and all of the creation joined in the as the living quire! It felt wonderful, and as some people came and joined me from their camps and joined in, it only got better. We shared a little, and soon we were sitting around a nice hot fire and having some kind of fun, just us and the Lord Yah now we could feel the presence of creation joining in. I supplied the guitar and God supplied the worshippers.

Walking through the Avenue of the Giants is an experience that I will not ever forget. Like most people that visit here, I have driven through, stopped, and walked through these groves before. But it was quite humbling to be in such a single part of creation among the Giant Redwoods that I was only starting to enter and walk through. What a fool I have been realizing the sorrowful misunderstanding of God's power, Majesty and Love. Who am I, that God would choose to reveal his awesome creation in such a real way? It was mid-September now, and the once bustling avenue was empty of vacationers while I was walking through. It was as if the great trees themselves were welcoming as I entered deeper and deeper. Welcome as a trueson of our Lord. The whispering of the Giants all around me was; "Finally, a worshipper has come! Welcome!" That was their beckoning call. In the silence, I could hear and understand the soft and gentle worship of God's creation all around me. Getting deeper into the forest, there were some human aspects added, of little gingerbread houses displaying hobbits, trolls, witches, goblins, and all types creatures, from man's imagination to the worship of all types of false idols. I felt that it was an aberration within the perfect beauty of God's natural setting. Certainly we missed the mark of what was evident.

We have misrepresented one of God's great attributes. And in doing so we have become

utter fools. Again let's have a look at: these are not my words this is from the first Apostles first generational understanding!

Romans 1

For the wrath of God is revealed from heaven against all ungodliness and unrighteousness of men, who by their unrighteousness suppress the truth. For what can be known about God is plain to them, because God has shown it to them. For his invisible attributes, namely, his eternal power and divine nature, have been clearly perceived, ever since the creation of the world, in the things that have been made. So they are without excuse. For although they knew God, they did not honor him as God or give thanks to him, but they became futile in their thinking and their foolish hearts were darkened. Claiming to be wise, they became fools, and exchanged the glory of the immortal God for images resembling mortal man and birds and animals and reptiles.

One example where science has suppressed the truth was by trying to use tree rings to prove that the world is billions of years old. Findings in 2007 have disproved this theory, because the trees grew much faster than they thought they would, and the rings fluctuate in width due to differences in growth rates between a wet and dry season.

All too often today's scientists are distorting truth for the purposes of being noteworthy and getting "published". This is what keeps them employed by agencies, how they are reviewed, and what gets them invited to conferences, which in turn brings in research money in a never-ending cycle of self-promotion. How far will God allow us to go down this path of deep suppression of the truth? I am as much to blame as everyone else—for I realize I am a man of unclean lips in a land of people with unclean lips. I have no great wisdom compared to the ever-living God, and all of his creation cries out in deep groaning, for the Sons and daughters to stand up and take our rightful place. That was what God himself was revealing to my heart while walking through the forest.

Romans 8
God's Everlasting Love

What then shall we say to these things. If God is for us, who can be against us? He who did not spare his own Son but gave Him up for us all, will he not also with Him graciously give us all things? Who shall bring any charge against God's elect? God justifies. Who is to condemn. Christ Jesus is the one who died more than that, who was raised who is at the right hand of God, who indeed is interceding for us. Who shall separate us from the love of Christ? Shall tribulation, or distress, or persecution, or famine, or nakedness, or danger, or sword separate us? As it is written, "For your sake we are being killed all the day long; we are regarded as sheep to be slaughtered." No, in all these things we are more than conquerors through him who loved us. For I am sure that neither death nor life, nor angels nor rulers, nor things present nor things to come, nor powers, nor height nor depth, nor anything else in all creation, will be able to separate us from the love of God in Christ Jesus our Lord.

Prophecy comes in strange ways and, just before reaching Myers Flats, I "prophetically" got a flat tire. I had lost my spare inner tubes and air pump in the fire, and I was completely stranded, realizing I was miles from any resemblance of a bike shop! The closest one being back in Garberville, it was right at that moment when an elderly couple immediately stopped to ask what my message was, and what the cross was all about. So I talked with them. I explained that I was walking as a witness of our Lord, and praying for people in need. These wonderful grandparents were worried about certain members of their family lost in the drug culture in the area. And we shared and prayed for protection and deliverance for their family members.

They saw I was in need of a new inner tube and a pump. I shared with them about the fire, and the couple asked if they could help! They drove all the way to Garberville to help me get going again. While they were gone, I got some lunch, and people were asking me all types of questions, including my political views. I answered in accordance with my heart: being a Navy man, I am a patriot. I noticed the faith of the couple that had such concern for their family that they stopped and asked me (a complete stranger) to pray for their family. Their willingness to help me in a time of personal distress tells me we still are a great Christian nation. And we are still a community of brothers and sisters, standing up for Christ and our families in unity of heart and oneness of spirit.

I know it doesn't seem that way in the world but I have witnessed it repeatedly over the last 1000 miles covered while walking the length of California. Returning to the cart, my new friends soon showed up with all the necessary parts. I thanked them for their generosity and time, yet words were not enough; they were a real blessing and a miracle from the Lord. Again, God showed up for me in this wonderful couple, and he is involved in our every need.

What was the chance these wonderful people would pull over for prayer, just as I got a flat, and meanwhile, allowing me the chance to get lunch and discuss politics? I did not know how to thank them and they said no need, thanks were not necessary. I pray God would answer their prayers, bless their whole family, and protect them!

It was getting a little late so I found a campsite just south of Myers Flat and stayed there the night. The people in the campground were friendly and helpful. The man in the office was a WWII Vet and we shared military stories—no atheists in foxholes, was the largest topic discussed between us. That came out of our conversation—it was great speak with a WWII vet, men and women that paid such a high price for our freedom. I really appreciate the men that fought and served in the military. Most people today have missed the knowledge and wisdom found in the American military. Calling us names and baby killers who is the baby killers now look around. Not the Military it is you.

The next morning, I got a hot shower and a cup of coffee. My friends and I said our good byes and I was off.

57

Headed to Weott

Weott was the next city on the "Avenue" and I reached there at about 9am. Once I got there a young woman in a Volkswagen Van stopped to talk. She was interested in hearing all about the pilgrimage and the adventures I had encountered along the way! She was a spiritualist, believing that all faith leads to God. "Really?" I responded. As this young woman was quite adamant about her belief, I silently asked God the Father for a word of wisdom for her, and it came once again. I began to explain that Buddhism, for instance, was a philosophy, starting about 200 years B.C. This line of teaching most likely has its roots from the Law of Moses. Buddhism, itself, spread during the reign of Alexander the Great who built the first real empire, as he captured lands from Greece to India, eventually covering much of the middle-east. That battle was fought by Buda's general father fighting for India at the time of Buddha's life.

Greek style education is older than the coming of Our Lord, by some 500 years, and it has had a massive impact on our modern culture

Buddha's teaching was theologically based on the way to live a peaceful and kind life. He never said he was a God, he was only a very good extremely kind and intelligent man, thus making it more of teaching than a religion.

Buddhist teaching evolved by incorporating folklore and sto-ries. At some point, a paradigm shift occurred, and led people to question the God of the Jews,—Moses, Isaac, and Jacob. It accomplished this by planting a seed of philosophical doubt; as it begged the question, "Has God ever said that He was a religion, or requested He be at the center of it?" Saying there is no path to heaven, humanity's goal is to obtain only a peaceful euphoric feeling through gentle action that leads to worldly perfection.

A subtle switch, but a basis for rebellion and deception; rebel-lion such as this was the start of all mankind's problems in the Garden of Eden: questioning God and His supremacy. Like any distraction from the straight and narrow, it can lead to a path of satanic influence.

Hinduism had similar origins that were influenced by the Law of Moses and Judaism of the Torah. It's about the same time period. Life in the Kingdom of Jerusalem was the greatest influ-ence under the messianic teaching for about 1500 years before Hindu and Buddhism.

Alexander the Great's kingdom was the first major empire comprised of the entire Middle East and most of India—about 500 years before the birth of Christ our Lord, and also was the precursor to the coming of the roman empire.

Alexander's vision was to change the world through higher education based on the teaching of the great Grecian theolo-gians. Alexander's vision was so far-reaching, we still feel that higher education is the answer to the world's problems, not Jesus the Christ.

This mind set is so prevalent it greatly influences our modern culture today. And in today's colleges we are teaching his same theological dribble, placing it over faith and knowledge of God, because our hearts can become deceitfully wicked and we are always fighting to deny the truth of a real God the Father, Son and the Holy Spirit!

And that faith in the—Trinity—is real religion—not every wind of doctrine or false teaching. If we read our American colleges' founding charters, we would realize that all were established to equip pastors to teach and preach the good news of God, and His Son the Christ.

As for my spiritualist friend, I challenged her not to believe me but to truly study for herself by reading 1) the founding charters of the older colleges; 2) the state constitutions; and 3) the constitution of the United States. I challenge any historian or individual to research these documents and the proceedings in which they were created and not find Jesus Christ as the cornerstone of each and every one.

As far as these other religions being equivalent to Christianity, and that all methods can get people to heaven, I am not personally locked in book study alone. I have been to these countries and personally experienced the outcome of their religions and theologies, and their social ramifications. Ironically, many are leaving these age old beliefs and becoming Christians throughout the world—all over again—while we continue to adopt their old ways and fall into paganism here in America!

What do I mean by "all over again"? Christianity started in Jerusalem and finally reached the other side of the earth when it arrived at California's Pacific shores. Wars fought over centuries were usually waged to stop the evangelistic spread of Christianity. More recently, it seems there is a large swing back to Christianity on a global scale, if persecution is any indicator.

Most young people today are completely ignorant of the fact that China had a Catholic settlement, having been introduced to it in the year 635 AD. According to stone tablets unearthed in the early 1600s, a Nestorian monk named Aluoben entered the ancient capital of Chang'an (Xi'an), received ministers sent by the emperor, and was brought to the palace. The Tang emperor issued an imperial edict three years later allowing a monastery to be built there. Almost 150 years later, the Old and New Testaments had been translated into Chinese, and monasteries had been founded in several cities. But in 845, an imperial edict limited all foreign religion, triggering a period of persecution which ended most of Christianity by 907.

A significant presence did not reappear until the 13th century, for the greater part up to about 1943, when the government inhumanely marched Catholics out into the street and shot them, taking all of their lands and possessions, which helped fuel WWI & II.

This young woman was astounded because, in spite of her studies she read the history in class however; it never resonated to her heart in such a way. I said that God was reaching out to her heart. She received the Lord Jesus. She said she was from New York and on fire to find all the truth. She wanted to teach the people in her life the whole truth.

I said in the name of Jesus let it be so for you as you have asked, go forth and spread the gospel throughout the whole world! And she gave me a hug with tears falling. I know Christ changed her life that very moment. God bless our young people.

58

Heading to Redcrest

I was deep in the forest. Daylight was hidden by the heavenly canopy of redwood trees, accompanied by a coolness in the air. It was wonderful again to walk this path. Seeing a big school bus converted into a camper, it's owner approached. We talked about satanic activity that the occultists practiced here in the redwoods, and he mentioned human sacrifice and black masses were incorporated, as documented by police reports and the news. Black Mass is a dark form of satanic worship! So we joined hands and prayed that God would send Michael Archangel and all of heaven's armies to defend the area, and to bring deliverance to the people's souls that are so lost and deceived. Deceived by the satanic onslaught this type of occultism action brings, forward to the citizenship of the area. We prayed against the demonic powers that were called forth by the evil practices of theses' dark actions, and we sought God's willingness and power to deliver us from the powers of darkness. And it saddened me to hear about such things happening their today. It was not always so. I used to play in the red woods as a child before joining the armed forces. It was not the same spirit then. An awful lot of change to take place in such a short amount of time!

Now I remember as a young boy in Newport Beach in the 70's, when the satanic worship movement was just starting to appear out in the open. We used to pick fights with them whenever they came to our town, until I joined the Navy and became a Christian. I no longer needed to "beat" people over the head, because I know now that the lost souls of people are won by great Love. Most of these lost were engaged in the black arts because they desired friends, materials goods and physical attention from the opposite sex. Without marriage and dating rules this leaves people that are evolved in such action having no idea what ramifications would come from their actions! Today our nation is lost in the sin of Abortion, Lust of every kind, Rising of Gay community. Anger against God and holiness lessons learned from many other nations and history. Well these type of sin's cause destruction always. And if not repented of a great war will come in its time. This is a warning not chastisement. I am truly trying to help us all get on the right track. Yes we have come a long ways down the wrong road. The path back will not be easy. Turning from sin for what it is well it is so difficult. Seek God's forgiveness through Jesus. Even if you may have never tried, just ask Jesus to help! Seek a good church, and slowly you will see the freedom and change in your life for the better I say enough pain. Freedom is only a prayer away. Right prayer is what is required to end the satanic war. These people are opening doors that can attack you and your families. In addition, Christians are not reading their Bibles or praying.

in order to protect their families or close wicked doors that have been open. What do I mean? If we are not reading our Bibles, we do not know how to pray. Yet these black Bible occultists read, study their dark magic, and bring havoc into the community. We are failing miserably because we ignore and reject the only weapon that will protect us!

Demons are released against the People of Christ, and weak Christians as well as the "unformed" or faithless can become black mass followers. We the faithful of God need more than ever to read our Bibles and pray for God's deliverance. It also requires that we unite the Churches, and to work on getting over our doctrinal differences. This will require national repentance to make a moral round turn, and to personally make biblical life first in America or we may lose this battle, and our children will be forced to pick up the broken pieces. The cost will be more than we and all of humanity can bear. Study, pray, and let us watch God win this war for us.

59

Stafford to Eureka

In the morning, I was off to Fernbridge along US 101, walking out of the mountains, and back to the flat lands of Humboldt county coast line. It was very nice to be on flat ground!! Walking underneath bridges and walking over passes found along the 101 hwy, many of the town children of Fernbridge came out to see the cross walking by, and they would wave to me and yell down, "I love you" and "keep going!" It seemed our Lord was uniting people in a wonderful way. That is what America is all about, and the greatest message of all is the body of Christ, making a stand here in America. We are one nation under God living in Christ Jesus.

Truckers would drive by, some I could tell were blessed by the sight, and others would wave finger "gestures" at me, showing their **disapproval**. We as Christians are blessed for our persecution, and our persecutors are quite motivated as well!

1 Thessalonians 2
Paul Recalls His Visit to the
Thessalonians

For you yourselves know, brothers, that our visit to you was not a waste of time. As you know, we suffered persecution and were mistreated in Philippi. Yet we were encouraged by our God to tell you his gospel in spite of strong opposition. For our appeal does not spring from deceit, impure motives, or trickery.

Rather, because we have been approved by God to be entrusted with the Gospel, we speak as we do, not trying to please people but God, who tests our motives.

There it is! God called me because he trusted my motives. How does a man find words enough to thank God? Thank you My Lord, and May my motives always be your great pleasure as long as I live. All are called to minister the gospel of our Lord Jesus, to suffer persecution and remain faithful to God.

We all must run this race. As the body of Christ we are the light of the world, so let your light shine as brightly as possible and you will bring hope to a dying world. Let the peace, love, and joy of Christ, King of Kings, and Lord of Lords be with you always.

60

Reaching Fernbridge

I got a room at the local Super 8 Hotel. As nice as the forest was I must confess it was great to be in civilization once again. Some wonderful people from Calvary Chapel helped me secure my cart then pick me up some Kentucky fried chicken for dinner, we sat in the room together and shared all about the crosswalk, The adventures and people's attitudes along the journey so far. Together as a group praying for greater unity and it was the reality of a much larger church family. I shared with them a lot about the global church which I understood during my years in the navy. I spoke about the true persecuted churches of the eastern rights, of the Middle East, Russia orthodoxy and China's Catholic Church's so together we confessed the Love of Jesus! There was a Calvary Chapel Bible study in town, so we went and attended the teaching I enjoyed the spirit of fellowship, and joy of loving Jesus I witnessed that night. Then back I went to my room and just reflected for a while. I soaked in a hot tub, to warm my sore bones. After camping out for a week through the redwood forest, now I was back in civilization once again, and there were people to share with and serve. Again I realized I was going to be busy.

61

Headed to Eureka

B ack on US 101, the wind was blowing strongly, some ninety
miles per hour off Humboldt Bay. And it would blow all day.
I was having a hard time holding on to the cross, and still some
people would stop to sign and receive prayer. Humboldt County
is a beautiful place but there is a heavy marijuana culture there.
The Lord had me praying over the land for healing and deliverance. Finally, I reached the outskirts of Eureka and stayed in a
little Humboldt motel.

It was owned by an Indian Buddhist man. He had great
respect for my pilgrimage, and we became friends quickly. I sat
and talked with him at some length about the problems here in
America. He had moved here from India when he was a young
man. He told me a story of how the people of his small Indian
community gathered together to send him to America and helped
to purchase the property, and how that much of the money made
by the little hotel went back to the community to bless the poorer
people of India.

He also shared with me all the hard work people used to put
into living and working their property. He loved the America
he came to know by now he went on to say too many people are
becoming lazy, not wanting to work that hard. He and his wife
were older, probably in their sixties, if I had to guess. He went on
to say that the older members had to do all the daily work. His

children would not work in the family business. Again, he and his wife admired and respected what I was doing, and gave me a couple of nights stay for free.

He and his wife were going to retire soon because the motel was becoming too much work for them. And he went on to mention how their kids raised here in America had become so lazy. They did not want to give the hotel to them so he said he was going to sell the place.

I tried to witness to him but he was quickly on to me, so I backed off, and decided to love my new-found friend, right where he was.

Sometimes it just takes love and time to win people to Christ. Though we must accept other people's lives, we must never begin to follow their teaching or beliefs because that is idolatry! You see Love is our greatest tool in the great commission to seek the lost, and due to our modern Americans lust for distractions, we as a Christian nation have not been a very good witness to this family. By the moral down turn of our communities our nation as a whole is failing. Not wanting to truly work and grow both physically and mentally to maturity. Working to become a full rounded citizen focused to better our communities well what use is a person like this anyway.

If we really have a heart to win the lost here in America, we must recover our morality, which used to be America! Our once Christian infrastructure is falling apart, because of the separation of the Churches arguing over every conceivable wind of doctrine, rather than focusing on the central tenets of faith.

We can grow from a simple point of dialog in peaceful conversation between churches. In all points of view, remember that belief in Jesus Christ is the only requirement to being a part of Christ's body. We the people are the body, and being a Kingdom builder is the work we are called to act upon. Think about how pharisaical the modern Church's have become. What would Jesus do? He would overturn a few tables, I think. National repentance is required!

We must return to our solid American work-ethical roots and priorities. We must place God first, then the betterment of our family, church and country as our duty. We must not be afraid to publicly display crosses at work or pray at lunch. We must help others to become Christ-centered people, who make personal and business decisions with moral fortitude. We must be strong yet kind to the few Americans that are left which do not believe at all. They are few in number comparably speaking. Complete none believing community citizen's that is! Most of the bickering and bantering back and forth are caused by our children and church's which are poised against every other church over doctrine or prophecy. Well 33 years ago this was not so.

I know for a while we must suffer a little indifference and harsh words, perhaps even being displaced from work.

However if we do not act this drastically in America today, we will see war within our borders soon enough—just like Europe and many other countries I have seen! Today it is my prayer Christ will build our American workplace back to a Christ-centered society. It is our American heritage and Christ is what makes America beautiful.

Uncle Sam wants you to clean up and praise God! Bless all the people you can around you also pray for the restoration of our nation that God will heal our land!

The first step, however, is to stand united as one Christian body of Christ. We need to build our churches, teach our congregations how to be strong Christians, and live as American brothers and sisters, standing as one body in Christ! Living in Spirit and in Truth! Yes, I see many people worshipping beautifully in spirit, but where is the proof of it in the daily grind of life?

Then I was off on the last leg of my journey heading through Eureka. I spoke to so many individuals that were Christians but they were hurting and broken. I proclaimed to the people that the King of Heaven's armies were the answer, Jesus Christ, and that He would do battle for their broken hearts. I proclaimed this to the people. The youth were fed up with the drug culture; they could not even enjoy nature around them due to the danger of walking into some criminal's marijuana field, hidden within the nearby hills.

They've witnessed it and know that drugs could ultimately destroy their lives, possibly even killing them. From my walk I see our youth are looking at our mistakes and are disgusted with our generation's inability to help them form their future and destiny.

Wouldn't Jesus want us to ensure that our young people have a free America in which to live and work? Our Children are crying out to us—are you going to answer their call? We do not know the length of our days; we should live each day as if it's our last and make it count! These could even be the end-times, though God is the only one that knows the day, and the hour not even the Son knows. Isn't it our children who will ultimately suffer if we don't take action? When Christ does appear what will he find us doing? At the minimum, we should be tending to your faith and family parental duties, I would hope!

It was Sunday and I walked up Harris Street to find a beautiful Baptist Church for Sunday services. The inspirational message was about the body and the gifting of God our Father. After the service, many of the congregation came out to pray and sign the cross of Christ's peace. We prayed for unity of the body and asked our Father to build earth as it is in Heaven! We all pray this in the Lord's prayer! I shared with every one that I was Catholic and the work of unity went over very well.

At 10 am I was off once again turning north on J St. I met so many more children, mostly from broken homes, with all kinds of questions about Jesus, and some gave Him their hearts. On the corner of 14th St. there was a boy, about 13 if I had to guess, and he was in a foster home, as a ward of the state. He wanted to sign the cross but was unable to come outside. By his story, he was locked behind his "prison walls", which was the fence of the back yard of the home. This young Boy had no freedom to do anything.

So I got close to the fence so he could sign the cross and we shared a little prayer. He was in tears as he told me he was unable to go to Church because his housemother did not believe in God. And he was in the home because his only parent was on drugs and in a sober living home. How sick has our land become so quickly? No one is immune to the fruit of this situation, and all are culpable for what happens, right where you live. Now is not the time to ask, "Who is my neighbor?" Is this young man's testimony enough to get you to pray, fast and serve in ministry? As we preach, God is watching. I am writing about what he sees.

Jesus Denounces
the Scribes and the Pharisees

"How terrible it will be for you, scribes and Pharisees, you hypocrites! You shut the door to the kingdom of heaven in people's faces. You don't go in yourselves, and you don't allow those who are trying to enter to go in. How terrible it will be for you, scribes and Pharisees, you hypocrites! You travel over sea and land to make a single convert, and when this happens, you make him twice as fit for hell as you are."

This is the problem with some of today's missionary efforts, particularly the short-turnaround trips. I spent 33 years in all of the world's mission fields and for the most part, people appeared to be on vacation. Many long-term missionaries are doing great work, really "in the trenches" with people. However, too many are on vacation for a couple of weeks, to proclaim to the world that they are missionaries, or to return with nice stories to tell their friends! What's more, we are not attending to our own nation's dilapidated state of affairs! How can we help others when our own house is not in order? That is why I am evangelizing right here at home. We have fallen so far we need churching up more than any nation I have been to, that is what this scripture is explaining to us.

Matthew 28

> *Then Jesus came up and said to them, "All authority in heaven and on earth has been given to me. Therefore, as you go, disciple all the nations, baptizing them in the name of the Father, and of the Son, and of the Holy Spirit, teaching them to obey all that I have commanded you. And remember, I am with you every day until the end of the age."*

We are to make disciples; not just converts. They must be converted and taught how to obey all that Christ commanded. Fill them with the teaching of the Gospel in order to bring them to apostolic appointments, before sending them out. And we must always lead by example. This is a big question in the Church of America today. Which brings me back to the rights of the young Boy trapped behind the fence; how are we meeting his needs, right here in America?

Turning north on 7th St., headed north out of town, a woman came running out of her house, and asked me to pray for her husband and family. We sat on her front porch and talked for about an hour. We had a great time, and I could see that this woman had so much faith. She told me her husband had much more faith than she, and how he was a wonderful father, minister and a priest to his family! She went into her house while I waited on the porch and she packed me a whole bag full of groceries. We prayed once again and off I went. Soon I found myself back on U.S. 101 and on my way to the next adventure. The last leg of the journey…

62

Eureka to Crescent City

At the Bayside cut off, there was a KOA campground where I planed to stay the night before entering Arcata. Just as I was walking into the entrance of the campground, I met a man that was quite unpleasant, and averse to the very site and message of the cross. He was reading an eclectic selection of science fiction novels, New Age spiritualism, and politically-correct historical opinion pieces. We can feed our souls with scripture and light, or fill up on the moral equivalent of worldly "junk food", and this type or reading will determine our emotional and spiritual health. Just a challenge If instead, of researching one side of an issue I suggest a well-rounded study. This will require much more homework to discover all the facts. Test me on this we will find a much different story of the foundation of everything, even the factual history of the Indians living here in California. Being a 9th generation Californian and a historian of sorts, I easily lost this man in fact not fiction. Not to mention that I had just walked through the missions themselves and there is no evidence in support of the harsh mistreatment of the Indians by the Church.

This is not to deny that bad things did occur. For it is true there were bad people but as it is today for the better part of humanity is good just living and raising their families and all that entailed. Moreover, it was the greed of the Gold Rush Era and that of the modern protestant movement which was far more

313

devastating to the demise of the native Indians. This was brought by the insatiable greed of the early homesteaders and Gold rushers into the state in the mid 1800's.

I myself come from a little piece of Californian Indian heritage and my great-grandparents understood the truth of the growth of California better than the modern textbooks claimed.

Ok some Californian history. On June 15, 1846, some 30 non-Mexican settlers, mostly Americans Indians and rancheros, staged a revolt, seized the small Mexican garrison in Sonoma, and captured Mexican general Mariano Vallejo. They raised the "Bear Flag" of the California Republic over Sonoma. And the local people voted in the ratification of the state of California September 9 1850. Though apparently well-read, this man was receiving misinformation.

It was not the man that was at fault, with his misperception as he simply believed misguided information that established wrong thinking! Deception can be carefully couched within interesting facts, as part of the enticement. Of course, it also sells books! And in the case of Science it is run amuck.

Entertainment has replaced good study habits! Teaching revisionism transforms our own people into a bunch of followers. This makes it easier for socialistic communism to take root, where people are unable to think on defend themselves. Misguided understandings can enslave our people; instead, we need to teach facts and allow our students to make personal choices. It is difficult to foster independence when people are in dire circumstances, i.e. the boy behind the fence.

This is the dimming of America. This is the problem with current-affairs study, and even our school's history books are written in current-affairs jargon. Textbooks of today point out that a person lived and did specific exploits but remove the context within which they occurred. So much of history has evolved around Christian and Islamic conflicts; though this facet is largely glossed over; for example any textbook will refer to Islamic conflicts using a variety of terms, such as muslims, moors, Barbary Coast "barbarians"—but this adds to confusion since it separates related movements. Remove the reasoning behind the person's motivation for one's actions, and it becomes jargon. It is then left to the imagination of humanity, and we "spin it" all over the place. Our so-called history books have become trivialized. We must tell the hard truth in all aspects of learning, and let people draw their lines where they will. The truth will set us free, and we can begin to recapture our American, Christ-centered nation once again. The goal is not to control social environments through education, but to avail free, open-minded thinking. From teaching freely about our world, without the elimination of Christian history, we will find peace. Strong faith will emerge when truth is taught.

John 8 Freedom and Slavery

> *So Jesus said to those Jews who had believed in him, "If you continue in my word, you are really my disciples. And you will know the truth, and the truth will set you free."*

We confess to be a free people but we placed our selves into bondage when we took the Bible out of our schools, in the United States! And even worse, we gave our school system over to socialistic and even Islamic influences, under the guise of "global-thinking" and tolerance. In the secular fight against imperialism, racism and ethnocentric viewpoints, which had some redeeming moral value, we've thrown the baby out with the bathwater, promoting other faiths and blatantly teaching them in our textbooks

It was not hard to understand the fallen nature of this man. Our culture has accepted the false belief in social engineering that all trains of thought get us to utopia. That my brethren, is lunacy, since it is an ideal that does not exist! Utopia literally means "nowhere." After our discussion, the gentleman I was speaking with walked away angry.

If there is one thing I have learned while on this walk, it is that in general, atheists, agnostics, and even Christians who are unwilling to study their own faith, lack substantive knowledge to explain themselves. They are typically very controlling and angry people.

I suppose one could say the same about me. I am carrying a huge Cross, yet I did not come up to him. Attracted to the cross, he sought me out to ask questions, seeking help. He arrived angry when he walked up to me, his point of questioning was quite argumentative, and remained so afterwards. Sad to say, when people claim to be studied, analytical and cerebral, yet they appear to be very emotional, it shows quite the opposite of a refined education. Living life based upon their human emotions has placed them into bondage.

Most of the problem is deeply hidden away in the dark corners of our own hearts, locked away somewhere for some personal reason, and is unable to break free. Study and see the truth for what it is.

John 8

Jesus answered them, "Truly, truly I tell you that everyone who commits sin is a slave of sin. The slave does not remain in the household forever, but the son does remain forever. So if the Son sets you free, you will be free indeed!"

Then I walked into the KOA campsite. A local Church had recently bought the site, and the congregation was running the little resort. It was very friendly and clean so many or the people and families which were camping there came out to pray and sign the cross. Perhaps just the respite and encouragement I needed after the last encounter actually this was true always along the walk darkness, and light right next to each other. So it has always been in our world!

They had little bungalow cabins at their resort, and I asked for one of them to stay in just for the night. They blessed me and gave me a nice discount. I got settled in while I was doing some laundry a young woman came into the camp and got a little site across from my cabin. When I was finished with my laundry, I walked back over to my place, and put everything away. Then a knock on the door: this young woman was interested in the message of the cross. I asked if she would like to sign it, so she said a little prayer and wrote her name.

She looked a little preoccupied to me, so I asked if she would like to join me in a little worship music, and she accepted. The cabin had two little porch swings facing across from each other. I asked how old she was, and she said she was 22 years old. I said that is a wonderful age to be, and that God of all creation loved her very much. I asked if she liked the song 'God of Wonders' and she said, 'yes' and we started singing from there. After a couple of songs, I asked why she was camping all alone. She began to reveal a story of young love in a new age America and that a young man wished to marry her. That she was out camping alone to reflect on the situation before saying yes. Well I asked if she and her beau were Christians but she replied that they were not practicing, and believed all faith was good. She was meditating as Buddha would in order to gain some special wisdom on what to do. I replied that the one true God established marriage, and she agreed. Well, outside of the true faith, there are no real marriage vows to worry about are there?

She said that it made sense. I replied of course it does! Then I ask why she wanted to marry this man in particular. She replied that she actually did not want to get married at all yet. She wanted to finish school and take more time. Well, thank God. There is the answer to the question. Then I shared this scripture with her!

Ephesians 5

Look carefully then how you walk, not as unwise, but as wise, making the most of the time, because the days are evil. Therefore do not be foolish, but understand what the will of the Lord is. And do not get drunk with wine, for that is debauchery; but be filled with the Spirit, addressing one another in psalms and hymns and spiritual songs, singing and making melody to the Lord with all your heart, always and for everything giving thanks in the name of our Lord Jesus Christ to God the Father.

Now pay close attention to the next few verses!

Be subject to one another out of reverence for Christ. Wives, be subject to your husbands, as to the Lord. For the husband is the head of the wife as Christ is the head of the Church, his body, and is himself its Savior. As the Church is subject to Christ, so let wives also be subject in everything to their husbands. Husbands love your wives, as Christ loved the Church and gave himself up for her, that he might sanctify her, having cleansed her by the washing of water with the word, that he might present the Church to himself in splendor, without spot or wrinkle or any such thing, that she might be holy and without blemish. Even so husbands should love their wives as their own bodies. He who loves his wife loves himself. For no man ever hates his own flesh, but nourishes and cherishes it, as Christ does the Church, because we are members of his body. "For this reason a man shall leave his father and mother and be joined to his wife, and the two shall become one flesh." This mystery is a profound one, and I am saying that it refers to Christ and the Church; however, let each one of you love his wife as himself, and let the wife see that she respects her husband.

Do you want to have a husband like this and a real lasting marriage in which to raise your children? Yes, she said. I don't know of a woman that doesn't want a marriage like that.

CROSSWALK

Well I asked if she knew that Christ is her Husband right now. She said no. Well he is, and he is Lord over all things and did she think that we met by chance? She said no. She felt it was an anointed appointment that we were supposed to meet. I said yes that is true! Because God the Father is in the little things, as well as the big things! And I said that based on what she had said that she needs to really go back to a good Christian Church, find God and learn how to let Jesus be her husband and to become His spouse first.

We also shared with her that I was a Catholic, and suggested she attend a solid Christian teaching college in order to seek out a solid education in accordance to the Holy Scriptures.

It would seem that our educational system has disintegrated into debauchery, and that somewhere along the path, God would bring the right man along her path of life. And I replied that there was no life worth living without Christ in it.

She began weeping and said she wished her father would teach her such things. I said it was probably not his fault because the battle that is destroying America's educational system from within has defiled the last 5 generations (decades? Since WWII We have stopped reading, and teaching the word of God to our families, which is the instruction Booklet to live. This was more likely do to the devastation WWII should our world. Many a solders life was damaged beyond repair some turning from God some removing God out of their lives all together. And who can blame them. I shared with her that I had written a story of American faith, based upon historical facts, and asked if she would like to hear it? She said yes very much and here is just a peace of it.

America

America starts with the family, so let's reenact what it would be like to be an English family in Portsmouth England in the early

1600's. Our model family resides in a small British home on Piccadilly center. It's a traditional home with smoke rising out of the long chimney made of brick with iron stovetops. There is a street master walking the cobblestone street lighting all the iron, wood-burning streetlights that were placed along the abbey. He was calling out the time as was the custom of the era.

It is early spring in Britannia, the year of our Lord 1625, and the country is in a state of unrest. The church is broken between the Roman Catholic Church, the Church of England, and the Protestant reformation movement, the latter of which protested both of these. However there is a new excitement, certain uneasiness with the discovery of the new world. Settlements have started to take root over the past 100 years, and families are on the move! What is it about, this new land causing people to leave or sell all they own, and move to this new America?! It was an idea fraught with peril. In crossing the Atlantic Ocean, one faced the danger of pirates or war with the French, only to live upon this new land of unknown promise in America!

Entering our home on # 2 Piccadilly Center, we find it alive and full of good cheer! There is a brilliant fire burning upon the foggy evening. Now picture if you will a young man of 27 years, Lt. Luke Drake, a strong man serving His Majesty's Naval Service and his grandfather John Drake sitting before a brilliant fire. Granddad is telling Luke of old war stories about his involvement in the crusades with Islam: For the reestablishment of Israel and the protection of Christendom; from the Zairian and Moorish hordes; of the roads that were traveled; and the murderous hardship, leading into mighty wars between Britain, France and Spain. He also told of the brutal Janissaries soldiers made up of Spanish male babies captured by Islam, raised in prison camps to later fight for Islamic Holy War, and rumors of war as running rampant in these earlier days. Treaties were broken, and deceit descended from the hearts of tyrannical leadership. Pride, greed and power became the driving force of this time in history.

An age-old story of frail humanity, however, it was the love of our fellow man and absolute faith in our Lord Jesus that saw the warriors through these battles. Imagine the treacheries and perils they had to endure! Entire generations were lost in seemingly insurmountable odds at war with Islam. There were new terrifying advancements in war technologies that would instill fear in today's modern warfare.

Back to John's stories, Christian men that could read would pass down fabled stories and lessons found in the bible, because the printing press and paper were almost out of reach for the average household, as it had only been invented a few years before. But mighty and powerful stories they were, coming from the mouth of a beloved and trusted grandfather. This was the normal interaction of families which brought forth strong tradition both for fun and for learning Christ's principles in this time! Just think of the long hours spent enjoying the love and fellowship of families.

Now Martha their mother, Sondra, their 18 year old daughter, and Sarah, Luke's wife are in the kitchen baking bread and making dinner in an open hearth furnace. There's a big iron pot boiling on the open fire! There is also an iron stove baking oven set in stone over the fireplace. It was warm and cozy in those old kitchens filled with love and memories.

It was just then that Paul Drake the husband and father storms in from a day of working on the docks. Paul was the dock master of Portsmouth harbor. A tall master ship has entered Portsmouth harbor upon this day, hailing from the Americas! Luke was quick to ask his father of any news.

Paul hears his son but does not answer right away, as was the way with Paul, slow to speak that is. He would ponder his answers in silent prayer, seeking wisdom before answering a thought. (This action is true wisdom! And this is wisdom for our time as well! We should be slow to speak seeking the answers by discerning the Holy Spirit.) So Paul sits before his son and his father in his favorite chair as he did most often upon damp and cold evenings found in mid winter in Portsmouth, England. Then Paul picks up an old scribed pipe imported through the Southeastern trading company and lights it with a piece of kindling wood. The aroma of East Asian spiced tobacco quickly fills the humble home. Paul then begins to answer: The HSMS Endeavor has arrived, and the captain took me aboard to share the wondrous things brought back, gifts for King James the sixth. With a grin Paul told them about the spoils brought back from the new land. Such things have never been seen in Portsmouth, England before! Bone knives with pictures of strange looking animals scribed in the handles, and some kind of headdress worn by savage kings. He had never seen such things in all his years. The strong chinned man then looked up and with bright sparkling eyes, shown somewhat squinted by the light of the brilliant fire from the old fireplace. He smiled and asked his son, are you and your wife Sarah ready to serve his Majesty as the new magistrate in the Americas, when the Endeavor returns to the bay at Chesapeake? Luke and John looked across the heavy black oak coffee table.

Luke ponders on his father's question for a moment to reflect upon his loving wife Sarah; they had been married for three years. Sarah was carrying their first born. Sarah is a little hesitant about the months at sea aboard ship. There is sure to be hardship, his grandfather grumbles! Then he reminded her that we were the mightiest Navy in the entire world, and that our ships were made of the strongest oak. It would be Ol'e right and there was nothing to fear of a life in Christ. She is still a little frightened. Paul answers, "Yes I am sure your right about that. However I am excited about my new appointed station as magistrate in the new frontier, kind of like the crusades that Grandfather and I were just sharing about, before you got home father." Spoken in a tone with honor and respect, from a loving and grateful grandson.

CROSSWALK

Right then Martha comes in announcing that dinner was ready and on the table. So the men got up, and the family took their seats around the table Paul asks for quiet. And the family members softly bow their heads in reverence, then Paul begins to pray, "Let us take sallies of the day to our Lord to whom we give thanks…"

All Mighty Father we praise your holy name, and I thank you for my most precious family. It is to you we pledge our faith and it's You Lord God we serve. We give thanks unto you for the fine meal set before us You have blessed us this day and we praise your Son our dear Lord Jesus! And Father we ask that you bless our King James, and that you would set mighty angelic hosts around us to protect us through the night. And I praise you for Martha all the help of the women in our home for their labor. And I thank my family for their love and strong faith in Christ our Lord! Amen!

And as it was every night in the Drake home, this was the reminder of their faith in the living God. When was the last time you set a daily standard of faith for your family? Then ask yourself, is the Family dinner table important in your home?

63

Somewhere in the Great Ohio Valley
Year of our Lord 1625

Rests a little wood and mud thatched home, nestled high in the sparsely settled prairie, set in a field just off a lake fed by the Ohio river. The French were first arriving in what would become the city of Dayton in 1796. This little home in a hollow nestled in morning dew, ever so slightly surround the family dwelling. And there is smoke gently ascending from the simple chimney. The year 1625, the day unsure. They seldom had visitors which spoke French that had any better knowledge of the day. Frances, a French settler, and his Iroquois Indian friend Ochoa, were walking home from a successful day's hunt of fat pheasant.

For what hopefully was to be their dinner that night. It was a fruitful hunt for his family, and Ochoa was their dinner guest. Now inside this humble American home a little baby is crying. It's still early morning and Bernard, their 6 month old boy, was named after his grandpapa who was still living in France. Bernard was crying out for his mother Alice. She was working in the small wild garden of fresh American vegetables that their new friend Ochoa taught them to grow.

Alice hears her son crying and runs to him. She opens her blouse, and pulls out her breast to suckle the young child a sweet breakfast of mother's milk. The tender mother and child are bonding as is good unto heaven. Then she does something wonderful: Alice starts singing songs of rejoicing unto her Lord for the wonderful life without interruption or worry, not a care in the world, about anything. Pure and undefiled Freedom? Francis and his young family had been living in their new land for seven years, in their new home that Francis and Ochoa built out of nature that was supplied around them, in order to cover and protect them from the harsh environment. This new and wondrous land had become their home, these Americas some 7,000 miles away from all they had known—and all they had loved. Bernard is one of the first Americans to live out their lives in this brave new and wonderful land, with nothing but stories of France and the old ways of Christendom. Holy wars with Islam seemed far off, over the holy city of Israel & the great holy city of Constantinople of modern Christendom, now modern day Istanbul.

As it would be, the only thing that survived the long and hard journey was sitting in a corner of the house. There sat a solid oak pulpit where a large family Bible rested, open to the first Book of John, the only piece of the old world remaining in their all new surroundings. This was real Freedom! And God was rejoicing with them there in their quiet, humble place. There were many hardships to endure in their new Eden. Harsh, rarely-seen tornadoes, lightning storms, blistering cold winters and snow storms, and hot sun scorched summers! Summer days were always good for swimming in the cool, fresh-water fed lake. Only a few minute's walk from their cabin home. The lake was full of bass big as you have ever seen. This little young family living off the land had befriended the Iroquois who taught them how to survive in their new home.

By this time Francis and Ochoa were walking across the open field to where the little home rested. Francis starts running to the house with Ochoa close behind. Francis yells out, "Alice, we are back." He enters and kisses Alice full on the lips, and gives

Bernard a great hug. "Ochoa and I were blessed today with field fattened pheasant for our table tonight."

By this time Alice had a hearty fire burning in their cobblestone fireplace. With a steaming broth made of the fresh vegetables she had picked in the garden earlier. Francis and Ochoa sat at the new simple table which Francis had made. Ochoa thought tables were a good thing and loved helping Francis with making theirs. Alice placed a wooden wash bowl at the table for the men to clean the birds for dinner. After that chore was over, Francis went over to his pulpit and sat in his chair. He started reading from first John the second chapter verse 1

> *My little children, these things write I to you. That ye sin not, and if any man sin, we have an advocate with the father Jesus Christ the righteous: And he is the propitiation for our sins: and not for ours only, but also for the sins of the whole world.*

Alice truly enjoyed the peace that reading brought to their home and Francis loved to read from God's word. He could read for hours in the evenings to his friend and family. Ochoa had never seen a person spend so much time staring at a tablet, speaking out loud, seemingly to himself! Ochoa had to laugh even though he tried not to.

Then dinner was ready. They joined hands and asked God the father to bless their humble home and thanked God for the fruitful hunt of the morning, to bless the meal and to protect them through the night. A very young and strange group it was, an Iroquois Indian and a French family together in Christ Jesus.

These are stories of fiction based on the truth and faith people possessed at that time! It was the faith of the early settlers that made this land of ours a great nation. God bless America land that I love stand beside her and guide her with the light that guides us from above. We have to once again begin to practice the faith of the people that founded Our Nation under God! It is my only hope that you will find a starting place for your life's pursuit in order to find your inner fire and inspiration Remember. I am only a man crying out in the wilderness of a technological mundane society. It is going to take great action, love, kindness, and caring for our fellow citizens and the Hope we still have in Christ our Lord. Once again looking past ourselves and meeting the needs of others, then God can deliver us out of our communal bondage. There is our purpose and humanity's higher calling.

John the beloved writes to us in his first epistles

And hereby we do know that we know him, if we keep his commandments. He that saith, I know and keep not his commandments, is a liar, and the truth is not in him. But who so keeps his word, in him verily is the love of God perfected: hereby know we that we are in him. He that saith he abides in him ought himself also to walk, even as he walked. Brethren, I write no new commandment to you, but an old commandment which ye had from the beginning. Again a new commandment I write unto you, which thing is true in him and in you: because the darkness is past, and the true light now shines. He that saith he is in the light, and hates his brother, is in darkness even until now. He that loves his brother abides in the light, and there is no occasion of stumbling in him. But he that hates his brother is in darkness, and knows not where he goes, because that darkness has blinded his eyes. I write to you, little children because your sins are forgiven you for his name sake. I write unto you fathers, because ye have known him that is from the beginning. I write unto you, young men, because you have overcome the wicked one. I write unto you little children, because ye have known the Father.

We the righteous fathers of our Nation should be looking into the hearts of men, and women of our American brethren to light a flame of faith, morality, truth, and humility. This is the fiber of morality needed to recover our land! Needed also is our inner conviction and strength, enough to bring about effective change. The goal is to reinstate a nation under God!

America our land of the free and home of the brave. It was paid for with a mighty cost. So if you live and reside in the borders of this nation under the United States Flag, then first know this.

Why is our flag Red White and Blue? The red is representative of the shed blood of Christ our Lord over our entire nation, and it's the cornerstone of our Nation the white represents the purity of Gods Holy Spirit set to reside over our land. Ask yourself Why America has lead in technology of the World being the youngest Nation on earth? And the blue back ground represents the cleansing flow of Gods amazing grace over this land. So that is why we don't let the flag touch the ground or allow the ends to be frayed or worn. It has been out of a heart after Christ our Lord honor is missing today.

The president of Our United States knows that He is always reigning from on high, and watches over us. Ask yourself what does He see in your life? Then think why we have an elected President and not a dictating Kingship!

So the next time you see a fellow American disgracing our flag remind them the cost. What does our flag mean to you? It's not by pride that we stand in faith, but love in a wonderful Father that promises us that he will not leave or forsake us. But he can't bless us if our lives are not a living worship unto Him! Yes fathers, mothers, sons and daughters, we are all enlisted in God's army. From the day you were conceived we are born to serve in some capacity here in our country. The whole rest of the world calls us the Christian West, many of us are strongly aware of this simple truth but there are too many of us wanting to live for our own self-serving purposes. Change starts within us! Ask yourself where is your relationship with God today?

Then it starts by getting involved at home get your family in order, find a Christ centered Church and read Your bible to hold yourself and others around you to live out its teaching! When America begins to pray constantly once again standing on the word of God, then she will be healed! So you must read it for yourselves and aloud to your family book by book. It won't be easy to turn off the television and become involved in raising your children in the faith, but that is why we are the land of the brave!

Now back to the young Lady (Chapter 63). I said that if she truly set her mind to do all I had said, she would start to win the husband, and father she wants, by her witness. I went on to explain to stop having sex all together, and set her sights on Jesus and her life would become more abundant and fruitful than she could ever imagine. She gave her heart back to Jesus, and we sang some more worship songs, and she left and went to sleep.

I was tired and I knew another mountain range was waiting for me in the morning. So I also got some sleep in my little cabin. The next day I was headed into Arcata and Mckinleyville.

As I was walking into Arcata, a woman pulled off the 101 to bless me and she was serious, saying I was in the devil's den.

In this area, people had forgotten all about God and his commandments, and she was praying to rock the foundation of evil in their city. Well, I prayed that God would never forsake his people and felt he was about to show up.

I mentioned that God speaks about the land some 1575 times in the Bible, and I felt she was interested in the promises of God about healing our land in the name of Jesus.

She was a member of a start up Church in the area, and all were looking to God to move mightily in their town and surrounding area. I knew that the marijuana drug culture was the main cause for the dilapidated state of affairs in the area. I said that we Christians needed to take a stand by retaking the territory in the name of Jesus.

Walking into town, I witnessed what she was conveying to me. It was dark in spirit; sadly the people were laughing and mocking the witness of the Holy Cross and God himself, right to my face. Women openly cursed at me, proffering their wares of hatred. Whether they were harassed by evil, or fully a possessed, it was hard to tell.

CROSSWALK

Yet still there were people of light coming up and wanting to sign the cross. People that had lived there to an old age began to realize the filth that had changed the little town. JA righteous anger welled up inside of me. I couldn't contain the pain I felt for the people that had their little home decimated by the witchcraft, which had nearly taken over in this place.

I asked God to bless the Churches in the area and to pour out a blessing of evangelism, which would bring clear and present change to the area! I thought about all the severed Churches along the walk. If we could only get past our differences and stand together, we would squash this filth and get our people back on track! What will it take to inspire unity, other than the external enemy? It remained that way most of the day, what could be said really about the persecution? It was hard but I moved through it. And soon I was approached by a couple of Jehovah Witnesses; they were the first to approach me along the entire walk.

If they really loved Jesus, wouldn't you think they would at least show more interest in what I was doing? It is a shame the path Satan has led them down, with all the manipulated scriptures. They tried to defend their stand in the word of God, with multiple verses and misinterpreted scripture. I love them that are lost, spending a lot of time in chapter and verse with them. Apparently, outside of their trained line of thought, they never studied openly by themselves and that they had no personal relationship with God whatsoever; it was doctrine alone.

Just a bunch of scripture verses to prove a point—that is where I could witness to their lost stand best. By questioning them using chapter and verse, working throughout the entire word of God, in order to reveal whole truth upon doctrinal differences. That is why it is crucial to have a vivid and firm understanding of the Gospels and the whole Bible, because old and new testaments reaffirm its true doctrines and statutes repeatedly. That is where I took these two, running all through scripture after scripture book after book, and it was instantly evident that they had not studied, but were trained in a particular line of manipulated understanding.

This should not be done by picking on these poor deceived souls, but rather I was using loving apologetics. I was sowing them a true life in Christ and that we communicate our relationship with the Holy Trinity by deeply studying the entire word of God. I showed them how dangerous it is for their souls that their limited knowledge can get them into deep trouble. I did not try to win them in a prayer but rather sent them with an assignment. I am confident if they study for themselves Our Lord will reveal himself to them, and they might even lead a few of the followers out of their deception.

However, many Christian Churches have done this repeatedly, memorizing a hand full of scriptures out of the Bible and saying good to go. Sadly my church is in need of some bible study as well. I realize we all start somewhere and I know many Jehovah Witnesses know and love the Lord and this is an isolated conversation. Here is the problem it's that many confessing people can be and probably are saved but still lost, and as deceived as the day they confessed Christ Jesus as Lord because they do not know God's word. This is Satan's tool of deception, to stop us from studying the word, which is Christ Jesus. So Christendom how are you going to stand, if you don't even know how? Think about it, if these people came to you, how would you have answered their cry for truth?

They are well trained, and Christians that are not well versed are their prey. I just walked on through the rest of Mckinleyville. And standing by the airport where again I prayed with a bunch of people then back down onto the coast walking a very long strand of empty beach.

The surf was good and no one was out. Probably because the water was so cold, so I enjoyed just watching the big empty waves break while walking into the small town of Trinidad. Once I got there, I stopped to get some dinner. I talked with another young woman that was a sold-out humanist for some time, by the word of her own testimony.

She was a nice person, and great to talk with, but this poor woman had a lot of anger once again. It seems to me that the humanistic person is looking for absolute agreement without question; as if they had some sort of patent on correctness. I could go along, if all that was being proclaimed was backed up. If they are correct, where is the fruit of it? The fruit is their anger.

Relying on theoretical science is not complete. Often times, scientific discoveries have to be rescinded, or "re-evaluated." When we build society on misinformation, it gives people who trust scientists fear and worry. Then, that turns into mistrust, when the facts are not fully addressed. Then look around at the fires we have to put out.

As for the peacefulness offered by New Age Movements, it is the same old lie of Babylon retold in a new fashion. Look at the witch trendy clothes, brought by wiccan followers, in the name of artistic freedom. It's all from the old school. There is nothing new about any of it. Yes, it is intriguing, there is power in it but I would highly suggest doing some deep comparative studying. How has it worked out in other cultures, over centuries of practice in the areas of the world, where these social theologies are practiced? You will find that where healthy society thrives, there is a strong longstanding Christian community. Where other systems have been practiced for centuries, we find third world actions, such as maiming, wife burning, acid burns or hacking women to pieces with swords. Study to show yourself—it's all in the library.

Christians follow the way, the truth and the life through Christ, who resides in us. This is His Holy Spirit. We are sent as God's messengers to proclaim the Good News and to bless those who curse you, and to stand in our faith. And the fruit of the spirit is Love, Peace, Kindness, and great Joy. She said, "There is no absolute truth," and that everything was as a person perceives it. I asked her, are we sitting in a building with a roof? She answered of course we are. Ok, then it is an absolute fact that we are sitting in a house and if it rains, we will stay dry.

The building, as an absolute truth, is what I surrendered for proof against her argument. She indicated that she was talking about History and Social Studies. I began to explain that history, and science, and all the rest are just as absolute. The problem lies in the fact that it requires a lot of travel, study, experience and wisdom from the Holy Spirit. Seek to read original documents, and actually stand in a place where an event took place—these are necessary in order to realize the absoluteness of it. Once the work is accomplished, you will be able to uncover so many absolute truths that you will be enticed to learn more. Is a flower actually a flower? Taste it! It will be bitter and nasty to the taste that will signify its authenticity.

Moving on, I camped at the beautiful park of Patrick's Point. The people in the area were all sold out to Buddhism, hence the young girl I met in the café. No absolute truth—what are we thinking?! I suggest that a person should fly to foreign countries and observe these philosophies before biting into any other teaching. In other words, a person with any knowledge would inspect, and then wash a piece of fruit before biting into it. Yet we subject our minds and our lives to all types of dangerous thought patterns without testing or ascertaining the harm or the benefit of a philosophy or culture. Such as would be the drug culture that has descended upon our nation over the past 50 years or so.

The study of philosophies, false religions and the occult are far more dangerous. They harm the health of a society more than any weapon ever formed. If these philosophies are so good, why are most of the countries still third world societies, where these same teachings have been practiced for over 2500 years? These are valid points; you look both ways when crossing the street, don't you?

That night, I had been robbed, and most importantly, my jacket was missing. The next morning was colder because a fog bank had settled in, and I was shivering head to toe. I asked

CROSSWALK

the Lord to please help. I had reached Patrick's Point rest area and I was going to seek some shelter until it warmed up a little. Unnoticed by me, a nice man seemed to come out of nowhere, and gave me his jacket. I hardly had time to thank him and he was gone.

A Miracle or answered prayer? I would say so. This location was completely deserted, very rural, and there wasn't a car in the rest area anywhere. Where did my friend come from and where had he gone? I sat and thanked the Lord. Soon I was warm again, and I was off walking to Orick. I was walking through Humboldt Lagoon, which is a beautiful state park. I was praying aloud because there was no one around for miles.

About 5 more miles I came to some state road workers and they had a warning for me. About 2 ½ miles of narrow winding road was coming up and it could be dangerous. I said it would be what it will be. Two of the men signed the cross and we shared a little. And on I went. Just before I entered the narrow, windy strip of highway, I was approached and warned again by two more men. After having walked ¾ the way through, there were two more men, with a different warning: they said that they did not want that Southern Californian "stuff" around their lands, referring to the cross. Just then, the tire on my cart came off on the backside of a tight turn; it pulled me, the cross and the cart into the shoulder, and laid me tightly against the cliff on the side of the road. At that very instant, a huge logging semi came barreling around the same turn, directly where my path had been. Had the tire not come off, I would have certainly been run over. It was amazing to experience God's perfect protection. Scripture states that no weapon fashioned against us shall prevail, and I am living proof.

Right after that a young Christian couple pulled over to help me and they had a big van. The tire was off and I was stranded, so they helped me load the whole thing in their van and drove me the last 26 miles into Crescent City. The area appeared to be void of population anyway, so I got a motel room. The young couple and I prayed together for their baby that was "still in the womb." We prayed that the child would have a wonderful nation and home in which to grow, and that he or she would have a fine future and a hope for its coming life here in America. God Bless America!

All of the different events that I encountered repeatedly showed forth God's grace.

In summary, I am not against higher education or the study of theology. I have lived a full life, and obtained only a piece of God's truth on Earth. If a person has questions, seek and you will find, knock and it will be opened to you. It is not supernatural. There is a wealth of wisdom to be studied and understood!

I was carrying a huge cross so the events and questions were about Christ of course. We are on an Island continent. We are really separated from the rest of humanity and history, which formed civilization as we know it today. For all the knowledge of our great civilizations today, no one has been able to prove Darwinism, and disprove God. However not all of that misappropriation was without fruit. We have reached the point that the word of God is the only truth, it just fits. Tantrums of emotion will not wash the power of fact away! 150 years ago learned men launched a science campaign to prove beyond a doubt the truth of our beginning. I now concede all that was discovered!

Genesis 1
The Beginning of Creation

In the beginning, God created the heavens and the earth. The earth was without form and void, and darkness was over the face of the deep. And the Spirit of God was hovering over the face of the waters.

The Six Days of Creation

And God said, "Let there be light," and there was light. And God saw that the light was good. And God separated the light from the darkness. God called the light Day, and the darkness he called Night. And there was evening and there was morning, the first day.

And God said, "Let there be an expanse in the midst of the waters, and let it separate the waters from the waters." And God made the expanse and separated the waters that were under the expanse from the waters that were above the expanse. And it was so. And God called the expanse Heaven. And there was evening and there was morning, the second day. And God said "Let the waters under the heavens be gathered together into one place, and let the dry land appear." And it was so. God called the dry land Earth, and the waters that were gathered together he called Seas. And God saw that it was good.

And God said, "Let the earth sprout vegetation, plants yielding seed, and fruit trees bearing fruit in which is their seed, each according to its kind, on the earth." And it was so. The earth brought forth vegetation, plants yielding seed according to their own kinds, and trees bearing fruit in which is their seed, each according to its kind. And God saw that it was good. And there was evening and there was morning, the third day.

DNA science has proven this to be the fact all of things created.

And God said "Let there be lights in the expanse of the heavens to separate the day from the night. And let them be for signs and for seasons, and for days and years, and let them be lights in the expanse of the heavens to give light upon the earth." And it was so. And God made the two great lights—the greater light to rule the day and the lesser light to rule the night—and the stars. And God set them in the expanse of the heavens to give light on the earth, to rule over the day and over the night, and to separate the light from the darkness. And God saw that it was good. And there was evening and there was morning, the fourth day.

And God said "Let the waters swarm with swarms of living creatures, and let birds fly above the earth across the expanse of the heavens." So God created the great sea creatures and every living creature that moves, with which the waters swarm, according to their kinds, and every winged bird according to its kind. And God saw that it was good. And God blessed them, saying, "Be fruitful and multiply and fill the waters in the seas, and let birds multiply on the earth." And there was evening and there was morning, the fifth day.

And God said, "Let the earth bring forth living creatures according to their kinds—livestock and creeping things and beasts of the earth according to their kinds." And it was so. And God made the beasts of the earth according to their kinds and the livestock according to their kinds, and everything that creeps on the ground according to its kind. And God saw that it was good.

Then God said, "Let us make man in our image, after our likeness. And let them have dominion over the fish of the sea and over the birds of the heavens and over the livestock and over all the earth and over every creeping thing that creeps on the earth." So God created man in his own image, in the image of God, he created him; male and female he created them.

And God blessed them. And God said to them, "Be fruitful and multiply and fill the earth and subdue it and have dominion over the fish of the sea and over the birds of the heavens and over every living thing that moves on the earth." And God said, "Behold, I have given you every plant yielding seed that is on the face of all the earth, and every tree with seed in its fruit. You shall have them for food. And to every beast of the earth and to every bird of the heavens and to everything that creeps on the earth, everything that has the breath of life, I have given every green plant for food." And it was so. And God saw everything that he had made, and behold, it was very good. And there was evening and there was morning, the sixth day. God Rested.

64

The End of Crosswalk California

God is in the little things, which we do in our daily lives, if we do them out of love. His love brings love, His peace brings peace.

So whether we are at work or play together we can plan and build a brighter world with our joy in Christ. So my brothers and sisters let your Joy shine brightly, and watch and see if America won't get better, one life at a time. You see outside nations have descended upon us once again, and their fruit is divisionism and separatism. This will never fit in our free culture. Do you want to divide America, and the Church? Yes, the Church has thrown up walls in the name of shepherding, protecting a flock as it were, yet we cling so tightly that we lose the very freedom we have all fought so hard to possess.

Freedom can only be lived in communal, open, joyful loving neighborhoods, with strong, Christ-focused American values and work ethic. Now this is where I see a strong tool in my catholic faith. It has been shown over the past 20 centuries that building communities is the heart of Catholicism and society and we need this age Old Catholic understanding. In order to heal our nation and build communities, we need to do it God's way. Agape is the Love of God, and with Christ as our joy so Agape Love is to be given away through us into our communities, in our workplace and everywhere we go. Some pastors teach that we are leaky vessels and we are, so let your light shine and let your vessels leek the blessing of Christ's love all over your community! What do I mean? Love is the Tool of healing, more important than political parties, views or moral agendas. It is a power for change.

Now look at your children—what do you really want for them? My personal thoughts seeing the northern coast from the van I just wanted to go surfing and running along the beach. As I surfed there often during my high school surf safari days; I would have to if my surfboard hadn't been burned back in Redway. "O" well it is what it is after having learned so much about people's thoughts, while spending so many years defending our Nation. I can see too many Americans have lost their faith for so many reasons! None of which were presented from a defendable educated point of view. As we can read they fall short. I never did get a phone call from the professor I spoke with back in Venice Beach. I often wonder where he stands today on creationalism. It was so wonderful meeting America face to face in such a blessed and wonderful fashion. It is my prayer that we can begin to study objectively all of the facts of our world. All who will persist in this challenge in all honesty will find God and his creation the only answer. Well I was very happy when I reached the Oregon border. I enjoyed a hot bath and a soft bed at the finish of such a long journey. However a new journey was just a head of me I was later to find out I was to walk across the United States of America that will be another book.

Good-bye for now and until next time, may God bless America and May Our God richly bless you, all my Brothers and Sisters, and may He bring you Peace and great Joy! To all Christians, Jew's and all other people no matter their faith beliefs or thoughts.

References & Topical Index

- Chinese Christianity, roots of:
  http://www.pbs.org/frontlineworld/stories/china_705/history/china.html
- Founding Fathers' Christianity
- College Charters and Christianity
- Stillwell, Don, Spirit of America, #234
- Tree Rings and Earth's Age
- In the spirit of Unity I used Bible verses from many versions.
- Catholic new American
- NIV new American
- American New Standard
- King James
- Other sources
- Roman Missile
- Catholic Catechism